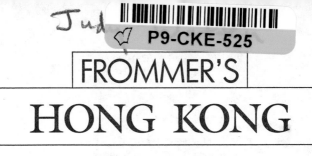

Jud P9-CKE-525

FROMMER'S

HONG KONG

BETH REIBER

1ST EDITION

PRENTICE HALL

New York □ London □ Toronto □ Sydney □ Tokyo □ Singapore

Published by Prentice Hall Trade Division
A Division of Simon & Schuster Inc.
15 Columbus Circle
New York, NY 10023

ISBN 0-13-332826-0
ISSN 1045-9332

Manufactured in the United States of America

CONTENTS

MAPS

A Disclaimer

Readers are advised that prices fluctuate in the course of time and travel information changes under the impact of the varied and volatile factors that affect the travel industry. The author and publisher cannot be held responsible for the experiences of the reader while traveling. Readers are invited to write the publisher with ideas, comments, and suggestions for future editions.

INTRODUCING HONG KONG

Like most Asian cities, Hong Kong wears many faces. There's the face of its sophisticated first-class hotels and restaurants, its international face, looking much like what you'd find in Paris or New York. There's its financial face, the Wall Street of Asia with its banking, international insurance, advertising, and publishing concerns. Hong Kong's Central District shows the face of an optimistic future, with its innovative architecture, designer boutiques, and an ever-increasing number of high-rises. A British colony, Hong Kong was founded as a place to conduct business and to trade, and it has done so aggressively and successfully ever since. The British face is evident everywhere in Hong Kong, from its schools to its government, from rugby to double-decker buses, from English pubs to three-piece suits.

And then there's the other face, the Chinese face, the one of crowded marketplaces, streetside vendors, lively dim sum restaurants, colorful festivals, and the love of neon signs. There are Chinese medicine shops, snake shops, and the old men who take their caged birds for walks in the park. There's the noise, the chaos, the vibrancy of city life, and the diversity. This British colony is overwhelmingly Chinese, and yet it's a city molded by the British and transformed through the decades by floods of Chinese refugees.

Ever-present in Hong Kong is also the face of the visitor, faces from around the world, five million of whom come to Hong Kong annually. Tourism is Hong Kong's third-largest industry, and shopping is one of the main reasons people come here. At first glance, Hong Kong does seem rather like one huge shopping center, but there's much more to Hong Kong than shopping. There's dining, wining, and sightseeing, and there are even isolated places to get away from it all.

Yes, Hong Kong wears many faces, but bridging all worlds is that most famous of Hong Kong's sights, the Star Ferry, as it glides across the harbor, carrying businessmen buried in their newspapers, wide-eyed tourists with cameras hanging from their necks, vendors with straw bags full of wares. From the polished wooden railings of the Star Ferry, views of Hong Kong fuse together, as futuristic highrises blend with gigantic housing projects, neon signs blink beneath towering windswept hills, narrow alleyways melt into busy thoroughfares, and ocean liners pass small wooden boats guided by wizened women in straw hats.

Being in Hong Kong is like being in the middle of an epic drama, where there are a myriad of actors, settings, plots, and interpretations. In 1997 when the British colony is handed over to the mainland Chinese, a new chapter of Hong Kong will begin.

1. The Lay of the Land

Hong Kong is located at the southeastern tip of the People's Republic of China, some 1,240 miles south of China's capital of Beijing. It lies just south of the Tropic of Cancer at about the same latitude as Mexico City, the Bahamas, and Hawaii. Most people who have never been to the Orient probably think of Hong Kong as an island—and they'd be right if it were 1841. But not long after the colony was first established on Hong Kong Island almost 150 years ago, the British felt the need to expand, which they did by acquiring more land across the harbor on the Chinese mainland. Today Hong Kong Island is just a small part of the entire territory, which covers 404 square miles and measures only 23.5 miles north to south and 31 miles east to west.

Hong Kong can be divided into four distinct parts: Hong Kong Island, the Kowloon Peninsula, the New Territories, and 235 outlying islands. Since most of Hong Kong's residents are concentrated in the city proper, in housing projects and villages, much of the New Territories and outlying islands remain unpeopled and open. The fact that Hong Kong is more than just a city surprises many first-time visitors to the colony.

Hong Kong Island is where it all began, when a small port and community was established by the British in the 1840s. Named Victoria in honor of the British queen, the community quickly grew into one of Asia's most important financial and business districts. Today the area is still Hong Kong's nerve center for banking and business and is now known as the **Central District.**

West of the Central District is one of the most fascinating areas of all of Hong Kong, the **Western District.** This is where you should wander if you're searching for things quintessentially Chinese—from snake shops and herbal-medicinal stores to ginseng wholesalers or coffin makers. East of the Central District are **Wanchai,** formerly the reputed haunt of the fictitious Suzie Wong and women of the night, and **Causeway Bay,** an area of restaurants, shops, and Japanese department stores. **Victoria Peak** crowns the center of the island, and beyond that on the southern coast is **Aberdeen** with its population of boat people, **Repulse Bay** with its long stretch of beach, the **Ocean Park** amusement park, and **Stanley** with its famous clothing market.

North of Hong Kong Island across Victoria Harbour is the **Kowloon Peninsula,** the tip of which is called **Tsimshatsui** (also written Tsim Sha Tsui). Tsimshatsui has the colony's greatest concentration of hotels, restaurants, and tourist shops. **East Tsimshatsui,** built entirely on reclaimed land, contains a growing number of new hotels and restaurants. North of Tsimshatsui is an interesting area called **Yaumatei** (also spelled Yau Ma Tei), where you'll find the Jade Market by day and the fascinating Temple Street market by night.

The **New Territories** stretch north of Kowloon all the way to the border of China. Once a vast area of peaceful little villages, fields, and duck farms, in the past couple of decades the New Territories have witnessed a remarkable mushrooming of satellite towns with huge public-housing projects. As for Hong Kong's 235 **outlying islands,** most of them are barren and uninhabited, but those that aren't make for excellent exploration into Hong Kong's past. Lantau, Lamma, and Cheung Chau are three of the colony's best-known and most easily accessible islands, where a gentler, slower, and more peaceful life reigns.

2. A Brief History

Stone, bronze, and iron artifacts found on Hong Kong Island are proof that the island has been inhabited since ancient times, and more than 100 Neolithic and Bronze Age sites have been identified throughout the colony.

Hong Kong's modern history, however, begins a mere 150 years ago, under conditions that were less than honorable. It seems that back in the 1800s the British were crazy about Chinese silk and tea, and would do just about anything to get their hands on them. The Chinese, however, were not interested in anything the British offered for a trade. What's more, the Chinese forbade the British to enter their kingdom, with the exception of a small trading depot in Canton.

But then the British hit upon a commodity that proved irresistible to the Chinese, a drug so powerful that it enslaved everyone from poor peasants to the nobility. That drug was opium, and before long the country was being drained of silver traded to support a

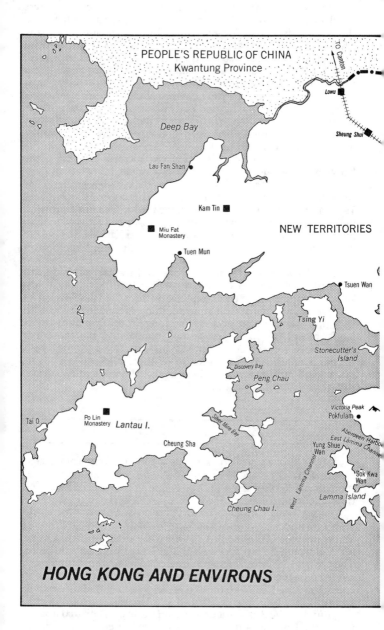

HONG KONG AND ENVIRONS

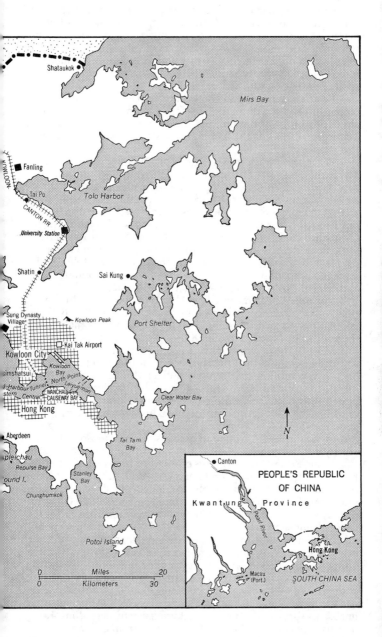

Shataukok

Mirs Bay

Fanling

Tai Po

Tolo Harbor

CANTON RR

University Station

Shatin

Sai Kung

Sung Dynasty Village

Kowloon Peak

Kai Tak Airport

Kowloon City

Port Shelter

Kowloon Bay

North Point

Lei-yue-mon

imshatsui

Harbour Tunnel

stem

Central

WANCHAI

CAUSEWAY BAY

Hong Kong

Clear Water Bay

Aberdeen

pleichau

Repulse Bay

Tai Tam Bay

ound I.

Stanley Bay

Chunghumkok

Potoi Island

Miles   20

Kilometers   30

Canton

PEOPLE'S REPUBLIC OF CHINA

Kwantung Province

Pearl River

Hong Kong

Macau (Port.)

SOUTH CHINA SEA

widespread drug habit. The Chinese emperor, fearful of the damage being wreaked on society and alarmed by his country's loss of silver, declared a ban on opium imports and confiscated the British opium stockpiles in Canton. The British, of course, declared war, and the Chinese lost the struggle. In a treaty it never recognized, China was forced to cede in perpetuity Hong Kong Island to the British as a spoil of the first Opium War in 1841.

Kowloon Peninsula and Stonecutters Island were added to the colony in 1860 as a result of the second Opium War. In 1898 Britain decided it needed more land for defense, so it leased the New Territories, including the 235 outlying islands, for 99 years, a lease that expires in 1997.

When the British moved in to occupy Hong Kong Island in 1841, the prospects for developing a thriving port did not look rosy. No one, including the Chinese, was much interested in the island, and many in the British government considered its acquisition an embarrassing mistake. The British Lord Palmerston dismissed it as "a barren island with hardly a house upon it." What's more, no sooner had the island been settled than a typhoon tore through the settlement. Repairs started immediately, only to be demolished five days later by another tropical storm. The storms were followed by fever and fire, and the weather grew so oppressive and humid it was as though the colony were enveloped in a giant steam bath.

But even though the number of headstones on the hillside multiplied like crazy, so did the number of the living. By 1846 the population was an astonishing 24,000. By the turn of the century the number had swelled to 300,000.

Most of the newcomers were mainland Chinese, who arrived with nothing more than the shirts on their backs and nothing to lose. Every turmoil that sent a shudder through China—famine, floods, or civil war—sent a new wave of farmers, merchants, peasants, coolies, and entrepreneurs into Hong Kong. Everyone's dream was to make a fortune; it was just a matter of timing and good *joss* (luck). The Chinese philosophy of hard work and good fortune found fertile ground in the laissez-faire atmosphere of the colony.

Hong Kong's growth in this century has been no less astonishing, in terms of both its trade and its population. In 1911 the overthrow of the Manchu Empire in China sent a flood of refugees into Hong Kong, followed in 1938 by an additional 500,000 refugees. Another mass influx of Chinese refugees took place after the fall of Shanghai to the Communists in 1950. From this wave of immigrants, including many Shanghai industrialists, emerged the beginnings of Hong Kong's now-famous textile industry. By 1956 Hong Kong's population stood at 2.5 million.

In 1978 Vietnamese refugees started pouring into Hong Kong at the rate of 600 a day, and a year later more than 550,000 Vietnamese were living in camps around the colony. Finding itself unable to support the strain of additional refugees, Hong Kong now has a policy whereby illegal immigrants from China are immediately sent back and Vietnamese are sent elsewhere as soon as possible.

3. The People

With a population of 5.5 million, Hong Kong is one of the most densely populated areas in the world. The *Guinness Book of World Records* lists it as the world's most populous colony, with 13,390 people per square mile. Little wonder that Hong Kong has worked so diligently to reclaim land from the sea. Much of the population is housed in satellite towns in the New Territories, in a forest of high-rises that leave foreign visitors aghast. But as unimaginative and sterile as these public housing projects may seem, they're a vast improvement over the way much of the population used to live. As recently as 1976 an area of Hong Kong called Mongkok, in north-western Kowloon, registered an astounding 652,910 people per square mile. One house designed for 12 people had 459 living in it, including 104 people who shared one room and 4 people who lived on the roof.

The vast majority of Hong Kong's residents—98%—are Chinese, more than half of whom were born in Hong Kong. But the Chinese themselves are a diverse people and they hail from different parts of China. The majority are Cantonese from southern China, hence Cantonese is one of the two official languages of the colony. Other Chinese include the Hakka (whose women are easily recognizable by their hats with black fringe) and the Tanka, the majority of Hong Kong's boat population.

Gregarious, noisy, and rather uninhibited, the Chinese are by nature a very hard-working, pragmatic people. There are many stories of refugees who arrived with nothing in their pockets, set up a small sidewalk stall, worked diligently until they had their own store, and then expanded it into a modest chain. In such a business-oriented society, success is everything and failure accounts for nothing. In a land with virtually no raw materials, it's the people themselves who have proved to be Hong Kong's greatest asset, geniuses at transforming imported raw goods into the electrical equipment, clothing, watches, toys, and other products that have made Hong Kong famous.

As for the other 2% that make up Hong Kong's population, they are mainly British, followed by Americans, Australians, Canadians, Indians, and other Asians. They are known in Cantonese as *gweilo* (or *gwailo*), which literally means "foreign devils." Once derogatory, the term is now used not only by the Chinese but by the foreigners who live here.

4. The Languages

Because Hong Kong is governed by the British, it should come as no surprise to learn that English is one of the two official languages. The other official language is Cantonese, a dialect of southern China in the area of Canton and Guangdong. Cantonese is a different language from the official language of the People's Republic of China, which is Mandarin. Although the two Chinese languages are completely different when spoken, they use the same Chinese characters for writing. Therefore, while a Hong Kong Chinese and a mainland Chinese may not be able to communicate orally, they can read each other's newspapers because the written language is the same. Chinese characters number in the tens of thousands; knowledge of at least 1,500 characters is necessary in order to read a newspaper.

Chinese is difficult to learn primarily because of the tonal variations. These differences in pronunciation may seem almost impossible to detect by a Western ear, but a slight change in tone changes the whole meaning. One thing you'll notice, however, is that Chinese is spoken loudly—whispering does not seem to be part of the language.

Despite the fact that English is an official language and is understood in hotels and tourist shops, few Chinese understand it outside these areas. Bus drivers, taxi drivers, and waiters in many Chinese restaurants do not speak English and will simply shrug their shoulders to your query. To avoid confusion, have someone in your hotel write out your destination in Chinese so that you can show it to the taxi or bus driver. Most Chinese restaurants—and all the ones in this book—have English menus. If you need assistance, try asking younger Chinese, since it's more likely they will have had English instruction in school.

---

5. Religion

The practical nature of the Chinese is probably most evident in the role religion plays in their lives. Most Hong Kong Chinese worship both Buddhist and Taoist deities, something they do not find at all incongruous. They also worship their family ancestors. There are about 360 temples scattered throughout Hong Kong; some are a mixture of both Buddhist and Taoist principles.

Whereas Buddhism is concerned with the afterlife, Taoism is a folk faith that believes in luck and in currying its favor. Tao, essentially, is the way of the universe, the spirit of all things, the force of nature, and as such cannot be perceived or seen. Taoist gods must be worshipped and its spirits appeased, and the most popular of these is Tin Hau, goddess of the sea and protectress of fishermen. There are at least 24 temples erected in her honor in Hong Kong.

Although not a religion as such, another guiding force in Chinese philosophy was Confucius, who lived in the 5th century before Christ and who devised a strict set of rules designed to create the perfect human being. Kindness, selflessness, obedience, and courtesy were preached, with carefully prescribed manners for how people should relate to each other—how women should act toward men or children toward their parents. Since the masses were largely illiterate, Confucius spread his teachings with easy-to-remember proverbs. Confucianism is a strong force in Chinese society even today.

But despite the fact that many Hong Kong Chinese are both Buddhist and Taoist, they are not a particularly religious people in the Western sense of the word. They are too practical for that, too busy earning money. Rather, religion in Hong Kong plays a much more subtle role and is evident more in philosophy and action than in pious ceremony. To the Chinese, religion is a way of life and one that determines everyday living.

Take, for example, the Taoist principle of *fung shui* (literally "wind-water"), in which one attempts to harmonize one's existence with the spirits of nature. Virtually every Hong Kong Chinese believes that before a house can be built, a tree chopped down, or a boulder moved, a geomancer must be called in to make certain that the spirits inhabiting the place are not disturbed. The geomancer determines the placement of buildings and doors, desks and even beds, so as not to anger the spirits residing there.

You'll see evidence of fung shui everywhere. Mirrors are hung up to deflect the path of evil spirits. The Hang Seng Bank has diagonally positioned main doors. Office workers never place their desks with their backs exposed to the room's door. Even the Regent Hotel has a massive glass wall facing the harbor—supposedly to allow the resident dragon easy access to the water beyond.

Almost every home or shop has a small shrine, where lighted joss sticks are thought to bring good luck. In New Year celebrations, door gods are placed on the front door for good luck, and all lights are switched on to discourage monster spirits. On New Year's Day, homes are not swept for fear of whisking away good luck. And during a full moon or major festival, housewives will often set fire to paper creations of homes, cars, or fake money to bring good luck.

6. The Future

As a Crown Colony governed by the British, Hong Kong has always lived very much in the present. However, at midnight on June 30, 1997, Britain will transfer all of Hong Kong to Chinese Communist rule. The future of Hong Kong is very much on everyone's mind.

According to the Sino-British Agreement of 1984, China guarantees that it will preserve Hong Kong's capitalist lifestyle and social system for at least 50 years after 1997. It will become a "Special Administrative Region," largely self-governing, and its people will retain their property and the right to travel in and out.

That's the agreement, but whether Hong Kong will nevertheless undergo a drastic change under Communist China's hegemony is a subject of hot debate in the Crown Colony, especially in light of the brutal manner in which the Chinese authorities quashed its student uprising in 1989. China's actions toward the rebellion sent shock waves through Hong Kong and rounds of angry protest. Nearly half of Hong Kong's Chinese are refugees from the mainland, and as one Hong Kong Chinese told me, his family fled China to escape Communist rule—why remain after 1997? Hong Kong residents were not consulted about their future or the agreement, but then, this is a colony.

Thus, many Chinese who can afford to emigrate have already done so or are looking for viable new homes. In addition, as Britain pulls out, many of Hong Kong's foreign community will go as well.

The vast majority of Chinese, however, will stay. They hope that China will recognize how much it has to gain by keeping Hong Kong as it is. Actually, Hong Kong has had a strong relationship with China for a long time, and even now is dependent on the mainland for much of its food and water. China has already invested quite a lot in Hong Kong, with hotels, banks, and department stores. As one of Asia's most important financial and manufacturing centers, capitalist Hong Kong has been and could continue to be very important to the People's Republic.

---

7. Recommended Reading

If you want to know something about Hong Kong before setting out on your trip, I recommend reading *Fragrant Harbour: A Short History of Hong Kong* by G. B. Endacott and A. Hinton, which gives a thorough account of the history of the colony from its beginnings to the mid-1960s. Hong Kong's days during the opium trade are chronicled in Nigel Cameron's *The Cultured Pearl.* One of the best books to come out on the British colony in recent years is Jan Morris's *Hong Kong,* which traces the evolution of the British colony from its birth during the Opium Wars to the present. Her book gives a unique perspective into the workings of the colony and imparts an astonishing wealth of information, making it fascinating armchair reading.

For an intimate view of Hong Kong, a standard reading is *Hong Kong: Borrowed Place, Borrowed Time* by Richard Hughes, a foreign correspondent who lived in Hong Kong for several decades and was said to have been the inspiration for some characters in John Le Carré's novels. Fictional accounts that depict the flavor of Hong Kong are Richard Mason's *The World of Suzie Wong* and Han Suyin's *A Many Splendoured Thing,* an autobiographical account of life in Hong Kong shortly after the Chinese revolution. James Clavell's *Taipan* is a novel about Hong Kong's beginnings; *Noble House* is its sequel. John Le Carré's *The Honourable Schoolboy* follows the actions of George Smiley, acting head of the British Secret Service in Hong Kong.

BEFORE YOU LEAVE HOME

1. SOURCES OF INFORMATION
2. PASSPORTS AND OTHER DOCUMENTS
3. CURRENCY AND CREDIT CARDS
4. WHEN TO GO
5. WHAT TO PACK
6. HEALTH PREPARATIONS

Much of the anxiety associated with travel comes from a fear of the unknown. Not knowing what to expect—or even what a place looks like—can give even seasoned travelers butterflies. This chapter will help you prepare for your trip to Hong Kong, but don't stop here. Reading through the other chapters before leaving home will also help you plan your travels. Just learning that Hong Kong has hiking trails, for example, may prompt you to pack your hiking boots.

1. Sources of Information

The **Hong Kong Tourist Association (HKTA)** is one of the best-organized and most efficient tourist offices I've come across. They have a wealth of free information available for travelers, including brochures on everything from hotel listings and restaurants to walking tours and sightseeing.

If you'd like information and literature before leaving home, contact one of the HKTA offices in the United States: 590 Fifth Avenue, New York, NY 10036 (tel. 212/869-5008); Suite 2400, 333 North Michigan Avenue, Chicago, IL 60601 (tel. 312/782-3872); Suite 404, 360 Post Street, San Francisco, CA 94108 (tel. 415/781-4582); and Suite 1220, 10940 Wilshire Boulevard, Los Angeles, CA 90024 (tel. 213/208-4582). There are also HKTA offices at 347 Bay Street, Suite 909, Toronto, Ontario, Canada M5H 2R7 (tel. 416/366-2389); 125 Pall Mall, London SW1Y 5EA, England (tel. 01/930-4775); and National Australia Bank House, 20th Floor, 255 George Street, Sydney, N.S.W. 2000, Australia (tel. 02/251-2855).

2. Passports and Other Documents

A valid passport is the only document most tourists, including Americans, need to enter Hong Kong. Americans can stay up to one month without a visa. Australians, Canadians, and other British Commonwealth citizens can stay for three months without a visa, while those from the United Kingdom can stay for six months. If you wish to stay longer or have any questions once you're in Hong Kong, contact the **Hong Kong Immigration Dept.,** 61 Mody Rd., East Tsimshatsui (tel. 7333111).

3. Currency and Credit Cards

The basic unit of currency in the colony is the **Hong Kong dollar.** Two local banks, the Hongkong Bank and the Standard Chartered Bank, both issue notes in denominations of HK$10, HK$20, HK$50, HK$100, HK$500, and HK$1,000. In 1985 new notes were introduced that are smaller than the older notes, which you may still see. As for coins, they're minted in England in bronze for HK$.10, HK$.20, and HK$.50 pieces and in silver for HK$1, HK$2, and HK$5.

Throughout Hong Kong you'll see the dollar sign ("$"), which refers to Hong Kong dollars, not to U.S. dollars. To prevent confusion, this guide identifies Hong Kong dollars with the symbol **"HK$."** Although rates flucuate a little, all conversions in this book are based on HK$7.70 to $1 U.S. (and then rounded off), a rate that has remained fairly constant for the past several years. If the exchange rate changes drastically, however, plan your budget accordingly.

To help you deal with money in Hong Kong, we have provided a currency conversion chart in the Appendix at the back of this book.

CHANGING MONEY
When exchanging money in Hong Kong, you'll get the best deal at banks, because they don't charge a commission except on traveler's checks. The exchange rate can vary among banks, however, so it may pay to shop around if you're exchanging large quantities.

Hotels give a slightly less favorable exchange rate but are convenient because they're open at night and on weekends. Money changers are found in the tourist areas, especially along Nathan Road in Tsimshatsui. Avoid them if you can. They often charge a commission or a "changing fee," or give a much lower rate. Check exactly how much you'll get in return *before* handing over your money. If you exchange money at Kai Tak Airport, you'll be charged a 5% service fee. Therefore, if you want to exchange cash or cash American Express traveler's checks at the American Express office at the airport, change only what you need to get into town—$10 (U.S.) should be enough.

CREDIT CARDS

Many of the smaller shops in Hong Kong will give a better price if you pay in cash, but you'll also want to take along credit cards to avoid carrying large amounts of bills. Most shops accept international credit cards, although some of the smaller ones do not. Look to see whether there are credit-card signs displayed on the front door or in the shop. Credit cards readily accepted include American Express, VISA, and MasterCard. Note, however, that shops have to pay an extra fee for transactions that take place with a credit card—and they will try to pass on that expense to you. Keep this in mind if you're bargaining for something (more on this later in the shopping chapter), and make sure the shopkeeper knows whether you're going to pay with cash or plastic. All the major hotels and better restaurants accept credit cards, but the budget establishments often don't.

CASH MACHINES

American Express cardholders have access to Jetco automated-teller machines and can withdraw local currency or traveler's checks at the Express Cash machine at the New World Tower, Central. Holders of VISA cards can obtain local currency from the Hongkong Bank "Electronic Money" machine located at the airport and approximately ten other convenient locations.

4. When to Go

Hong Kong's peak tourist season used to be in spring and autumn, but now tourists are flocking to the territory all year round. No matter when you go, therefore, make hotel reservations beforehand, particularly if you're arriving during the Chinese New Year or one of the festivals described below.

CLIMATE

Because of its subtropical location, Hong Kong's weather is generally mild in winter and hot and humid in summer, with an average annual rainfall of 89 inches. The most pleasant time of year is late September to early December, when skies are clear and sunny, temperatures range in the 70s, and the humidity drops to 70%. January and February are the coldest months, with temperatures often in the 50s. In spring (March to May), the temperature can vary between 60°F and 80°F and the humidity rises to about 84%, with fog and rain fairly common. That means there may not be much of a view from the cloud-enveloped Victoria Peak.

By summer, temperatures are often in the 90s, humidity can be 90% or more, and there's little or no relief even at night. This is when Hong Kong receives its most rain; it's also typhoon season. However, Hong Kong has a very good warning system, so there's no need to worry about the physical dangers of a tropical storm. The worst that can happen is that you may have to stay in your hotel room for a day or more or that your plane may be delayed or diverted. It has never happened to me, but it happened to a friend of mine—she was glad she was staying at the Regent instead of Chungking Mansion, since she was confined to her hotel for an entire weekend.

Average Monthly Temperatures in Hong Kong

	Jan	Feb	Mar	Apr	May	June	July	Aug	Sept	Oct	Nov	Dec
°C	15	15	18	22	25	27	29	29	27	25	21	18
°F	59	59	64	72	77	80	84	84	80	77	70	64

FESTIVALS

If you're lucky, your trip might coincide with one of Hong Kong's colorful festivals or annual events. Because most of them follow the Chinese lunar calendar, they don't fall on the same date each year. The only time shops and offices close for festival time is during the Chinese New Year, though many in Tsimshatsui remain open to cater to tourists.

Below are the most popular festivals, including Chinese festivals and festivals of the arts. Other celebrations worth catching include Buddha's Birthday, usually in late May, and the Festival of the Hungry Ghosts, held at the end of August when offerings of food and carefully crafted paper replicas of life's necessities are burned at roadsides to appease the ghosts that are allowed to come back for one day to roam the earth.

Chinese New Year

The most important Chinese holiday, this is a family festival with visits paid to friends and relatives. Falling in either late January or February, it's a time for settling debts, visiting fortune tellers, and worshipping ancestors. Most shops (except those around tourist areas) close down for two to three days, streets are decorated, and a fireworks display is held over the harbor. Since this festival is largely a family affair (much like the Christian Christmas), it holds little of interest to the tourist. In fact, you should remember that if you're planning a side trip into China, this is the worst time to go, since all routes to the mainland are clogged with Hong Kong Chinese going back to their homeland to visit relatives. Dates for the Chinese New Year are January 27 in 1990 and February 15 in 1991.

Hong Kong Arts Festival

Held in January or February, the Hong Kong Arts Festival is a month-long celebration with performances by world-renowned orchestras, early music to pop and jazz ensembles, and dance and theater companies, as well as art exhibitions. Contact the Hong Kong Tourist Association for exact dates and a list of performances.

Hong Kong International Film Festival

Held usually in April, the International Film Festival has been gaining recognition and popularity for the scope of its films. Again, contact the HKTA for a list of this year's films.

Tin Hau Festival

This is one of Hong Kong's most colorful festivals. Tin Hau, Hong Kong's most popular deity among fishing folk, is goddess of the sea. Legend has it that Tin Hau was a fisherman's daughter who braved a terrible storm to lead a fishing fleet to the safety of shore. To pay her tribute, fishing boats are decorated with colorful flags and family shrines are carried to shore to be blessed by Taoist priests. There are big celebrations at Joss House Bay and the temple at Yuen Long. This festival falls on April 18 in 1990 and on May 7 in 1991.

Cheung Chau Bun Festival

Held in May on the island of Cheung Chau, this week-long affair is thought to appease restless ghosts and spirits. Originally held to placate the unfortunate souls of people murdered by pirates, it features a street parade of lions and dragons, as well as floats with children seemingly suspended in the air, held up by cleverly concealed wires. The end of the festival is heralded by three scaffolds erected in front of the Pak Tai Temple which are covered with buns. These buns supposedly bring good luck to those who receive them. The 1990 and 1991 dates for this festival have not been set as we go to press. The HKTA may have more information by the time you plan your trip.

Dragon Boat Races

Races of long and narrow boats, gaily painted and powered by oarsmen, are held every year in June. It's an exciting event, and tour operators run cruises so that visitors can watch the events from a junk, ferry, or cruiser. This festival dates from ancient China, when legend has it that an imperial advisor drowned himself in a Hunan river to protest government corruption. His faithful followers, wishing to recover his body, supposedly raced out in the river in boats, beating paddles on the surface of the water and throwing rice to distract sea creatures from his body. Upcoming dates for this event are May 28, 1990, and June 16, 1991.

Mid-Autumn Festival

Held in early autumn, this festival celebrates the harvest and the brightest moon of the year, and is sometimes referred to as the Moon Festival. In honor of the event, the locals light lanterns, gaze at the moon, and eat mooncakes (sweet rolls with sesame seeds, duck eggs, and ground lotus seeds). The mooncakes commemorate the 14th-century uprising against the Mongols, when written messages calling for the revolt were concealed in cakes smuggled to the rebels. Today the Urban Council organizes lantern carnivals in parks on both Hong Kong Island and Kowloon, where you can join the Chinese for strolls under hundreds of lanterns. Popular places for viewing include Victoria Park in Causeway Bay and on Victoria Peak. This festival falls on October 3, 1990, and September 22, 1991.

HOLIDAYS

Hong Kong has 17 public holidays a year, including some of the festivals described above. Although some of them are British holidays, the majority are Chinese and therefore are different each year according to the lunar calendar. Since many shops and restaurants remain open except perhaps during Chinese New Year, the holidays should not cause any inconvenience to visitors. Public holidays are: New Year's Day (January 1); Chinese New Year (January 27–30, 1990, and February 15–18, 1991); Easter (Good Friday, Easter Sunday, and Easter Monday); Ching Ming Festival (April 5); Dragon Boat Festival (May 28, 1990, and June 16, 1991); Liberation Day (last Saturday and Monday in August); day following the Mid-Autumn Festival (October 4, 1990, and September 23, 1991); Christmas (December 25); and Boxing Day (December 26).

---

5. What to Pack

Since Hong Kong has European and Asian department stores, you can probably find anything you might need during your stay. In fact, the best advice I can give is to arrive with an empty suitcase, because you're going to leave Hong Kong with a lot more than you came with. I now buy virtually all my clothing in Hong Kong, so I arrive with practically nothing. And if you plan to stay more than three days, you can have clothes custom-made. (See "Tailors" in the shopping chapter for more information.) You can even buy a reasonably priced suitcase here if you end up with too much—something I've had to do once or twice myself.

The Chinese, especially the younger generation, can be quite fashion-conscious, so you might feel underdressed in thongs and shorts. Still, young travelers, fresh off the beaches of Thailand or Bali, arrive in Hong Kong dressed exactly so, and no one gives them a second glance. Since Hong Kong's climate is subtropical, you can get away with light clothing most of the year. It's fine to dress casually and comfortably, especially during the day for sightseeing, but you'll want to bring something dressy for evening wear. The finest restaurants require coat and tie for the men and comparable attire for women. If you're coming on business, you should dress for the part, even if it's summer. After all, Hong Kong is still British, and you can bet that the British will be dressed for success.

Summers are hot and stuffy, so you'll be best off wearing light cottons or linens (if you're sensitive to air conditioning, bring a light, long-sleeved shirt). If you're coming in spring or autumn, be sure to bring a light jacket for cooler nights, because the weather can be unpredictable. In winter you'll definitely need a jacket or sweater, since cold winds sometimes blow in from China. And no matter what the time of year, you'd be wise to pack an umbrella, particularly if you're going to be here in the wetter summer months.

I also wear a moneybelt in Hong Kong for my passport and money, though almost all hotels have safety-deposit boxes. As for my trusty Swiss army knife, I've learned to pack it in my check-in luggage, not my carry-on; otherwise it will be confiscated at the x-ray security machine and returned after the flight. I guess the airline doesn't want me to hijack a plane wielding my scissors or can opener.

Otherwise, let common sense prevail when packing for your trip: comfortable walking shoes, sunglasses, personal medications, etc. But as I said, the only things you absolutely must bring with you to Hong Kong are your plane tickets, passport, and credit cards. All the rest is available here.

---

6. Health Preparations

No shots or inoculations are required for entry to Hong Kong from the United States, but you will need proof of a vaccination against cholera if you have been in an infected area during the 14 days prior to your arrival. Check with your travel agent or call the Hong Kong Tourist Authority if you are traveling through Asia before reaching Hong Kong.

If you need a prescription from a Hong Kong doctor filled while in Hong Kong, there are plenty of drugstores in the territory. They will not, however, fill prescriptions from elsewhere. Refer to the "Fast Facts About Hong Kong" section of Chapter IV for specific addresses.

TIPS FOR THE DISABLED

If you are in a wheelchair, contact the Hong Kong Tourist Association to ask whether you can receive a free booklet called "A Guide for Physically Handicapped Visitors to Hong Kong." It lists more than 200 sites with information on vehicle access, how many steps the entrance has and whether there's a ramp, whether toilets are equipped for the handicapped, access to public telephones, seating, etc. Included is information on individual hotels, restaurants, shops, movie theaters, performing arts venues, libraries, museums, places of worship, and recreational facilities.

GETTING THERE

1. BY AIR
2. BY TRAIN
3. BY SHIP

With more than 30 airlines and half a dozen cruise lines serving Hong Kong, it's certainly not difficult to get there. Your itinerary, the amount of time you have, and your pocketbook will probably dictate how you travel. Below are some pointers to get you headed in the right direction.

1. By Air

Airlines that fly between North American and Hong Kong include **Canadian Airlines International** (tel. toll free 800/426-7000), **Cathay Pacific Airways** (tel. toll free 800/233-2742), **China Airlines** (tel. toll free 800/227-5118), **Japan Airlines** (tel. toll free 800/525-3663), **Korean Air** (tel. toll free 800/223-1155), **Northwest Airlines** (tel. toll free 800/225-2525), **Philippine Airlines** (tel. toll free 800/435-9725), **Singapore Airlines** (tel. toll free 800/742-3333), **Thai Airways International** (tel. toll free 800/426-5204), and **United Airlines** (tel. toll free 800/241-6522).

AIRFARES
Depending on your ticket, prices—especially the cheapest fares—will probably vary according to the season. The most expensive time to go is usually during peak season, which is June through August and then again the last couple of weeks in December. The lowest fares are available January through March. Fares in between the two extremes, known as the shoulder season, are available in April and May and again from September to the middle of December. To complicate matters, each season also has different rates for both weekday and weekend flights.

APEX (Advance Purchase Excursion) fares are also available if you purchase your ticket in advance and comply with certain restrictions. Reservations, ticketing, and payment for the APEX fare must be completed usually no later than 21 days prior to departure, but rules vary depending on the airline. There's often a minimum time you can stay in Hong Kong, as well as a maximum stay.

Many airlines and tour operators also offer occasional **promotional fares** with tight restrictions, as well as package tours, which might be the cheapest way to go because packages include hotels, transfers, and more.

You might also consider including several **stopovers** on your trip to Hong Kong. One of the most popular routes is to purchase a ticket for Hong Kong that allows a stopover in Tokyo.

While **fares** may have changed by the time you plan your trip, as we go to press, year-round first-class round-trip fares are $4,580 from New York and $3,880 from the West Coast; business class is $2,720 from New York and $2,138 from the West Coast; and economy fares (with no restrictions) are $2,350 from New York and $1,768 from the West Coast. Round-trip APEX fares (with all their restrictions) can run as high as $1,459 for flying on a weekend in high season from New York to as low as $935 during the week in low season from the West Coast.

A Warning: Remember that all fares, rules, and regulations are subject to change. Be sure to contact your travel agent or the airlines for current information.

Since prices can vary according to your gateway, your route, the number of days spent abroad, the days you travel, and whether you travel first class or economy, your best bet is to shop around. As people living on the U.S. West Coast travel more frequently to Asia (those on the East Coast are more apt to go to Europe), it's a good idea to purchase a West Coast newspaper such as the *Los Angeles Times* to look over the advertisements for cheap fares. Call various travel agencies to inquire about charter flights, Super-APEX fares, or special promotional flights.

DISCOUNT TRAVEL AGENCIES

There are also companies that provide deeply discounted tickets (some more than 50% less than economy and 30% less than APEX) with no restrictions, depending on availability. You can buy your ticket through them well in advance as well as at the last moment, if you're lucky. Among the firms that deal with travel to Hong Kong (usually with a stop in Tokyo) are **Nippon Travel** (tel. 202/362-0039), **Japan Associates Travel** (tel. 202/939-8853), and **Japan Express Travel** (tel. 202/347-7730). Another large discount firm is **Euro-Asia Express** of Millbrae, California (tel. 415/692-9966, or toll free 800/782-9623 outside California). If you are a full-time student under 33 years of age with an International Student ID Card, try **STA Travel** of Los Angeles (tel. 213/934-8722 in Los Angeles, 617/266-6014 in Boston, 212/986-9470 in New York, or 415/391-8407 in San Francisco; or toll free 800/777-0112 from anywhere except Los Angeles County and New York City).

Consolidators like C. L. Thompson Express International in San Francisco and CNH International and Star Tours, Inc., in Los

Angeles also sell discounted tickets, but only through travel agents.

Note: When you arrive in Hong Kong, remember that you must confirm your ongoing or return flight reservation 72 hours prior to departure or you will loose your seat.

2. By Train

It's unlikely that you'll arrive in Hong Kong by train, unless of course you've been traveling the length of China. What's more likely is that you'll want to take a short trip into China (for which you'll need a visa) once you arrive in Hong Kong. Although the easiest way to spend a couple days in China is to join an organized tour, you can also travel to and from China on your own via the Kowloon-Canton Railway (KCR). (For more information on traveling to China, see Chapter X, Section 3.) In any case, if you're traveling to Hong Kong via train, you'll pass through Customs at Wo Lu, the border station, before continuing on the KCR to Hung Hom near East Tsimshatsui. The round-trip fare between Lo Wu and Hung Hom is HK$38 ($4.95). The Hung Hom station is practically in the middle of the city, though if you have a lot of luggage you might want to take a taxi to your hotel.

3. By Ship

Luxury cruise liners are a common sight in Hong Kong's harbor, anchored conveniently right next to the territory's largest shopping mall at Ocean Terminal. U.S.-based cruise lines that include stopovers in Hong Kong on journeys through the Orient include **Pearl Cruises** (tel. toll free 800/426-3588), **Princess Cruises** (tel. 213/553-1666), **Royal Cruise Line** (tel. 415/956-7200), and **Royal Viking Line** (tel. toll free 800/422-8000). Information on cruises can also be obtained from your travel agent.

GETTING TO KNOW HONG KONG

1. ORIENTATION
2. GETTING AROUND
3. FAST FACTS ABOUT HONG KONG

Hong Kong is an easy city to get to know because it's surprisingly compact and the streets are all clearly marked in English. Public transportation here is not only well-organized and a breeze to use, but the Star Ferry and the trams are themselves sightseeing attractions. However, walking the streets is the best way to see everything, particularly some of the fascinating lanes and alleys where transportation cannot go.

This chapter will tell you how to get to and from your hotel, explain the layout of the city and how to get around it, and provide you with facts about everything from airport information to weather and weights and measures.

---

1. Orientation

ARRIVING AT KAI TAK AIRPORT

Unless you've joined a luxury liner or are trekking across China, most likely you'll arrive in Hong Kong by plane. Hong Kong's Kai Tak Airport is one of the world's few airports right in the middle of a city. Located in the densely populated Kowloon Peninsula, it has one of the most spectacular runways in the world—built right out into the middle of the bay.

Upon arrival at Kai Tak Airport (tel. 7697531), one of the first things you'll want to do is stop by the counter of the **Hong Kong Tourist Association (HKTA)** in the arrivals hall, where you can pick up a map of the city, sightseeing brochures, and a wealth of other information. It's open from 8am to 10:30pm daily.

Next to HKTA is the counter of the **Hong Kong Hotel Association,** where you can book a room in one of its 60-some member hotels free of charge. Its hours are 7am to midnight every day. Note, however, that they do not have information on rock-bottom establishments; they can, on the other hand, book rooms in several low-priced lodgings and the YMCAs.

If you plan on traveling to Macau, you should also stop by the **Macau tourist information counter,** also in the arrival lobby. It's open from 9am to 10:30pm daily.

You can also **exchange money** at the airport, but since you'll be charged a 5% service fee you should exchange only what you need to get into town. About $10 (U.S.) should do it, and be sure to tell the bank officer that you need small change if you plan on taking the airport bus described below.

If you need to leave luggage at the airport, there are **luggage-storage counters** on both the departure and arrival floors. Other facilities at the airport include restaurants, pay phones, a police station, a post office, and a Cable and Wireless office for long-distance calls and telegrams.

A Note on Departure: The x-ray machines at the security gates in Kai Tak Airport are notoriously bad for film, so all photographers I know always ask for a hand inspection of film when leaving the country. In addition, keep in mind that when you leave Hong Kong you'll have to pay an airport departure tax of HK$100 ($13) for adults and HK$50 ($6.50) for children. Also, remember to reconfirm your ongoing or return flight reservation at least 72 hours before departure or you may loose your seat.

Customs

You're allowed to bring into Hong Kong duty free a 1-liter (34-ounce) bottle of alcohol, 200 cigarettes or 50 cigars, and a reasonable quantity of cosmetics and perfumes in opened bottles for personal use.

Getting to Your Hotel

Because Kai Tak Airport is so conveniently located, it's only a 20- to 30-minute ride to Tsimshatsui and a 40-minute ride to Central. During rush hours, however (8 to 9:30am and again from 4 to 6:30pm), it can take as long as an hour.

The cheapest and one of the easiest ways to travel between the airport and Hong Kong's major hotels is by the **Airbus coach service** (tel. 7454466). There are three different routes serving various hotels, with buses traveling every 15 minutes between 7am and 11pm. To find the buses, follow the "Airport Bus" signs from the arrivals lobby or ask at the HKTA counter. Note that *the Airbus requires exact fare.* Each bus stop generally services a cluster of hotels in the same vicinity, so make sure you know where to exit the bus for your particular hotel.

Airbus A1 travels through Kowloon and costs HK$6 (80¢). Take this bus if you're going to the Ambassador, Empress, Grand, Holiday Inn Golden Mile, Holiday Inn Harbour View, Hong Kong, Hyatt Regency, Imperial, International, Kowloon, Miramar, New Astor, New World, Nikko, Park, Peninsula, Ramada Inn Kowloon, Ramada Renaissance, Regal Meridien, Regent, Royal Garden,

Shangri-La, Sheraton, or Windsor Hotel, the YMCA on Salisbury Road, or Chungking Mansion.

The other two bus routes service Hong Kong Island, and both charge HK$8 ($1.05). Airbus A2 travels through Wanchai and Central before terminating at the old Macau Ferry Pier, making stops at or near the Furama, Harbour, Harbour View International House, Hilton, Mandarin Oriental, New Harbour, Ramada Inn Hong Kong, and the Victoria. Airbus A3 serves hotels in Causeway Bay, including the Caravelle, Excelsior, Lee Gardens, and Park Lane.

In addition to the Airbus, there are also **hotel shuttle buses** that pick up arriving passengers at Kai Tak and deliver them to the front doors of major hotels by three different routes. Fares vary depending on how far you're going, but it cost me HK$30 ($3.90) to get to Tsimshatsui. These air-conditioned coaches leave every 15 minutes from 7am to 11pm. To return to the airport, ask at your hotel about pickup points and departure times or call 7454466.

The easiest way to travel, of course, is by **taxi,** which is very cheap in Hong Kong. A taxi to Tsimshatsui costs about HK$30 ($3.90), while a taxi to Central District costs HK$60 ($7.80) because of the extra charge levied for crossing the harbor tunnel. There's also an extra luggage charge of HK$2 (25¢) per piece of baggage.

TOURIST INFORMATION

There are four **Hong Kong Tourist Association (HKTA)** offices ready to serve you in Hong Kong. As mentioned above, one is in the arrivals lobby of Kai Tak Airport, open from 8am to 10:30pm daily. Another convenient office is located in Tsimshatsui right in the Star Ferry concourse, and hours here are 8am to 6pm daily. If you're in East Tsimshatsui, there's a new office on the ground floor of the Royal Garden Hotel, 69 Mody Rd., open from 9am to 6pm weekdays and 9am to 1pm on Saturday and Sunday.

On the Hong Kong Island side you'll find the main office for HKTA in the basement, Shop 8, of the Jardine House (formerly the Connaught Centre), in the Central District. It's located to the right as you exit the Star Ferry and is the tall building with all those round windows. It's closed on Sunday and public holidays but otherwise is open Monday through Friday from 8am to 6pm and on Saturday until 1pm.

If you have a question about Hong Kong, you can call the **HKTA hotline** (tel. 7225555). This service is available from 8am to 6pm daily. If you call after office hours, an answering machine should ask for your telephone number so that a staff member can return your call the next day.

The HKTA is prolific in turning out a great variety of **free literature** about Hong Kong. You'd be wise, therefore, to make the tourist office your first stop, which is easy because there are so many locations. Brochures I find particularly useful are "Quick Guide to Hong Kong," "Places of Interest by Public Transport," "Museums & Arts & Crafts," "Outlying Islands," and "The Official Guide to Shopping, Eating Out and Services in Hong Kong."

You can also get a **free map** of Hong Kong from HKTA, which gives closeups of Tsimshatsui, the Central District, Wanchai, and Causeway Bay.

The Official Hong Kong Guide, published monthly, is available free in guest rooms of most upper- and medium-range hotels and has a lot of practical information and sightseeing advice on the colony. It's also available at HKTA offices for HK$10 ($1.30).

Two tourist tabloids distributed free in hotel lobbies and tourist places are *Hong Kong* and *Orient.* Although filled mostly with advertisements, they're published weekly and have some information on what's going on in Hong Kong. *Hong Kong Visitor,* published by the *South China Morning Post,* is also valuable for information on what's happening in the colony.

CITY LAYOUT

Most of Hong Kong's hotels, restaurants, nightlife entertainment, shops, and businesses are located in four areas: Tsimshatsui on the Kowloon side; and Central District, Wanchai, and Causeway Bay, all of which are on Hong Kong Island. Because these areas are so compact, the city must rank as Asia's most accessible and navigable city.

Hong Kong Island

If there is a heart of Hong Kong, it surely lies in the **Central District,** referred to by the locals as simply **Central.** It's the financial and commercial center of the city, and if Hong Kong did have such a thing as a "downtown," Central would be it. Located on the northern coast of Hong Kong Island, it has the island's concourse for the Star Ferry and its own subway station, both of which connect it to Tsimshatsui across Victoria Harbour. In addition, Hong Kong's two-tiered trams run right through the heart of Central on their way from Causeway Bay to the Western District, and it's here that buses depart for Stanley, Ocean Park, Aberdeen, and other attractions on the island's south side. The most important streets that bisect Central are **Des Voeux Road Central** with its tram line, **Queen's Road Central, Pedder Street, Ice House Street,** and **Connaught Road Central.**

The Central District boasts a handful of first-class hotels, a few department stores and expensive shopping centers, office buildings, and restaurants and pubs that cater to Hong Kong's white-collar workers, but banks are so important to the Central District that their impact is highly visible—the Hongkong Bank and the Bank of China are just two examples of modern architecture that have dramatically transformed the Central District's skyline in the past decade (the Bank of China, by the way, is the innovation of I. M. Pei, an American-Chinese architect who also designed the new glass pyramids for the Louvre in Paris). In fact, if it's been 20 years since you've seen Hong Kong, you won't be able to recognize Central, so drastically has its skyline changed.

But even though the Central District is where you'll find many of Hong Kong's most futuristic high-rise buildings, fashionable boutiques, and expensive restaurants, it's also riddled with tradi-

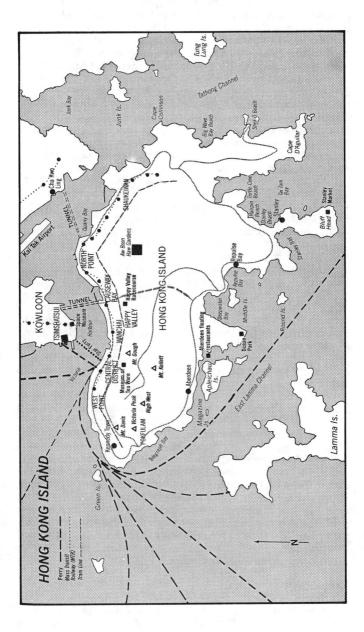

HONG KONG ISLAND

Ferry — — —
Mass Transit
Railway (MTR) ·········
Tram Line — — —

HONG KONG ISLAND

Green Is.

Magazine Is.

Telegraph Bay

Mt. Davis △
△ Victoria Peak
High West △

POKFULAM
WEST POINT
Kennedy Town

CENTRAL DISTRICT
Museum of Tea Ware ■
Mt. Gough △
Mt. Kellett △

Aberdeen ●
Apleichau Is.

Aberdeen floating restaurants
Ocean Park ■

Deepwater Bay
Middle Is.
Round Is.

Repulse Bay
Repulse Bay ●

East Lamma Channel

Lamma Is.

Stanley Bay
Stanley Market ■
Stanley ●
Stanley Beach
Bluff Head ■

Chung Hom Kok Beach
Turtle Cove Beach

Tai Tam Bay

Cape D'Aguilar

Shek O Beach
Big Wave Bay Beach

Cape Collinson

HONG KONG ISLAND

Aw Boon Haw Gardens ■

Happy Valley Racecourse
HAPPY VALLEY
WANCHAI
CAUSEWAY BAY
NORTH POINT

SHAUKEIWAN

Quarry Bay

TUNNEL

Cha Kwo Ling ●

Junk Bay

Junk Is.

Tathong Channel

Tung Lung Is.

Kai Tak Airport

KOWLOON
TSIMSHATSUI
Space Museum ■
Star Ferry
Victoria Harbour
TUNNEL

N →

tional Chinese restaurants, outdoor markets, and the neon signs of family-run businesses. It even has its own burgeoning nightlife district, along Lan Kwai Fong Street and D'Aguilar Street.

To the south of Central are the Zoological and Botanical Gardens and the famous Victoria Peak with its spectacular 360° view of most of the territory and the outlying islands in the China Sea.

Although there isn't much in Central that reflects the colonial days of the past, its neighbor, called the **Western District,** is one of the most fascinating areas of Hong Kong Island. One of the first communities settled by colonialists back in the 1800s, ironically it's now the island's most Chinese district. This is one of my own personal favorites in the entire colony, and I've spent days wandering its narrow streets and inspecting shops selling traditional herbs, medicines, dried fish, antiques, and other Chinese products.

On the other side of the Central District to the east is **Wanchai,** which became notorious after World War II for its sleazy bars, easy women, tattoo parlors, and sailors off the ships looking for a good time. Richard Mason's 1957 novel, *The World of Suzie Wong,* describes this bygone era of Wanchai, which later during the Vietnam War also served as a popular destination for American servicemen on R&R. Although some of the nightlife entertainment remains, Wanchai has slowly become respectable with the addition of new hotels, more high-rises, and the Hong Kong Arts Centre.

If you follow any of the major thoroughfares—Hennessy Road, Lockhart Road, Jaffe Road, or Gloucester Road—all the way through Wanchai to the east, you'll soon come upon another important neighborhood of Hong Kong Island, **Causeway Bay.** It gets its name from the fact that the whole area was once indeed a bay, until land reclamation turned water into soil several decades ago. A busy area of Japanese department stores, boutiques, nightclubs, and restaurants, this is where you'll find Food Street, a pedestrian lane lined with both Western and Chinese eateries popular with Hong Kong locals. On its eastern perimeter is the large Victoria Park, and beyond that the colorful Aw Boon Haw (Tiger Balm) Gardens.

The south side of Hong Kong Island has its own attractions. Once a fishing village, but now studded with high-rises and housing projects, **Aberdeen** is still known for its hundreds of sampans, junks, and boat people, and its huge floating restaurants. Just to the east, in **Deep Water Bay,** are Ocean Park with its botanical gardens, impressive aquarium, and a re-creation of an old Chinese village called Middle Kingdom, and Ocean World with its beaches and pools open in summer. There are more beaches farther east in **Repulse Bay,** and finally there's **Stanley,** once a fishing village and now a lively center for discount markets selling everything from overrun designer jeans to rattanware.

Kowloon

North of Hong Kong Island, across **Victoria Harbour,** is the Kowloon Peninsula. Kowloon gets its name from *Gau Lung,* which means "nine dragons." Legend has it that about 800 years ago a boy emperor named Ping counted eight hills here and remarked that there must be eight dragons living here, since dragons were known to inhabit hills. His prime minister pointed out that in actuality there were nine dragons, since an emperor is also considered to be a dragon.

You'd have a hard time finding eight hills in Kowloon today. Less than 3½ square miles in size, Kowloon, once open countryside, has practically disappeared under the dense spread of hotels, shops, restaurants, and housing and industrial projects.

At the southern tip of Kowloon is **Tsimshatsui** (also spelled Tsim Sha Tsui), which, after Central, rates as Hong Kong's most important region. Both the Star Ferry and the subway connect Tsimshatsui with Central on the other side of the harbor, and buses departing from the Tsimshatsui **Star Ferry** concourse deliver passengers to other points in Kowloon and beyond.

Tsimshatsui is where most tourists spend the night and their money, since it has the greatest concentration of hotels, restaurants, and shops in the colony. In fact, some of my acquaintances living in Hong Kong avoid Tsimshatsui like the plague, calling it the "tourist ghetto." On the other hand, Tsimshatsui does boast the Space Museum, a new cultural center for the performing arts, one of the world's largest shopping malls, a good and varied selection of international restaurants, a jumping nightlife, and Nathan Road, appropriately nicknamed the "golden mile of shopping." Although you'd be foolish to spend all your time in Tsimshatsui, you'd be foolish also to miss it.

East of Tsimshatsui is an area called, appropriately enough, **East Tsimshatsui.** Built entirely on reclaimed land, this area is becoming increasingly important, with a rash of new hotels, entertainment centers, shopping and restaurant complexes, a coliseum, and on its eastern edge, the Kowloon Railway Station, terminus for the Kowloon-Canton Railway that carries passengers through the New Territories and beyond to China.

If you get on the subway in Tsimshatsui and go two stations to the north (or walk for about 25 minutes straight up Nathan Road), you'll reach the **Yaumatei** district (also spelled Yau Ma Tei). Like the Western District, Yaumatei is also very Chinese, with an interesting produce market, a jade market, and the fascinating Temple Street Night Market.

Farther north are the **New Territories** (see the "Exploring the Environs" chapter later on) and China itself.

FINDING AN ADDRESS

If you have a good map (aside from the maps in this book, the one distributed free at HKTA is adequate for Hong Kong's main areas), you should have no problem finding an address since the system is the same as in North America. Streets are all identified in English, and numbers of buildings progress consecutively. For the most part, streets that run east to west (such as Des Voeux Road Central, Hennessy, Lockhart Road, or Salisbury Road) all have the even-numbered buildings on the north side of the street and the odd-numbered ones on the south. From Central, roads running through Wanchai all the way west to Causeway Bay start with the lowest numbers near Central, with the highest-numbered buildings ending at Causeway Bay. On Nathan Road, Kowloon's most important thoroughfare, the lowest-numbered buildings are at the southern tip near the harbor; the numbers rise consecutively, with the evens on the east and the odds to the west.

The main thing to remember is that the floors inside buildings follow the British system of numbering. That is, what we would call the first floor in the United States is called the ground floor in Hong Kong. Our second floor, therefore, is called the first floor in Hong Kong. In addition, if you're trying to find a specific office or factory outlet in a big building, it's useful to know that a number 714 means it's on the seventh floor in Room 14, while 2312 means Room 12 on the 23rd floor.

2. Getting Around

If you've just been to Tokyo, Bangkok, or some other sprawling Asian metropolis, Hong Kong may seem just like home. For one thing, English is everywhere—on street signs, on buses, in the subways. In addition, the city of Hong Kong is so compact, and its public transportation system so efficient, it's no problem at all zipping from Tsimshatsui to Causeway Bay or vice versa for a meal or some shopping. Even the novice traveler should have no problem getting around, so extensive and easy is the public transport. It's also extremely cheap. Just remember that cars drive on the left hand side of the street, English style, so watch it when stepping off the curb.

One thing you should keep in mind, however, is that *buses and trams require the exact fare.* It's therefore imperative to have a lot of loose change with you wherever you go. Even though the ferries and subways will give change, you'll find it more convenient if you have exact change, especially during rush hours. If you plan to do a lot of traveling by public transport, pick up a brochure called "Places of Interest by Public Transport," available free at Hong Kong Tourist Association offices.

BY PUBLIC TRANSPORTATION

By Ferry

THE STAR FERRY A trip across Victoria Harbour on one of the white-and-green ferries of the Star Ferry Company is one of the most celebrated rides in the world. Carrying passengers back and forth between Hong Kong Island and Kowloon ever since 1898, these boats have come to symbolize Hong Kong itself and are almost always featured in travel articles on Hong Kong Island. They are all named after stars—such as the *Twinkling Star* or the *Meridien Star.*

They're very easy to ride. Simply drop your coin into a slot on the ancient-looking turnstile, follow the crowd in front of you down the ramp, walk over the gangway, and find a seat on one of the

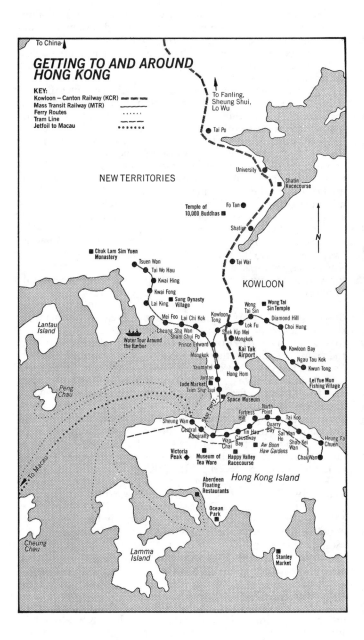

GETTING TO AND AROUND HONG KONG

KEY:
Kowloon – Canton Railway (KCR)
Mass Transit Railway (MTR)
Ferry Routes
Tram Line
Jetfoil to Macau

To China

To Fanling,
Sheung Shui,
Lo Wu

Tai Po

University

Shatin
Racecourse

NEW TERRITORIES

Temple of 10,000 Buddhas

Fo Tan

Shatin

N

Chuk Lam Sim Yuen Monastery

Tsuen Wan

Tai Wo Hau

Kwai Hing

Kwai Fong

Lai King

Sung Dynasty Village

Tai Wai

KOWLOON

Mei Foo

Lai Chi Kok

Kowloon Tong

Wong Tai Sin

Wong Tai Sin Temple

Diamond Hill

Lok Fu

Choi Hung

Lantau Island

Water Tour Around the Harbor

Cheung Sha Wan

Sham Shui Po

Prince Edward

Shek Kip Mei

Mongkok

Kai Tak Airport

Kowloon Bay

Ngau Tau Kok

Mongkok

Yaumatei

Jordan

Jade Market

Tsim Sha Tsui

Hong Hom

Kwun Tong

Lei Yue Mun Fishing Village

Peng Chau

Space Museum

Star Ferry

North Point

Fortress Hill

Tai Koo

Sheung Wan

Central

Admiralty

Wan Chai

Tin Hau

Causeway Bay

Quarry Bay

Sai Wan Ho

Shau Kei Wan

Chai Wan

Heung Fa Chuen

To Macau

Victoria Peak

Museum of Tea Ware

Happy Valley Racecourse

Aw Boon Haw Gardens

Hong Kong Island

Aberdeen Floating Restaurants

Ocean Park

Cheung Chau

Lamma Island

Stanley Market

polished wooden benches. A whistle will blow, a man in a sailor uniform will haul up the gangway, and you're off, dodging fishing boats, tugboats, and barges as you make your way across the harbor. Business people who live in Hong Kong are easy to spot—they're all buried behind their newspapers. The visitors are all crowded at the railing, cameras in hand.

The whole trip is much too short, only seven minutes. But that seven-minute ride is one of the best in the world, and it's also one of the cheapest. It costs only HK$.60 (8¢) for ordinary (second) class; if you really want to splurge, dish out HK$1 (13¢) for first class. First class is on the upper deck, with its own entryway and gangway (follow the signs in the ferry concourse), and is a good idea if it's raining or cold because it has glass windows surrounding it. Otherwise I find ordinary class much more colorful and entertaining because it's the one the locals use and the view of the harbor is much better. Signs admonish passengers to watch out for pickpockets, to refrain from spitting on the deck, and to remain seated until the ferry docks.

Star ferries ply the waters daily from 6:30am to 11:30pm between Hong Kong Island's Central District and the tip of Kowloon's Tsimshatsui. Ferries depart every few minutes, except for early in the morning or late at night when they leave every 10 minutes.

OTHER FERRIES Besides the Star Ferry above, there are also many ferries to other parts of the colony. Ferries from the Central District, for example, also go to Kowloon's Hung Hom, where you can catch the train to China at the Kowloon Railway Station, and to the Yaumatei Ferry Pier, close to Jordan Road. From Tsimshatsui a service operates to Wanchai.

In addition to ferries traversing the waters between Kowloon and Hong Kong Island, there's also a large fleet of ferries that serve the many outlying islands and the northern part of the mainland. If you want to go to one of Hong Kong's outlying islands, you'll find most of the ferries to the islands departing from the Outlying Islands Ferry Pier, located an easy walk west of Central's Star Ferry terminus. Operated by the Hong Kong Ferry Company Ltd. (HKF), these boats vary in size; some even have outdoor deck areas in first class. The latest schedules and fares are available in a list compiled by the Hong Kong Tourist Association (HKTA) or by calling HKF (tel. 5423081). One thing to keep in mind is that on weekends the ferries are unbelievably crowded with locals wishing to escape the city; and on weekends the fares also increase. It's best, therefore, to travel on a weekday. More information on ferries to specific islands is given in the chapter "Exploring the Environs."

By Tram

After the Star Ferry, the second most romantic way to get around is by tram, which is found only on Hong Kong Island. Set up in 1904 along what used to be the waterfront, these are old, narrow, double-decker affairs that clank their way in a straight line slowly along the northern edge of the island from Kennedy Town in the west to Shau Kei Wan in the east, with one branch making a detour to Happy Valley. Passing through the Central District, Wanchai, and Causeway Bay on Des Voeux Road, Queensway Road, and Hennessy Road, they can't be beat for atmosphere and are easy to ride since most of them go only on one line (those branching off to Happy Valley are clearly marked). In the zealousness of Central's modernization, it's a wonder that these trams have survived at all. Since the advent of the subway, there's talk of getting rid of these ancient trams, so ride them while you can.

Enter trams from the back and go immediately up the winding stairs to the top deck. The best seats in the house are those in the front row, where you have an unparalleled view of Hong Kong: laundry hanging from second-story windows, signs hanging over the street, markets twisting down side streets, food stalls, crowded sidewalks, and people darting in front of the tram who you'll swear couldn't have made it. This is one of the cheapest methods for a sightseeing tour of Hong Kong Island's northern side, and the fare is the same no matter how far you go. Once you've had enough, simply go downstairs to the front of the tram and pay the exact fare of HK$.60 (8¢) into a little tin box next to the bus driver as you exit. If you don't have the exact fare, don't have a heart attack—no one will arrest you for overpaying with a HK$1 (13¢) coin. Trams run from 5:40am to 1am.

By Subway

The Star Ferry and trams are so popular and crowded that it's hard to imagine what they must have been like *before* Hong Kong's subway system was constructed to relieve the human crunch. Hong Kong's **Mass Transit Railway (MTR)** is modern, efficient, clean, and easy to use, and it's also much faster than the older modes of transportation. The only hard thing about it is trying to remain seated on its slick, stainless-steel seats (you may laugh now, but wait till you've tried it). Also, take note that there are no public toilets at any of the stations or on the trains, and that smoking, drinking, and eating are prohibited. You'll probably want to avoid rush hours, unless you enjoy feeling like a sardine in a can. The MTR is in operation from 6am to 1am.

Built primarily to transport commuters in the New Territories to and from work, it runs under the harbor to link Hong Kong Island with Kowloon. There are only three lines on the 24-mile subway system, and stations are clearly marked in English, so you shouldn't have any problems finding your way around. The most important line for tourists is the one that starts in Central on Hong Kong Island, goes underneath Victoria Harbour to Tsimshatsui, and then runs north the length of Nathan Road to Tsuen Wan, with stops at Jordan and Yaumatei stations. Another line on the Kowloon Peninsula travels north and east to Kwun Tong. The Island Line, with 14 stations, operates on the north side of Hong Kong Island from Sheung Wan (where you'll find the Macau Ferry Pier) east to Chai Wan, passing through Central, Wanchai, and Causeway Bay.

Fares range from HK$2.50 (30¢) to HK$6 (80¢), depending

on the distance, but the most expensive ride is the trip underneath the harbor, which costs HK$4.50 (60¢) from Tsimshatsui to Central (still cheap, but outrageous when compared to the Star Ferry). Fares are posted in English above each vending machine, which, unfortunately, do not give change. They accept HK$2, HK$1, and HK$.50 coins, and if you put in too much the next person in line benefits (though you can cancel the entire operation and get back the whole amount you've put in). If you don't have the right amount, there are change machines close by for coins and information desks for bills.

In any case, your ticket is plastic and the size of a credit card, which you feed into a slot at the turnstile. It disappears and then shoots up at the other end of the turnstile. *Be sure to save your ticket for the end of your journey,* when you will again insert your ticket into the turnstile, only this time you won't get it back. Since these tickets are used again and again and have a magnetized strip, be careful not to bend or damage them.

If you think you're going to be doing a lot of traveling on the MTR, then buy the **MTR/KCR Tourist Ticket,** which can also be used for travel on the Kowloon-Canton Railway (KCR) described below. It saves you from having to buy another ticket each time you ride and costs HK$20 ($2.60) for HK$20-worth of transportation. It's used just like a regular ticket, and the computerized gate will figure out how much each journey costs and deduct it from the balance left on your card. Remember to collect your ticket from the turnstile after each journey.

You can purchase the MTR/KCR Tourist Ticket from any Hong Kong Tourist Association office, from all MTR and KCR station booking offices (except at Lo Wu Station) and from the Hang Seng mini-banks located inside major MTR stations. Be sure to bring your passport to show you're a bonafide tourist, and tickets must be purchased within 14 days of your arrival.

By Train

There's only one train line in Hong Kong and it goes from Hung Hom in East Tsimshatsui in Kowloon up to Sheung Shui in the New Territories. That is, Sheung Shui is where you have to get off if you don't have a visa to go to China. If you do have a visa, you can continue to the border, change trains, and travel all the way through China—and even Russia and Europe if you want to, ending up in London (but who knows how many years that would take). There are two different kinds of trains: the express for people going through to China, which goes to the border station of Lo Wu; and the local commuter service for those going to towns in the New Territories.

Known as the **Kowloon–Canton Railway (KCR),** it passes through Mongkok, Kowloon Tong, Tai Wai, Shatin, Fo Tan, University, Tai Po Market, and Fanling before reaching Sheung Shui. The easiest place to board the KCR is at Kowloon Tong, since it's also a subway stop and transfer is easy. At any rate, the whole trip on the train from Kowloon to Sheung Shui takes only a half hour on Hong Kong's new electric trains, so it's the easiest and fastest way to see part of the New Territories. It's also cheap, costing HK$5.40 (70¢) for ordinary (second) class and HK$11 ($1.45) for first class if you go all the way to Sheung Shui. Children under 12 pay half fare; those under 3 travel free. On horse racing days at Shatin, there's a flat-fare, round-trip ticket to the Shatin Race Course for HK$13 ($1.70). The MTR/KCR Tourist Ticket, which costs HK$20 ($2.60), allows HK$20-worth of travel on both the subway and ordinary class of the KCR. Trains run every 3 to 20 minutes from about 6am to midnight.

By Bus

Buses are good for traveling to places where other forms of public transport don't go, such as to the southern part of Hong Kong Island or up into parts of Kowloon and the New Territories. Depending on the route, buses run from about 6am to midnight, with fares ranging from HK$1.20 (15¢) to HK$9 ($1.15). *You must have the exact fare,* which you pay as you get on. Drivers often don't speak English, so you may want to have someone at your hotel write down your destination in Chinese, particularly if you're traveling in the New Territories. The two major bus terminals are at both ends of the Star Ferry, in the Central District on Hong Kong Island and in Tsimshatsui in Kowloon.

The HKTA has leaflets that give bus routes to most of the major tourist spots, indicating where you can catch the bus, where to get off, and how long the journey should take. Keep in mind that buses can get very crowded at rush hours and that some buses look pretty ancient—which can make the winding trip to Stanley in a double-decker bus a bone-rattling and exciting experience.

BY TAXI

As a rule taxi drivers in Hong Kong are strictly controlled and are fairly honest. If they're free to pick up passengers, a red "For Hire" flag will be raised in the windshield during the day and a lighted "Taxi" sign will be on the roof at night. You can hail them from the street, though there are some restricted areas, especially in Central. Probably the easiest place to pick up a taxi is at a taxi stand (located at all bus terminals) or at a hotel. Since many drivers do not speak English, it's a good idea to have your destination written in Chinese. Taxis are generally abundant anytime except rainy days, during shift change (which is usually at 4pm), and on horse-racing days from September to May.

Taxis on Hong Kong Island and Kowloon are red and start at a low HK$6.50 (85¢), plus HK$.80 (10¢) for each 275 yards. Waiting time is HK$.80 (10¢) for every 60 seconds, and if you go through the tunnel you'll be charged an extra HK$20 ($2.60). The luggage charge is HK$2 (25¢) per piece, and if you call for a taxi it's an extra HK$1 (15¢). For a tip, simply round off to the nearest HK$1. Although theoretically taxi drivers can service both sides of Victoria Harbour, they tend to stick to a certain neighborhood and often aren't familiar with anything outside their territory.

Taxis in the New Territories are green and white and fares start at HK$5.50 (70¢) at flag fall. They travel only in the New Territories.

If you have a complaint about a taxi driver, call the police at 5776866, but make sure you have the taxi's license number.

BY MAXICAB AND MINIBUS

These small buses are the poor-man's taxi and are very useful for the locals, but they're a bit confusing for the tourist. For one thing, although the destination is written in both Chinese and English, you almost need a magnifying glass to identify the English, and by then the vehicle has probably already whizzed by. And even if you can read it, you may not know its route or where it's going.

There are two types of services, distinguishable by color, and they both hold up to 14 people. The green-and-yellow ones, called **maxicabs,** follow fixed routes and range in price from HK$1 (15¢) to HK$4 (50¢), depending on the distance, and are paid for as you enter. The most useful ones on Hong Kong Island are probably those that depart from the Star Ferry concourse for Bowen Road and Ocean Park, as well as those that travel from City Hall (opposite the Furama Hotel) to Victoria Peak. In Kowloon, you can travel from the Star Ferry concourse in a maxicab to the Tsimshatsui East shopping district.

The red-and-yellow **minibuses** are a lot more confusing, because they follow no fixed route and stop when you hail them from the street (except for some restricted areas in Central). However, they're useful for traveling along Nathan Road or between Central and Causeway Bay. Fares range from HK$2 (25¢) to HK$6 (80¢) but are often higher on rainy days or race days, and you pay as you exit. Just yell when you want to get off.

BY RENTAL CAR

Rental cars are not advisable in Hong Kong. For one thing, nothing is so far away that you can't get there easily and quickly by taxi or public transport. In addition, there probably won't be any place to park once you get there. If you want a chauffeur-driven car, many of the major hotels have their own private fleet you can hire— you can even rent an air-conditioned limousine (a romantically minded friend of mine picked her arriving boyfriend up at the airport that way). If you're still determined to rent, the familiar, self-drive firms—Avis, Budget, and Hertz—have branches here, along with a couple of dozen local firms. A valid driver's license is required. Remember, traffic flows on the left hand side of the street.

BY RICKSHAW

Rickshaws hit the streets of Hong Kong in the 1870s and were once the most common form of transport in the colony. Now, however, they are almost a thing of the past—no new licenses are being issued. A few ancient-looking men hang around the Star Ferry terminal in the Central District, but they're usually either snoozing or reading the paper. I've never once seen them hauling a customer. Rather, they make their money by charging HK$20 ($2.60) to HK$50 ($6.50) to tourists who want to take their picture. If you do want to take a ride, they'll charge you about HK$50 ($6.50) to HK$100 ($13) to take you around the block, clearly the most expensive form of transportation in Hong Kong, and by the look of them that's about as far as they can go. But whether you're just taking a photograph or going for a ride, negotiate the price first.

ON FOOT

One of the great things about Hong Kong is that you can explore virtually the entire city proper on foot. You can walk from the Central District all the way through Wanchai to Causeway Bay in about an hour or so, while the half-hour walk up Nathan Road to Yaumatei is one all visitors should do.

In the Central District there are mazes of covered, elevated walkways to separate pedestrians from traffic, connecting office buildings, shopping complexes, and hotels. In fact, some roads are deserted of pedestrians because they're all using overhead passageways. You can, for example, walk from the Mandarin Hotel to the Prince's Building, Alexandra House, and Landmark all via covered bridges. Likewise, you can walk from the Star Ferry concourse all the way to the Macau Ferry Pier via walkway.

---

3. Fast Facts About Hong Kong

Arriving in a new city is never very easy, especially when it's on the other side of the world and you're confronted with a completely different language, culture, and way of doing things. This section is designed to answer some questions you might have before departing on your trip, to make your immersion into Hong Kong life easier and to help you with unforeseen questions or emergencies that might arise once you get there.

Remember that the concierge of your hotel is usually a valuable source of information for everything from where the nearest bank is to how to get to a certain destination. In addition, the Hong Kong Tourist Association (HKTA) is also very well equipped and eager to help visitors and answer their questions.

AIRLINES: You should reconfirm an ongoing flight at least three days prior to departure. Airline reservation telephone numbers in Hong Kong for some of the major carriers are: British Airways (tel. 8680303 or 3689255), Canadian Airlines International (tel. 8683123), Cathay Pacific (tel. 8841488), Japan Airlines (tel. 5230081 or 3113355), Northwest Airlines (tel. 8104288), Quantas Airways (tel. 8421450), Singapore Airlines (tel. 5202233 or 3694181), and United Airlines (tel. 8104888).

AIRPORT: For information regarding Kai Tak Airport and transportation to and from the airport, refer to the beginning of this chapter in Section 1, "Orientation." Remember that when you leave Hong Kong, you must pay a departure tax of HK$100 ($13) for adults and HK$50 ($6.50) for children.

AMERICAN EXPRESS: The most convenient office in the Central District is opposite Jardine House at 8 Connaught Road in the Swire House (tel. 5243151). On the Kowloon side it's at the Park Lane Shopper's Boulevard, a stretch of shops on Nathan Road opposite the Miramar Hotel at 111-139 Nathan Road (tel. 7391542). Hours for both are 9:30am to 4pm Monday through Friday and 9:30am to noon on Saturday.

BABYSITTERS: Most of the upper-class and many of the medium-range hotels have babysitting services. Check the accommodations chapter for hotels that provide this service. For a full list of hotels that have babysitters, contact the Hong Kong Tourist Association.

BANKS: The usual banking hours are from 9 or 10am to about 3pm Monday through Friday and 9:30am to noon on Saturday. Some of the larger branches, however, stay open longer. Both the Hongkong Bank and Standard Chartered Bank, two of Hong Kong's major banks, stay open from 9am to 4:30pm weekdays and 9am to 12:30pm on Saturday. The Hang Seng Bank, which I find often offers the best exchange rates, stays open from 9am to 5pm weekdays and from 9am to 1pm on Saturday. Keep in mind that some banks end transactions an hour before the actual closing time.

BOOKSTORES: Since English is an official language, there are plenty of English-language bookstores, particularly in Central and Tsimshatsui. Ask your hotel concierge for the one nearest you. If you're looking for a store with a large selection of travel guide books for countries around the world, try **Wanderlust,** 30 Hollywood Rd. on the edge of Central (tel. 5232042), open from 10am to 7pm Monday through Friday, 10am to 6pm on Saturday, and 1 to 6pm on Sunday.

BUSES: Information on buses is given earlier in this chapter in Section 2, "Getting Around."

BUSINESS HOURS: Most **business offices** are open from 9am to 5pm, with lunch hour from 1 to 2pm. Saturday business hours are generally 9am to 1pm.

Most **shops** are open seven days a week, although some department stores are closed on Sunday. Shops in the Central District are generally open from 10am to 6pm; in Causeway Bay and Wanchai, from 10am to 9:30pm; in Tsimshatsui, from 10am to 9 or 10pm, and some even later than that; and in East Tsimshatsui, from 10am to 7:30pm.

CLIMATE: See Chapter II for information on Hong Kong's climate and how to pack accordingly.

CLOTHING SIZES: Use the conversion chart in the Appendix at the back of this book to help you find clothing in sizes that will fit you.

CONSULATES: If you need to contact a consulate with regard to applications for a visa, a lost passport, tourist information, or an emergency, it's a good idea to telephone first to find out the hours of the various sections. The visa section, for example, may be open only during certain hours of the day.

The **American Consulate** is at 26 Garden Road, Central District (tel. 5239011). Hours are 8:30am to 12:30pm and 1:30 to 5:30pm weekdays. If you need to go to the passport section, it's open only on weekdays, from 8:30am to noon and again from 1:30 to 5pm. The **Canadian Consulate,** Tower One, Exchange Square, Connaught Road, Central District (tel. 8104321), is open Monday through Friday from 8am to 4:30pm. The **Australian Consulate** is on the 23rd and 24th floors of Harbour Centre, 25 Harbour Road, Wanchai, on Hong Kong Island (tel. 5731881), and is open weekdays from 9 to 11:30am and 1 to 4pm. Matters pertaining to **Britain** are c/o Overseas Visa Section, Hong Kong Immigration Dept., Upper Basement, Mirror Tower, 61 Mody Road, East Tsimshatsui (tel. 7333111). Hours here are 8:45am to 4:30pm Monday through Friday and 9 to 11:30am on Saturday.

In case you decide to travel onward in Asia and wish to know about visa requirements, other consulate and commission telephone numbers that may help are: **Burma** (tel. 8913329), **India** (tel. 5284028), **Indonesia** (tel. 8904421), **Japan** (tel. 5221184), **Korea** (tel. 5294141), **Malaysia** (tel. 5270921), **New Zealand** (tel. 5225120), **Philippines** (tel. 8100183), **Singapore** (tel. 5272212), and **Thailand** (tel. 5216481).

For information on visa applications to mainland **China,** contact a tour operator such as China Travel Service (tel. 5252284). For **Nepal,** telephone the Royal Nepalese Liaison Office (tel. 8633253). For **Taiwan,** call Chung Hwa Travel (tel. 5258315).

CURRENCY: The **Hong Kong dollar (HK$),** its equivalence to the U.S. dollar, and credit cards are discussed in Section 3 of Chapter II. The currency conversion chart in the Appendix at the back of this book, based on HK$7.70 to $1 U.S., will help you deal with money in Hong Kong. U.S. dollar conversions given in the text of this book have been rounded off.

DENTISTS AND DOCTORS: Most first-class hotels have in-house doctors or can refer you to a doctor or dentist (see Chapter V on accommodations for hotels that have in-house physicians). Otherwise, call the HKTA for more information. If it's an emergency, refer to the "Hospitals" listing later in the section.

DRUGSTORES: There are no 24-hour drugstores in Hong Kong, so if you need something urgently in the middle of the night you should contact one of the hospitals listed below.

One of the best-known pharmacies in Hong Kong is **Watson's,** which first opened in the 1880s. Today there are more than 30 Watson's drugstores in Hong Kong, most of them open from 10am to 7:30 or 9pm. Locations of some of them are: Star House, next to Star Ferry on the Kowloon side (tel. 7301832); Haiphong Road in Tsimshatsui (tel. 3686381); Paterson Plaza on Paterson Street, Causeway Bay (tel. 8954008); the Hilton Hotel, and the Pedder Building on Pedder Street (tel. 5215531), both in the Central District.

ELECTRICITY: The electricity used in Hong Kong is 200 volts, alternating current (AC), 50 cycles. Most hotels have adapters to fit shavers of different plugs and voltages, but for other gadgets you'll need transformers and plug adapters (Hong Kong outlets take plugs with three round prongs). Better yet, buy travel hairdryers or irons that can be used both in the United States and abroad.

EMERGENCIES: All emergency calls are free—just **dial 999** for police, fire, or ambulance.

EYEGLASSES: Hong Kong is a good place for inexpensive frames, and you'll see shops everywhere, particularly along Nathan Road and in the huge shopping malls. Ask your hotel for the shop nearest you.

HAIRDRESSERS: It seems that every luxury and first-class hotel has both a barbershop and beauty salon on its premises, and they're probably your best bet.

HOLIDAYS: See Chapter II's "When to Go" section for a list of Hong Kong's holidays and festivals. Although there are several bank holidays during the year, the only time the shops close as well is during the Chinese New Year, which falls according to the Chinese lunar calendar in either late January or in February. Some restaurants and shops, however, do stay open even then to cater to tourists, especially in Tsimshatsui.

HOSPITALS: The following hospitals can help you around the clock: **Queen Mary Hospital,** Pokfulam Road, Hong Kong Island (tel. 8192111); **Hong Kong Adventist Hospital,** 40 Stubbs Road, Hong Kong Island (tel. 5746211); and **Queen Elizabeth Hospital,** Wylie Road, Kowloon (tel. 7102111).

INFORMATION: Locations for various offices of the Hong Kong Tourist Association (HKTA) are given in the "Orientation" section at the beginning of this chapter.

LAUNDRY: Most hotels provide same-day laundry service. Otherwise, ask your hotel concierge where the nearest laundry is.

LOST PROPERTY: If you've lost something in Hong Kong, your best bet is to contact the Hong Kong Tourist Association (HKTA). Items found on the street are generally turned in to that district's closest police station.

MAIL DELIVERY: If you don't know where you'll be staying in Hong Kong, you can still receive mail. Have it sent to you "Post Restante" at the General Post office, 2 Connaught Place, Central District, Hong Kong Island, which is located just to the right as you exit from the Star Ferry. They'll hold your mail for you here for two months, and the counter is on the ground floor.

MAPS: You can pick up a free map of Hong Kong from the HKTA, which shows major roads and streets for Kowloon and Tsimshatsui, the Central District, Western District, Wanchai, and Causeway Bay. It should be adequate for locating most hotels, restaurants, shops, and bars mentioned in this book, but if you want to explore Hong Kong in more detail you can purchase one of several maps. One of the most extensive is an entire book with maps of the city region and areas in the New Territories called *Hong Kong Guide Maps,* but you'll only need this if you live here or are writing a guide book.

METRIC WEIGHTS AND MEASURES: In Hong Kong you will run into the metric system. To become familiar with it, turn to the "Weights and Measures" chart in the Appendix at the back of this book.

MONEY: The conversion rate used in this book is HK$7.70 = $1 U.S. (rounded off). Other details concerning money matters, including credit cards, are discussed in Section 3, "Currency and Credit Cards," in Chapter II. The currency conversion chart in the Appendix at the back of this book will help you deal with money in Hong Kong.

NEWSPAPERS: Four English-language newspapers are printed in Hong Kong: the *South China Morning Post,* the *Hong Kong Standard,* the *Asian Wall Street Journal,* and the *International Herald Tribune.*

POLICE: You can reach the police for an **emergency** by dialing 999, the same number as for a fire or an ambulance. There's a **crime hotline** (tel. 5277177), a 24-hour service that also handles complaints against taxis. On the streets, **English-speaking policemen** are identifiable by a red patch worn under their shoulder number.

POLITICS: Hong Kong is a British Crown Colony, though the British prefer to use the word "territory" since the term "colony" carries imperialistic connotations. You will therefore also see Hong Kong referred to as a "British Administered Territory." In any case, this colony/territory is governed by a governor appointed by the Queen, who is assisted by two constitutional organs: the Executive Council and the Legislative Council.

In 1997 Hong Kong will revert to Chinese Communist rule, and according to the pact drawn up for the transfer, Hong Kong will be allowed to pursue its capitalist lifestyle and social system for at least another 50 years.

POST OFFICES: All the major hotels will mail letters for you. Otherwise, there are plenty of post offices throughout the territory. The major ones are open from 8am to 6pm Monday through Saturday; closed Sunday and holidays. The **main post office** is on Hong Kong Island at 2 Connaught Place, right next to the Star Ferry concourse, where you'll find stamps sold on the first floor (what we would call the second floor in the United States). On the Kowloon side, post offices are located at 405 Nathan Road between the Jordan and Yaumatei subway stations, and at 10 Middle Road, which is one block north of Salisbury Road.

RADIO AND TELEVISION: There are two English-language television channels broadcasting from mid-afternoon to late in the evening with a selection of local programs and those imported from Britain, America, and Australia. In addition, many first-class hotels have in-house video movies.

There are also several English-language radio stations, including Radio 3, broadcasting on 567 kHz (AM); Radio 4, mainly classical music, at 91 and 100 mHz (FM); and Commercial Radio, at 1044 kHz (AM). The BBC World Service is broadcast on 96 and 105 mHz (FM) from 6 to 6:45am and from 5pm to 2:30am.

REST ROOMS: The best place to find public facilities in Hong Kong is in its many hotels. Fast-food restaurants and shopping malls are other good bets. There may be an attendant on hand, who will expect a small tip, about HK$1 (15¢). Note that there are no public facilities at any of the MTR subway stations.

SAFETY: Hong Kong is relatively safe for the tourist, especially if you use common sense and stick to such tourist areas as Tsimshatsui or Causeway Bay at night. The main thing you must guard against are pickpockets. Although on the decline, they often work in groups to pick men's pockets or slit open a woman's purse, quickly taking the valuables and then relaying them on to accomplices who disappear in the crowd. Favored places are those that draw the most tourists—Tsimshatsui, Causeway Bay, and Wanchai. To be on the safe side, keep your valuables in your hotel's safety-deposit box. If you need to carry your passport or are carrying large amounts of money, it's a good idea to conceal everything in a moneybelt. It's your responsibility to be aware and alert when you travel.

STUDENT INFORMATION: If you're a student, the **Hong Kong Student Travel Bureau** can help you with sightseeing tours of the city, visas and trips to China, cheap flights to other destinations, and even rail passes for both Europe and Japan. Even if you're not a student, you can still take advantage of some of their services. They have two conveniently located offices: on the 10th floor of Star House in Tsimshatsui, next to the Star Ferry concourse (tel. 7303269), open from 9am to 7pm Monday through Saturday; and on the 13th floor of the Entertainment Building, 30 Queen's Road,

Central District (tel. 8107272), open the same hours.

TAXES AND SERVICE CHARGES: Hotels will add a 10% service charge and a 5% government tax to your bill. Restaurants and bars will automatically add a 10% service charge. There's an airport departure tax of HK$100 ($13) for adults and HK$50 ($6.50) for children aged 2 to 11. If you're taking the boat to Macau, you have to pay a Hong Kong departure tax of HK$15 ($1.95).

TAXIS: See the "Getting Around" section, earlier in this chapter, for information on Hong Kong's taxis.

TELEPHONES AND TELEGRAMS: If you want to call Hong Kong from elsewhere in the world, the **international country code** for Hong Kong is 852.

Hong Kong used to have **telephone prefix numbers,** similar to our area codes. However, these have recently been discontinued. All telephone numbers now have seven digits. But if you still see a number with a "3-," "5-," or "0-" as a prefix, count the digits in the telephone number itself; disregard the prefix if the number has seven digits, but incorporate the prefix if it has six digits (for example, 3-1234567 becomes simply 1234567, while 5-123456 becomes 5123456).

Local calls made from homes, offices, shops, restaurants, and most hotel lobbies are free, so don't feel shy about asking to use the phone. From hotel lobbies, hotel rooms, and public phone booths, a local call costs HK$1 (13¢). For **directory assistance,** dial 108.

Most hotels in Hong Kong will handle overseas calls and offer direct dialing. Otherwise, **long-distance calls and telegrams** can be made from the Cables and Wireless offices. Open 24 hours a day, including public holidays, is a convenient Cables and Wireless office at Room 102A, Exchange Square Tower 1, Connaught Place, Central District. On the Kowloon side there's an office in the Hermes House, Middle Road, Tsimshatsui.

There are also **international direct-dialing public phones** that accept either coins or telephone cards. They are located on both sides of the harbor near the Star Ferry and at the airport. For information on international calling information and phone locations, call 013. If you want to make a **collect call,** you can make one from any public or private phone by dialing 011.

TIME: Hong Kong is 13 hours ahead of New York, 14 hours ahead of Chicago, and 16 hours ahead of Los Angeles. Since Hong Kong does not have a daylight savings time, subtract one hour from the above times if you're calling in the summer. Because Hong Kong is on the other side of the International Date Line, you lose one day when traveling from the United States to Asia. Don't worry—you gain it back when you return to North America, which means that you arrive back home the same day you left Hong Kong.

TIPPING: Even though restaurants and bars will automatically add a 10% service charge to your bill, you're still expected to leave your small change for the waiter. A general rule of thumb is to leave 5%, but in most Chinese restaurants where meals are usually low cost it's acceptable to leave change up to HK$2 (25¢). In the finest restaurants you should leave 10%.

You're also expected to tip taxi drivers, bellboys, barbers, and beauticians. For taxi drivers, simply round up to the nearest HK$1 or add a HK$1 (15¢) tip. Tip people who cut your hair 5% or 10%, and give bellboys HK$10 ($1.30) to HK$20 ($2.60), depending on the number of your bags. If you use a public rest room with an attendant, you may be expected to leave a small gratuity—HK$1 (15¢) should be enough. In addition, chambermaids and room attendants are usually given about 2% of the room charge.

USEFUL TELEPHONE NUMBERS: Some numbers you might need include: **emergency services,** for ambulance, fire, and police (tel. 999); **HKTA Tourist Enquiry Hotline** (tel. 7225555); **Police Hotline** and taxi complaints (tel. 5277177); **telephone directory information** (tel. 108); **time check and temperature** (tel. 1152).

WATER: It's perfectly safe to drink Hong Kong's water, though Europeans usually insist on bottled water.

WEATHER: If you want to check the day's temperature, dial 1152. Otherwise, if a storm is brewing and you're worried about a typhoon, tune in one of the radio or television stations described above.

WEIGHTS AND MEASURES: In Hong Kong you will run into the metric system. To become familiar with it, turn to the "Weights and Measures" chart in the Appendix at the back of this book.

WHERE TO STAY IN HONG KONG

1. THE VERY EXPENSIVE DELUXE HOTELS
2. THE EXPENSIVE HOTELS
3. THE MODERATELY PRICED HOTELS
4. THE BUDGET CATEGORY
5. ROCK-BOTTOM CHOICES
6. YOUTH HOSTELS AND CAMPSITES

Except for the cost of getting to Hong Kong, your biggest expenditure is likely to be a place to lie down at night. Hotels are not cheap in Hong Kong, especially when compared with many other Asian cities. Rather, prices are similar to what you'd pay in New York or any other major Western city. On the brighter side, however, dining and shopping in Hong Kong remain very much a bargain.

For many years hotel managers in Hong Kong have been in the enviable position of having too many guests and not enough rooms to accommodate them. Because of this high demand and low supply, prices for hotel rooms skyrocketed a few years back, and many hotels continue to raise their room rates as much as 20% a year. But the astonishing thing is that new hotels are still going up like mushrooms, as though there were no 1997. In December 1985 the Hong Kong Tourist Association reported a total of 18,180 hotel rooms in the colony. By the end of 1991, when the last of the new hotels has been completed, this figure is expected to rise to an incredible 38,121. Some 20 new hotels are opening in 1990 alone.

Luckily for visitors, more hotels mean more rooms, which also means that more and more hotels are going to have to compete for the tourist's dollar. Almost all the older hotels have remodeled in the past few years to keep up with the newer ones, and the new ones keep getting more sophisticated.

Generally speaking, the price of a room in Hong Kong is governed by its view and location—the size of the room often has little to do with price. Not surprisingly, the best and most expensive rooms are those with a sweeping view of the famous Victoria Harbour, as well as those on the higher floors. Many hotels, especially those that cater to a large business clientele, also offer special "executive floors" with their own lounges, where guests usually receive complimentary breakfast, cocktails, and other amenities.

Unless otherwise specified, you can expect all rooms in the deluxe through budget category to have air conditioning and to come with private bath. In addition, most also have a color television, telephone with international direct dialing, and a stocked refrigerator complete with a mini-bar (you can assume that if a room has a mini-bar, it has a refrigerator as well). Many hotels also offer chauffeured limousine service to Kai Tak Airport, though prices are much higher than for a taxi.

Keep in mind that prices listed below are for *room rates only*— with the exception of some of the budget and the rock-bottom accommodations, a 10% service charge and 5% government tax will be added to your bill. Since a 15% increase can really add up, be sure to take it into account when checking in. It would also be prudent to check the room rate when making your reservation, since prices in Hong Kong only go up.

The biggest hotel crunches occur twice a year, from March to early June and again from October to early December, but you'd be wise to reserve a hotel room at least two months in advance no matter when you plan on coming. If you're traveling off-season, it doesn't hurt to bargain for a cheaper rate, or at the very least to ask whether you can be upgraded to a better room. Ask also whether there are any special offers, since many of the more expensive hotels offer weekend packages and other incentives.

Most of the hotels I am including in this chapter are members of the **Hong Kong Hotel Association (HKHA),** as well as the Hong Kong Tourist Association (HKTA). All of Hong Kong's expensive and moderately priced hotels and the best of the budget hotels are members of these organizations. The benefit of staying in one of these hotels is that if you have a complaint, you can lodge it directly with the Hong Kong Tourist Association. In addition, the HKHA maintains a counter at Kai Tak Airport where you can reserve a room in one of its member hotels at no extra charge. Incidentally, if hotels in this book are all full, try one of the new hotels opening by 1990. They include the upper bracket New World Harbour View Hotel atop the Convention and Exhibition Centre and the Grand Hyatt Hotel, both in Wanchai, and the Conrad Hotel on Queensway at the edge of Central. In the medium range are Luk Kwok Hotel in Wanchai and Chung Hing Hotel on Nathan Road in Kowloon, which are reopening after extensive remodeling. Consult a travel agency or contact the Hong Kong Tourist Association for a complete list of hotels and rates.

Realizing that HKHA hotels are among the first to fill up during peak season, I am also including what I consider to be a few good alternatives in the budget range, as well as some rock-bottom recommendations.

1. The Very Expensive Deluxe Hotels

All the deluxe hotels in Hong Kong offer rooms with great views of the famous Victoria Harbour. As expected, prices for these rooms are higher than those that face inland. The range of prices given below, therefore, are from the lowest-priced rooms that face inland to deluxe rooms that face the harbor. *Note:* All rooms in this category have a private bath.

KOWLOON

- The **Peninsula**, Salisbury Rd., Tsimshatsui (tel. 3666251). 188 rms, 22 suites. `A/C` `MINI-BAR` `TV` `TEL`

This is Hong Kong's most famous hotel, an imposing and grand edifice facing Victoria Harbour. Built back in 1928, it exudes more of a colonial atmosphere than any other hotel in Hong Kong and is where you should stay if you are an incurable romantic, have a penchant for the historical, and have enough money to afford its high prices. Maintaining one of the largest fleets of Rolls-Royces in the world, the Peninsula prides itself on service, and room attendants will even draw your bath if you ask them. Its lobby, reminiscent of a Parisian palace with high gilded ceilings, pillars, and ferns, is Hong Kong's foremost spot for people-watching, so you might want to put on your finest and come here just for a cup of coffee.

All the high-ceilinged bedrooms were totally redecorated in 1987 in English country-house style with green carpets and floral-patterned spreads and drapes. The windowed bathrooms have two sinks, stall showers, baths, and separate rooms for the toilet. Toiletries, scales, robes, and slippers are provided, and hairdryers are located at the dressing tables in the bedrooms. Two in-house movies and Telerate's financial services are available in addition to the four Hong Kong television channels. There are special outlets for your computer (if you don't bring yours, they will be glad to get one for you), and each suite has its own fax machine. Unfortunately, the hotel's view of the harbor was largely pre-empted by the Space Museum built on reclaimed land across the street.

In early 1990, construction will begin on a new tower, but guests are unlikely to be disturbed as the rooms at the back of the hotel will be closed off to act as sound buffers.

Dining/Entertainment: The hotel's premier restaurant is its French restaurant, Gaddi's, with live music and dancing in the evenings. Another good choice is presented by the Verandah Grill. Head for the Chesa for traditional Swiss food, the Inagiku for Japanese cuisine, and Spring Moon for Cantonese specialties.

Services: 24-hour room service, Rolls-Royce limousine service, babysitting, laundry service, same-day/overnight film-processing service, house doctor, complimentary welcoming tea.

Facilities: Shopping arcade, beauty salon, barber.

RATES: HK$2,400–HK$3,300 ($312–$429) single or double; from HK$4,500 ($584) suite. AE, CB, DC, MC, V. MTR: Tsimshatsui.

- **Regent,** Salisbury Rd., Tsimshatsui (tel. 7211211). 531 rms, 71 suites. `A/C` `MINI-BAR` `TV` `TEL`

The Regent has usurped the Peninsula as having the best view of the harbor. In fact, you can't get much closer to the water than the Regent—the hotel is located on a projection of reclaimed land and sits on more than 120 pylons sunk into the harbor. Built in 1981, it boasts a lobby and restaurants with magnificent views of the harbor and a spectacular free-standing staircase of white Carrara marble.

All rooms come with sunken bathtubs, separate rooms for both shower and toilet, three phones, and a butler for every six rooms. As many as 70% of its rooms command sweeping views of the harbor.

Dining: The Plume is one of Hong Kong's finest French restaurants, while Lai Ching Heen is an elegant Cantonese restaurant. The Harbour Side offers a harbor view along with its inexpensive snacks and meals throughout the day. Steaks and salads are served at the Steak House.

Services: 24-hour room service, house doctor, babysitting, limousine service, laundry service, complimentary welcoming tea.

Facilities: Outdoor swimming pool, business center, health spa, shopping arcade, beauty salon.

RATES: HK$1,680–HK$2,600 ($218–$338) single or double occupancy; from HK$2,700 ($350) junior suite. AE, CB, DC, MC, V. MTR: Tsimshatsui.

- **Shangri-La,** 64 Mody Rd., East Tsimshatsui (tel. 7212111). 689 rms, 30 suites. `A/C` `MINI-BAR` `TV` `TEL`

A Westin hotel, the Kowloon Shangri-La is situated on the waterfront of East Tsimshatsui and is a good choice for business travelers, who make up a large percentage of its clientele. Its two-story lobby is spacious, and the hotel is within walking distance of Tsimshatsui.

Rooms are large and luxuriously appointed, with ceiling-to-floor bay windows, and there's a no-smoking floor where even the room attendants are nonsmokers. Curtains, TV, lights, and other appliances are controlled by bedside panels. Its 21st floor is the executive floor, called Club 21, which offers a chauffeured limousine to and from the airport, personalized stationery, a pressing service open 24 hours a day, and other special services.

Dining/Entertainment: The Tiara Lounge is a great place for a cocktail with a view of the harbor, which can be followed by European cuisine at the Margaux or Chinese food at the Shang Palace. Other restaurants serve Japanese cuisine and steaks. The Music Room is a sophisticated lounge with deep carpets, plush chairs, mellow music, and a small dance floor.

Services: 24-hour room service, complimentary welcoming tea, house doctor, limousine service, babysitting, laundry service.

Facilities: Indoor swimming pool, health spa with sauna, business center, beauty salon.

RATES: HK$1,800–HK$2,760 ($234–$358) single; HK$1,950–HK$2,940 ($253–$382) double; HK$2,760–HK$3,100 ($358–$402) Club 21 executive floor; from HK$3,600 ($467) suite. AE, CB, DC, MC, V. MTR: Tsimshatsui.

CENTRAL DISTRICT

- **Mandarin Oriental,** 5 Connaught Rd., Central (tel. 5220111). 486 rms, 58 suites. A/C MINI-BAR TV TEL

Famed for its service and consistently rated as one of the top hotels in the world, the Mandarin Oriental maintains a staff of 1,000 for its 544 rooms and suites, which are the most expensive on Hong Kong Island. Located in front of the Star Ferry, it boasts a lobby decorated with a stunning glass light fixture and wood-carvings from China, and its restaurants are among the best in Hong Kong. Because of its location in Hong Kong's business district, its clientele is largely business travelers.

Spacious and decorated on an Oriental theme with an understated elegance, all rooms have balconies and include all the amenities you could possibly want—but if you are still in need of something, the staff will make every effort to fulfill your wishes.

Dining/Entertainment: Several of its restaurants have well-deserved reputations for serving excellent cuisine, including the Mandarin Grill for seafood, the Man Wah for Cantonese food, and the Pierrot for specialties from France. The Captain's Bar, just off the hotel lobby, is an intimate, cozy bar popular with Central's executive and professional crowd.

Services: 24-hour room service, laundry service, complimentary newspaper, house doctor, limousine service, babysitting.

Facilities: Indoor swimming pool, health center/sauna, business center, beauty salon, shopping arcade.

RATES: HK$1,800–HK$2,800 ($234–$364) single or double occupancy; from HK$4,800 ($623) suite. **AE, CB, DC, MC, V.** MTR: Central.

- **Hongkong Hilton,** 2 Queen's Rd., Central (tel. 5233111). 682 rms, 78 suites. A/C MINI-BAR TV TEL

Giving the Mandarin Oriental stiff competition as the hotel of choice among business travelers, the Hilton offers a great location, excellent service, and lots of amenities. Located at the junction of Queen's Road and Garden Road not far from the Victoria Peak tram, it's one of the few hotels on Hong Kong Island with an outdoor heated swimming pool. It also has its own 110-foot brigantine, a faithful reproduction of British pirate-chasers in the 1840s, which offers tours of Hong Kong's waters.

Rooms, decorated in mauve or smoky green, have large windows extending the full width of the exterior wall, three phones, a marble bathroom, a well-stocked mini-bar, and a sitting area with settee and desk. The Hilton offers six floors of "Executive Rooms," and there are also no-smoking floors.

Dining/Entertainment: Dining with a view is only one of the drawing cards of the Eagle's Nest, its excellent and acclaimed Chinese food being another. The luncheon buffet at the Dragon Boat has long been a favorite among those who work in Central and visiting business people.

Services: House doctor; limousine service; babysitting; packing, mailing, and gift-wrapping service; welcoming tea.

Facilities: Outdoor heated swimming pool, shopping arcade, health club/sauna, business center, beauty salon.

RATES: HK$1,740–HK$2,100 ($226–$273) single; HK$1,840–HK$2,290 ($239–$297) double or twin; from HK$2,290 ($297) double on the executive floor; from HK$2,600 ($338) suite. AE, CB, DC, MC, V. MTR: Central.

• **Marriott,** Pacific Pl., 88 Queensway, Admiralty (tel. 8108366). 565 rms, 42 suites. A/C MINI-BAR TV TEL

The Marriott is one of Hong Kong's newer hotels, having made its debut in 1989. Located about halfway between the Central District and Wanchai, it has a rather grandiose lobby with a three-story atrium, a waterfall that trickles down its own staircase, large windows with views of the harbor, and a jungle of imitation plants.

Rooms are all designed with right-angled "saw-tooth" windows to maximize views and are outfitted with bedside control panels that also operate the curtains (it's great waking up in the morning and having Hong Kong appear before you with a mere push of a button). Bathrooms have separate bath and shower areas, as well as their own phone and a mirror for near-sighted people. There are three executive floors with the usual complimentary breakfast and cocktails, as well as no-smoking rooms.

Dining/Entertainment: The Man Ho features gourmet Cantonese delicacies. J.W.'s Grill offers classic grillroom cuisine. Light fare for breakfast, lunch, and dinner is served at the Marriott Café.

Services: 24-hour room service, limousine service, laundry service, babysitting, newspaper delivered to room, welcoming tea.

Facilities: Outdoor swimming pool, health center/sauna, shopping mall, business center.

RATES: HK$1,650–HK$2,200 ($214–$286) single or double occupancy; HK$2,340–HK$2,460 ($304–$319) on the executive floor; from HK$2,760 ($358) suites. AE, CB, DC, MC, V. MTR: Admiralty.

---

2. The Expensive Hotels

As with the deluxe hotels, the most expensive rooms are those on upper floors with views of the harbor. In many cases there are also lower-priced rooms on lower floors that also have harbor views. The lowest rates are generally for rooms that face inland. *Note:* All rooms in this category have private bath.

KOWLOON

• **Ambassador,** 4 Middle Rd., Tsimshatsui (tel. 3666321). 313 rms. A/C MINI-BAR TV TEL

The Ambassador is a good example of an older hotel that has kept up with the times by renovating and upgrading its facilities. In fact, it used to be a moderately priced hotel until its lobby was smartly redecorated in brown and black marble and its rooms were totally refurbished a few years back. It has a great location between the Sheraton and Holiday Inn on Nathan Road, but there are no spectacular views of the harbor here.

Rooms are bright, cheerful, and roomy, with marbled bathrooms. Rooms facing the back of the hotel are cheaper; the more expensive face Nathan Road and are larger. There are two floors of special executive rooms, called the Ambassador Club, with complimentary breakfast, shoeshine, laundry, personalized stationery, and free cocktails.

Dining: The East Ocean Chinese Restaurant on the top floor is good for dim sum throughout much of the day and offers views of the city. Other restaurants serve light meals and international food.

Services: 24-hour room service, house doctor, limousine service, laundry service, babysitting.

Facilities: Business center, shopping arcade.

RATES: HK$1,170–HK$1,650   ($152–$214)   single; HK$1,300–HK$1,770 ($169–$230) double; from HK$1,770 ($230) double in the Ambassador Club. AE, CB, DC, MC, V. MTR: Tsimshatsui.

- **Holiday Inn Golden Mile,** 50 Nathan Rd., Tsimshatsui (tel. 3693111). 589 rms, 9 suites. A/C MINI-BAR TV TEL

Named after the so-called Golden Mile of shopping on Nathan Road, this Holiday Inn has a very good location right in the heart of Tsimshatsui. Maybe that's why its lobby is used as a departure point for a number of tours throughout the colony, which means that it's convenient if you want to join tours during your stay, but rather noisy and bothersome if you don't. Rooms are very clean and modern, but there are no harbor views.

Dining/Entertainment: Europe reigns in its restaurants, with Austrian and Continental foods served in Café Vienna and gourmet German cuisine in the Baron's Table. There's also a delicatessen with a take-out counter offering smoked meats, sausages, and baked goods.

Services: 24-hour room service, babysitting, laundry service, typewriters on request, secretarial service, doctor on call.

Facilities: Shopping arcade, rooftop swimming pool, health center/sauna/massage, beauty salon.

RATES: from HK$1,080 ($140) single; from HK$1,180 ($153) double; from HK$2,760 ($358) suite. AE, CB, DC, MC, V. MTR: Tsimshatsui.

- **Holiday Inn Harbour View,** 70 Mody Rd., East Tsimshatsui (tel. 7215161). 588 rms, 9 suites. A/C MINI-BAR TV TEL

Because of its close location to Hong Kong's coliseum, a number of stars have stayed here, including David Bowie, Elton John, and John McEnroe. As its name implies, it offers a harbor view from many of its rooms, and a plus here is its rooftop swimming pool. All rooms feature either double or king-size beds, and some even come equipped with sofa beds in consideration of female executives who might feel uncomfortable hosting a business meeting in a hotel room. The executive floors have the usual amenities of free breakfasts and free cocktails. The least expensive rooms have windows that open rather unceremoniously onto a facing windowless wall.

Dining: The Belvedere serves Continental cuisine, while the

Mistral specializes in Mediterranean foods. There are also Chinese and Japanese restaurants.

Services: 24-hour room service, laundry service, babysitting, doctor and dentist on call, limousine service.

Facilities: Outdoor heated swimming pool, fitness and health center/sauna, business center, shopping arcade, beauty salon.

RATES: HK$1,250–HK$2,100 ($162–$273) single; HK$1,350–HK$2,220 ($175–$288) twin; HK$150 ($19.50) supplement for the executive floor; from HK$3,240 ($421) suite. AE, CB, DC, MC, V. MTR: Tsimshatsui.

- **Hyatt Regency Hong Kong,** 67 Nathan Rd., Tsimshatsui (tel. 3662321). 706 rms, 17 suites. A/C MINI-BAR TV TEL

Located on Nathan Road only a five-minute walk from the Star Ferry and a one-minute walk from the Tsimshatsui MTR subway station, the Hyatt Regency was established in 1969 as Hyatt's first property in Asia. It has since undergone extensive renovation—its former red-and-gold lobby was redone in marble and natural teakwood paneling, and its rooms now feature colors of apricot and celadon with natural teakwood furniture. Hints of local culture are represented in guest rooms with a lacquered Chinese chest housing a television and Chinese brush paintings on the walls.

There are no harbor views here, but guest-room features include double-glazed windows and insulated walls to reduce outside noise, telephones in the bathroom and at bedside with an extra plug-in socket at the desk, and safe-deposit boxes large enough for a briefcase. Bathrooms, designed with Italian marble, all come equipped with hairdryers. The hotel's executive floor, called the Regency Club, offers the usual complimentary breakfast, cocktails, and personalized stationery. The Hyatt Regency even has an in-house fortune teller who will read your palm between noon and 6pm every day except Sunday.

Dining/Entertainment: The hotel boasts five food-and-beverage outlets, including the Hugo's steak house and the very trendy, elegant Chinese Restaurant, decorated in modern art deco style. There's nightly entertainment in the very popular Chin Chin Bar.

Services: 24-hour room service, babysitting, house nurse, limousine service, laundry service.

Facilities: Business center, use of nearby fitness center, shopping arcade.

RATES: HK$1,100–HK$1,700 ($143–$221) single or double occupancy; HK$1,950 ($253) Regency Club; from HK$3,800 ($493) suite. AE, DC, MC, V. MTR: Tsimshatsui.

- **Miramar,** 130 Nathan Rd., Tsimshatsui (tel. 3681111). 539 rms, 3 suites. A/C TV TEL

Farther up Nathan Road across from Kowloon Park, the Miramar is strategically located in the midst of a shopping area, including the Park Lane shopping arcade. An older hotel once known for its showy exterior and flashy gold-colored decor, it has joined the recent trend in renovating and updating its facilities and guest rooms. The lobby is now marble, with only stained-glass windows in its atrium ceiling as the last trace of its former flashy self. It caters largely to group tours, which is reflected in the fact that all but 18 of its rooms are twins and doubles, and none of its rooms has harbor views.

Dining/Entertainment: Its four restaurants include the Tsui Hang Village, a Chinese restaurant of note. In the basement is the Choice Food Centre, a cafeteria with various types of Chinese snacks and foods.

Services: Babysitting, limousine service, laundry service.

Facilities: Indoor swimming pool, health center/sauna, beauty salon, shopping arcade. •

RATES: HK$1,020–$1,380 ($132–$179) single; HK$1,150–HK$1,500 ($149–$195) twin; from HK$3,600 ($467) suite. AE, CB, DC, MC, V. MTR: Tsimshatsui.

- **Nikko Hongkong,** 72 Mody Rd., Tsimshatsui (tel. 7391111). 442 rms, 19 suites. A/C MINI-BAR TV TEL

An affiliate of Japan Airlines, the Nikko Hongkong is the farthest of a string of hotels that stretches from the Star Ferry through East Tsimshatsui and is only a two-minute walk from the Kowloon Railway Station. Its rooms, more than half of which face the harbor, are decorated with furniture carved from American maple and with either Japanese works of art or Dutch maps of the Far East. An electronic bedside panel enables guests to set the alarm, control the television, and open or shut the curtains. Bathrooms, finished in black-veined white Italian Carrara marble, come equipped with separate bathtubs and showers, hairdryers, bathrobes, and cotton kimono.

Dining/Entertainment: Restaurants serve Chinese, Japanese, and French cuisine, while the Sky Lounge on the 15th floor offers drinks, dancing, and a view of Hong Kong's lights.

Services: 24-hour room service, house doctor, limousine service, babysitting, laundry service.

Facilities: Outdoor swimming pool, fitness center/sauna, business center, barbershop.

RATES: HK$1,320–HK$2,220 ($171–$288) single; add HK$100 ($13) for double occupancy; from HK$3,360 ($436) suite. AE, CB, DC, MC, V. MTR: Tsimshatsui.

- **Omni Hongkong Hotel,** Harbour City, 3 Canton Rd., Tsimshatsui (tel. 7360088). 670 rms, 84 suites. A/C MINI-BAR TV TEL

A member of the Omni group of hotels, this hotel is as close as you can get to the Star Ferry and is connected via air-conditioned walkways to the largest shopping complex in Asia. Some of its rooms have unparalleled views of harbor activity, including the ocean liners that dock right next door. Its marbled lobby is spacious and comfortable, and guest rooms, all of which have queen- or king-size beds, combine both Western and Eastern decor in muted colors.

Dining: Eleven restaurants and bars. Tai Pan, which features international cuisine served to the accompaniment of a piano, is the hotel's premier restaurant. The Spice Market offers great Asian buffets with wonderful views of the harbor, but equally good is the Golden Unicorn, a Cantonese restaurant that also serves an exceptional dim sum lunch.

Services: Babysitting, laundry service, limousine service, medical and dental clinics, no-smoking rooms.

Facilities: Beauty salon, business center, outdoor swimming pool.

RATES: HK$1,300–HK$2,100 ($169–$273) single or double occupancy; HK$1,800–HK$2,700 ($234–$351) on the executive floor; from HK$2,280 ($296) suite. AE, DC, MC, V. MTR: Tsimshatsui.

• **Omni Marco Polo Hotel,** Harbour City, Canton Rd., Tsimshatsui (tel. 7360888). 382 rms, 55 suites. A/C MINI-BAR TV TEL

Not far from the Omni Hongkong Hotel is a companion hotel, the Omni Marco Polo. None of its rooms has harbor views; rather, room prices are based on height. It's a comfortable hotel located in the Harbour City shopping complex, and though it has no pool of its own guests can use that of the Omni Hongkong. It caters mainly to business travelers, so rooms feature desks with a large work space. If noise bothers you, ask for a room away from Canton Road.

Dining: Four bars and restaurants, including La Brasserie with French provincial cooking.

Services: Babysitting, house doctor, limousine service.

Facilities: Shopping arcade, swimming pool at the Hongkong Hotel, business center.

RATES: HK$1,300–HK$1,500 ($169–$195) single/double; from HK$2,220 ($288) suite. AE, DC, MC, V. MTR: Tsimshatsui.

• **Omni Prince Hotel,** Harbour City, Canton Rd., Tsimshatsui (tel. 7361888). 350 rms, 51 suites. A/C MINI-BAR TV TEL

The third in a row of Omni hotels on Canton Road, the Prince Hotel is also located in the huge Harbour City shopping complex. It's a small hotel with a gleaming-white marble lobby and rooms all feature queen-size beds. The lowest-priced rooms are on the lower floors, and although none of the rooms offers a harbor view as such, a few on the top floors have minute glimpses of the water.

Dining/Entertainment: Grilled foods and Continental cuisine are dished out at the Rib Room, decorated like the dining hall of an elegant European hunting lodge. There's also a coffeeshop and a bar.

Services: 20-hour room service (all but the wee hours), house doctor, limousine service, babysitting.

Facilities: Shopping arcades, business center, swimming pool (at the Omni Hongkong Hotel).

RATES: HK$1,300–HK$1,500 ($169–$195) single or double occupancy; HK$2,220 ($228) suite. AE, DC, MC, V. MTR: Tsimshatsui.

• **Ramada Renaissance,** 8 Peking Rd., Tsimshatsui (tel. 3113311). 474 rms, 27 suites. A/C MINI-BAR TV TEL

One of Tsimshatsui's newest hotels, the Ramada Renaissance is just a few minutes' walk from the Star Ferry. A cross between a deluxe and upper-class hotel, it's considered the top of the line of the Ramada properties and claims to be Hong Kong's "most intelligent hotel." A sophisticated bedside control panel allows guests to operate lights and curtains, adjust air-conditioning levels, select a TV or radio program, call up messages or the hotel bill on the television screen, and switch on a "do not disturb" light which automatically disconnects the door chime. As an added safety precaution, each guest receives an electronic key with a new combination, and staff keys are programmed for specific times only, thereby barring anyone from entering rooms after a shift ends. What's more, a printer records all hotel employee use, indicating when each key was used, where, and by whom. And as if that weren't enough, rooms also contain electronic safes. The most expensive rooms have harbor views.

The 11th and 12th floors feature the Renaissance Club, which can be reached only by inserting a special key in the elevator. Added amenities here include limousine transfer to and from the airport, a private lounge where complimentary breakfast and cocktails are served, facsimile machines in all rooms, free use of the health club, and personalized stationery.

Dining/Entertainment: The Capriccio may well be Hong Kong's most exclusive Italian restaurant, offering authentic northern Italian cuisine from Tuscany. The Bostonian is the talk of the town for its American-style seafood and oyster bar.

Services: 24-hour room service, house doctor, babysitting, laundry service, limousine service, no-smoking floor, welcoming tea.

Facilities: Rooftop outdoor swimming pool, squash court, health club/sauna, shopping arcade, hairdressing salon, tailor, business center.

RATES: HK$1,500–HK$2,000 ($195–$260) single or double occupancy; from HK$2,280 ($296) in the Renaissance Club; from HK$3,120 ($405) suite. AE, CB, DC, MC, V. MTR: Tsimshatsui.

• **Regal Meridien Hotel**, 71 Mody Rd., East Tsimshatsui (tel. 7221818). 589 rms, 33 suites. A/C MINI-BAR TV TEL

A French-owned property, the Regal Meridien does a smart job of blending the East and the West with reproduction 18th-century French antiques and Louis XV–style furniture standing alongside Chinese works of art. Rooms, all soundproof, also feature period furniture and are decorated in variations of soft pastels of peach and celadon green. The cheapest rooms face another building and have no view; the most expensive have a partial view of the harbor (in case you're wondering, a "partial harbor view" means either that other buildings are obstructing part of your view or that your windows do not squarely face the water).

Dining/Entertainment: Since it's a French hotel, it should come as no surprise that its chefs dish out French haute cuisine in Le Restaurant de France and French provincial cooking in La Brasserie. Other restaurants serve Cantonese food and Japanese specialties.

Hollywood East offers disco dancing, while Manhattan Transfer features live jazz. Le Rendezvous also offers live music nightly.

Services: Babysitting, house doctor, limousine service, laundry service, no-smoking rooms.

Facilities: Shopping arcade, business center, beauty salon, health spa.

RATES: HK$1,000–HK$1,800 ($143–$234) single or double occupancy; HK$2,010 ($261) executive room; from HK$2,400 ($312) suite. AE, CB, DC, MC, V. MTR: Tsimshatsui.

- **Royal Garden,** 69 Mody Rd., East Tsimshatsui (tel. 7215215). 339 rms, 34 suites. A/C MINI-BAR TV TEL

A small hotel with a lot of architectural surprises, it features a 15-story inner atrium, a concept it adopted from the traditional Chinese inner garden. Plants hang down from balconies ringing the soaring space, glass-enclosed elevators glide up the wall, a piano sits on an island in the middle of a pool, and the sound of rushing water adds a freshness and coolness. Its rooms, some of which offer partial harbor views, are decorated in an Oriental theme with Chinese furniture and dark russet colors.

Dining/Entertainment: The Falcon is an exciting venue, offering a roast beef lunch and dinner and then transforming into a popular and sophisticated disco at night. The Lalique is the hotel's top restaurant, named after René Lalique and serving French food in a setting of 1930s art deco.

Services: 24-hour room service, laundry service, free newspaper, house doctor, limousine service, babysitting.

Facilities: Health center/sauna, shopping arcade, business center, beauty salon, barbershop.

RATES: HK$1,260–HK$1,980 ($164–$257) single or double occupancy; from HK$3,000 ($390) suite. AE, CB, DC, MC, V. MTR: Tsimshatsui.

- **Sheraton Hong Kong Hotel & Towers,** 20 Nathan Rd., Tsimshatsui (tel. 3691111). 922 rms & suites. A/C MINI-BAR TV TEL

The Sheraton has one of the most envied locations in Hong Kong—near the waterfront on the corner of Nathan Road and Salisbury Road. It's an attractive hotel, whose rooms, many of which have great views of Victoria Harbour, are tastefully decorated in bright earth tones. Single rooms are available, though they are small and face an inner courtyard. If you feel like splurging, executive rooms on the top floors are known as the Sheraton Towers and include the usual extras such as complimentary breakfast and cocktails. The hotel's outdoor rooftop swimming pool, heated in winter, offers a spectacular views.

Dining/Entertainment: One of the most popular drinking spots in Tsimshatsui is Someplace Else, when it's elbow-to-elbow at the bar during happy hour. For more sophisticated and relaxed drinking, there's the Sky Lounge on the 18th floor, which can't be beat for its romantic view of the harbor. The Pink Giraffe, with a fine selection of seafood and international cuisine, also offers great views of the harbor, live entertainment, and dancing. Unkai offers superb Japanese delicacies.

Services: 24-hour room service, babysitting, laundry service, limousine service, house doctor.

Facilities: Outdoor rooftop swimming pool, health center/ sauna, shopping arcade, business center, beauty salon, barbershop.

RATES: HK$1,020–HK$1,600 ($132–$208) single; HK$1,140–HK$1,800 ($148–$234) double; Tower rooms, HK$1,200–HK$2,000 ($156–$260) single and HK$1,800– HK$2,100 ($234–$273) double; from HK$2,500 ($325) suite. AE, CB, DC, MC, V. MTR: Tsimshatsui.

CENTRAL

- **Furama Inter-Continental, 1** Connaught Rd., Central (tel. 5255111). 466 rms, 56 suites. A/C MINI-BAR TV TEL

Famous for its revolving restaurant on the 30th floor, the Furama is located in the heart of Central across from Chater Garden. All guest rooms are equipped with hairdryer, safe, and bathrobe, and have a view of either the harbor or Victoria Peak.

Dining/Entertainment: La Ronda, a revolving restaurant that offers a lunch and dinner buffet of European and Asian cuisine, offers changing vistas of one of the world's most spectacular cityscapes. Its French restaurant, the Rôtisserie, features live music in the evenings, as does the Lau Ling Bar.

Services: 24-hour room service, laundry service, house doctor, limousine service, babysitting.

Facilities: Shopping arcade, business center, beauty salon, health center.

RATES: HK$1,350–HK$1,900 ($175–$247) single or double occupancy; from HK$2,100 ($273) suite. AE, CB, DC, MC, V. MTR: Central.

- **Hotel Victoria,** Shun Tak Centre, 200 Connaught Rd., Central (tel. 5407228). 474 rms, 62 suites. A/C MINI-BAR TV TEL

Located in the same complex that also houses the Macau Ferry Terminal, the Hotel Victoria is a bit of a hike from the middle of Central, which isn't so bad since you can walk the entire 15-minute stretch from the hotel to the Star Ferry via an elevated walkway. Occupying the top 15 floors of a 40-story tower, the hotel commands an undeniably great view of the harbor. In fact, 75% of its rooms face the harbor and are blessed with large sitting areas close to the windows so you can enjoy the view. Since it caters largely to a business crowd, its writing tables are large and its marbled bathrooms have lots of room to spread out. Its executive floors are called the Dynasty Club.

Dining/Entertainment: Five bars and restaurants, including the Dynasty, an elegant Chinese restaurant, and Bocarinos Grill with Western cuisine. The Interlude, decorated in art deco, features cocktails, lunch from the carvery, and live bands.

Services: Complimentary in-house movies, laundry service, house doctor/dentist, 24-hour room service, coffee/tea-making facilities in room, babysitting, limousine service, shuttle bus to the middle of town.

Facilities: Shopping arcade, tennis court, fitness center/sauna, outdoor swimming pool, business center.

RATES: HK$1,380–HK$1,740 ($179–$226) single; HK$1,550–HK$1,900 ($201–$247) double; Dynasty Club executive floors, from HK$1,740 ($226) single and HK$1,900 ($247) double; from HK$2,760 ($358) suite. AE, DC, MC, V. MTR: Sheung Wan.

CAUSEWAY BAY

▪ **Excelsior,** 281 Gloucester Rd., Causeway Bay (tel. 5767365). 903 rms, 22 suites. A/C MINI-BAR TV TEL

Located on the waterfront not far from Food Street and a lively shopping area, the Excelsior belongs to the Mandarin Oriental group of hotels. This is a good place to stay if you like to jog, since it's close to 50-acre Victoria Park, Hong Kong's largest city park. All rooms are the same size with the same decor, but those that command a view of the harbor, the Hong Kong Yacht Club, and Kowloon are more expensive.

Dining/Entertainment: Talk of the Town is a stylish penthouse disco that offers a 180° panoramic view of the harbor. Open seven days a week, the Dickens Bar, an English-style pub, features a jazz band on Sunday and a curry buffet lunch on weekdays. Steaks, salads, and Cantonese and Peking foods are available in the hotel's other restaurants.

Services: 24-hour room service, house doctor, limousine service, hairdryer, babysitting, laundry service.

Facilities: Rooftop tennis courts, business center, beauty salon, shopping arcade.

RATES: HK$1,080–HK$1,600 ($140–$208) single or double occupancy; from HK$2,280 ($296) suite. AE, DC, MC, V. MTR:

▪ **Park Lane Radisson Hong Kong,** 310 Gloucester Rd., Causeway Bay (tel. 8903355). 825 rms, 25 suites. A/C MINI-BAR TV TEL

Located across from Victoria Park, this hotel offers rooms that feature king-size beds, marble tabletops, and marble bathrooms. Rates are based on location: the cheapest rooms are on the lower floors, and the more expensive are on the upper floors with a view of either the harbor in the distance or the park. Its best rooms are those on the Premier Club executive floor.

Dining/Entertainment: Parc 27, its premier restaurant, offers a view of the harbor along with Continental food and a buffet. Evening diversions include the Starlight Disco and several lounges and bars.

Services: 24-hour room service, laundry service, house clinic, babysitting, limousine service, same-day film processing.

Facilities: Fitness center/sauna/massage/steambath/Jacuzzi, business center, hair salon, shopping arcade.

RATES: HK$1,250–HK$1,800 ($162–$234) single or double occupancy; HK$1,900–HK$2,100 ($247–$273) Premier Club executive floor; from HK$2,800 ($364) suite. AE, CB, DC, MC, V. MTR: Causeway Bay.

AT THE AIRPORT

• **Regal Airport Hotel,** 30-38 San Po Rd., Kowloon (tel. 7180333). 389 rms, 11 suites. A/C MINI-BAR TV TEL

This is a good choice if you have only one or two nights in Hong Kong and you want to stay close to the airport. Linked directly to the airport by an air-conditioned conveyor-belt walkway, this hotel features rooms with soundproof windows and TV screens with flight information. A free shuttle-bus service transports guests to the Star Ferry about every half hour.

Dining/Entertainment: A sushi bar and a pub serving English food and snacks are just some of the food-and-beverage outlets that offer Asian and Western food. In fact, if you have a couple of hours to kill at the airport or your flight is delayed, this is a good place to come, since there are flight screens throughout the hotel and in its restaurants.

Services: 24-hour room service, babysitting, medical and dental clinics, shuttle bus into town, limousine service.

Facilities: Shopping arcade, business center, beauty salon, games room with snooker and darts.

RATES: HK$780–HK$1,440 ($101–$187) single; HK$780–HK$1,560 ($101–$203); executive rooms, HK$1,560 ($203) single and HK$1,680 ($218) double; from HK$1,800 ($234) suites. AE, CB, DC, MC, V.

---

3. The Moderately Priced Hotels

Note: All rooms in this category have a private bath.

KOWLOON

• **Empress,** 17-19 Chatham Rd., Tsimshatsui (tel. 3660211). 189 rms. A/C MINI-BAR TV TEL

Located at the corner of Chatham Road and Mody Road about a 10-minute walk from the Star Ferry, the Empress is a small, older hotel that has undergone extensive renovation the past few years. One of the best things about this hotel is that most of its rooms have a large balcony; those on the top floors facing the harbor even have views of the water. If you want to sit outside, you can request chairs from housekeeping.

Services: Laundry service, same-day film processing, house doctor, limousine service, secretarial service, babysitting.

Facilities: Coffeeshop.

RATES: HK$720–HK$1,080 ($94–$140) single; HK$780–HK$1,140 ($101–$148) double; from HK$1,800 ($234) suite. AE, MC, V. MTR: Tsimshatsui.

• **Hotel Fortuna,** 351-361 Nathan Rd., Kowloon (tel. 3851011). 176 rms, 10 suites. A/C MINI-BAR TV TEL

This hotel is located about a 15- to 20-minute walk from the Star Ferry. Although more than a quarter century old, this hotel has been so artfully renovated that you can't tell. Its clean, bright lobby is of marble with art deco lighting, and only the large size of its rooms with tall ceilings give away its age. Since the property is owned by the Wing On Corporation, hotel guests are entitled to a discount at the Wing On department store next door. Most guests are Asian, including tour groups. The cheapest singles don't have windows, so if you're claustrophobic you'll want to splurge on a higher-priced room.

Services: House doctor, babysitting, limousine service.

Facilities: Two restaurants serving Chinese and Western food, bar, business center.

RATES: HK$600–HK$1,020 ($78–$132) single; HK$840–HK$1,140 ($109–$148) double; HK$1,140 ($148) triple; HK$1,320 ($171) suite. AE, DC, MC, V. MTR: Jordan.

- **Grand Hotel,** 14 Carnarvon Rd., Tsimshatsui (tel. 3669331). 205 rms, 4 suites. A/C MINI-BAR TV TEL

One of Hong Kong's older hotels, the Grand, built in the 1960s and refurbished in 1985, is located right in the heart of Tsimshatsui off Nathan Road. Its rooms are simple but bright and cheerful, and its restaurant serves a popular lunch buffet for HK$70 ($9.10) from noon to 3 pm and a dinner buffet for HK$130 ($17).

Services: 24-hour room service, limousine service, secretarial service, house doctor, babysitting, laundry service, hairdryer, free tea- and coffee-making facilities.

Facilities: Coffeeshop and buffet restaurant, bar.

RATES: HK$790–HK$1,130 ($103–$147) single; HK$860–HK$1,200 ($112–$156) double; HK$1,800 ($234) triple. AE, DC, MC, V. MTR: Tsimshatsui.

- **Grand Tower,** 627 Nathan Rd., Mongkok (tel. 7890011). 545 rms. A/C MINI-BAR TV TEL

Part of the Grand Plaza shopping center, the Grand Tower is a relatively new hotel located in Mongkok at the northern end of Nathan Road (the only way to reach it from Kai Tak Airport is by taxi, a 15-minute ride). Its lobby, up on the sixth floor, is marbled and bright under a skylight, a big contrast to the chaos and jumble of the streets below. Its rooms are quite large and pleasant; the cheapest face an internal courtyard, while the most expensive are those on upper floors with views of the city. You could spend hours just staring out your room window at the bustle of Nathan Road.

Services: 24-hour room service, limousine service, house doctor, babysitting, laundry service, hairdryer, complimentary tea and coffee set-up.

Facilities: Business center; shopping arcade; restaurants serving Chinese, Japanese, and international dishes.

RATES: HK$820–HK$1,090 ($106–$142) single; HK$900–HK$1,170 ($117–$152) double; HK$1,560 ($203) triple. AE, DC, MC, V. MTR: Mongkok, a minute away.

- **Guangdong Hotel,** 18 Prat Ave., Tsimshatsui (tel. 7393311). 234 rms, 11 suites. A/C FRIDGE TV TEL

Only slightly older is the Guangdong Hotel, about a 10-

minute walk from the Star Ferry. Its marbled lobby is spacious and bare, reflecting the latest look in Hong Kong's hotels. Rooms are clean and pleasant, with rates based primarily on size and amenities. If you want to be away from the din of traffic, ask for a room on a higher floor.

Services: Babysitting, laundry service, limousine service, massage service, film processing.

Facilities: Two restaurants serving Japanese, Chinese, and Western food; business center.

RATES: HK$840–HK$1,080 ($109–$140) single or double occupancy; from HK$1,440 ($187) suite. AE, MC, V. MTR: Tsimshatsui.

- **Imperial Hotel,** 30-34 Nathan Rd., Tsimshatsui (tel. 3662201). 223 rms. A/C FRIDGE TV TEL

Occupying a great location on Nathan Road between the Sheraton and Holiday Inn, this is a simple, no-frills hotel. Its cheapest rooms face the back side of Chungking Mansion, notorious for its cheap and often uninviting rooms. Although the view is not exactly stunning, it is enlightening, with laundry strung everywhere and garbage piled up below, apparently tossed unconcernedly from the windows above. If that doesn't appeal to your sense of the picturesque, you can spring for a room that faces Nathan Road, though keep in mind that these rooms get the brunt of the traffic noise. Rooms on the top floors are high enough to offer glimpses of the harbor.

Services: 24-hour room service, laundry service, babysitting, limousine service, house doctor, secretarial service.

Facilities: One restaurant serving international dishes.

RATES: HK$700–HK$900 ($91–$117) single; HK$740–HK$950 ($96–$123) double. AE, CB, DC, MC, V. MTR: Tsimshatsui.

- **Kowloon Hotel,** 19-21 Nathan Rd., Tsimshatsui (tel. 3698698). 742 rms. A/C MINI-BAR TV TEL

Under the same management as the Peninsula Hotel, the Kowloon is a modern glass-walled structure located right behind the older edifice of the Peninsula, a great location in the heart of Tsimshatsui. Although its rooms are fairly small, they're built at such an angle that their V-shaped bay windows allow unobstructed views up and down the street, and rooms on the top floor even have views of the harbor. Televisions in each room also act as a kind of computer—equipped with a simplified keyboard, they allow access to computerized information files, including airline telephone numbers, the weather report, and tourist sightseeing information. At the touch of a button, guests can also call up messages and their hotel bills. In the more expensive rooms, the television even works as a word processor, with completed work transferred to the hotel's business center for printout. Finally, the hotel lobby has a computerized street directory for consulates, points of interest, and other addresses; its printout is in both English and Chinese to instruct taxi drivers.

Services: Limousine service, babysitting, laundry service.

Facilities: Three restaurants (including a popular pizzeria), business center, shopping arcade.

RATES: HK$880–HK$980 ($114–$127) single; HK$920–HK$1,040 ($119–$135) double; executive rooms, from HK$1,640 ($213) single and HK$1,710 ($222) double. AE, CB, DC, MC, V. MTR: Tsimshatsui.

- **Nathan Hotel,** 378 Nathan Rd., Kowloon (tel. 3885141). 173 rms, 13 suites. A/C FRIDGE TV TEL

More than 20 years old, the Nathan Hotel has been completely renovated. Rooms are large and clean with all the basics, and there's even a phone in the bathroom.

Services: House doctor, babysitting, limousine service, laundry service.

Facilities: Four restaurants.

RATES: HK$600–HK$720 ($78–$93) single; HK$780–HK$960 ($101–$125) twin; HK$960–HK$1,020 ($125–$132) triple; from HK$1,020 ($132) suite. AE, DC, MC, V. MTR: Jordan.

- **New World,** 22 Salisbury Rd., Tsimshatsui (tel. 3694111). 729 rms. A/C MINI-BAR TV TEL

This hotel is part of the New World complex, which includes more than 400 shops and boutiques. But even though it's situated in a prime location, right on the waterfront, not one of its rooms faces the harbor. Resembling a Japanese business hotel with economy rooms not much larger than its beds, the New World is modern, clean, and functional, and is conveniently located. For those who want to splurge, there are two executive floors, called the Dynasty Club.

Services: House doctor, babysitting, laundry service.

Facilities: Three restaurants, three cocktail lounges, a disco, shopping arcade, outdoor swimming pool, fitness center/sauna, beauty salon, business center.

RATES: HK$790–HK$1,500 ($103–$195) single; HK$860–HK$1,620 ($112–$210) double; from HK$1,880 ($244) in the Dynasty Club. AE, CB, DC, MC, V. MTR: Tsimshatsui.

- **Park Hotel,** 61-65 Chatham Rd. South, Tsimshatsui (tel. 3661371). 410 rms. A/C FRIDGE TV TEL

Built in the 1960s, the Park Hotel is one of the best-known medium-priced hotels in Kowloon. Especially popular with Australians, it has what are probably the largest rooms in this category, a plus if you're tired of cramped quarters. Renovation has kept it abreast of the times. It's a comfortable and clean hotel—you can't go wrong staying here.

Services: House doctor, babysitting, limousine service.

Facilities: Five restaurants and bars, shopping arcade, beauty salon.

RATES: HK$840–HK$1,200 ($109–$156) single; HK$960–HK$1,300 ($125–$169) double. AE, DC, MC, V. MTR: Tsimshatsui.

- **Ramada Inn Kowloon,** 73-75 Chatham Rd. South, Tsimshatsui (tel. 3111100). 206 rms. A/C MINI-BAR TV TEL

Popular with the individual business traveler, this hotel offers a convenient location and rooms that feature TV with remote control, safe (except in the cheapest rooms), and hairdryer in addition to the usual amenities. The electricity is activated in your room when you insert your key into a special slot by the door, which means that you don't have to search for your keys when you leave. Room service is available until 2 am.

Services: Limousine service, babysitting, laundry service, free newspaper.

Facilities: One restaurant serving Western and Asian food, one bar, business center.

RATES: HK$910–HK$1,200 ($118–$156) single or double occupancy. AE, DC, MC, V. MTR: Tsimshatsui.

- **Ritz Hotel,** 122 Austin Rd., Kowloon (tel. 3692282). 60 rms. A/C MINI-BAR TV TEL

Located a good 20-minute hike from the Star Ferry, the Ritz is a small, personable hotel, a favorite with visiting businessmen from Europe and Southeast Asia. In fact, it's such a popular choice with a high number of repeat guests that it's almost mandatory to reserve a room here at least a month in advance, particularly during peak times. Its rates are among the lowest in this category, offering good value for your money.

Services: House doctor, babysitting.

Facilities: One coffeeshop.

RATES: From HK$720 ($94) single; from HK$820 ($106) double. AE, DC, MC, V. MTR: Jordan, two minutes away.

- **Royal Pacific Hotel & Towers,** 33 Canton Rd., Tsimshatsui (tel. 7361188). 643 rms & suites. A/C MINI-BAR TV TEL

One of Tsimshatsui's newest hotels, this hotel is actually two hotels in one, each with its own lobby, concept, and room rates. The Royal Pacific Hotel is the more moderately priced and is geared to tour groups from Japan, Korea, and Taiwan. Its rooms are rather small, but have all the usual comforts, including three phones (one in the bathroom), a safe, and hairdryer. The Tower is more up-market, catering to individual travelers and business people and offering more personalized services. Only the Tower offers views of the harbor. The only disadvantage of staying here is that it's a 15-minute walk from the Star Ferry; on the other hand, it's located practically on top of the new China Ferry Terminal, where boats depart for Macau and China.

Services: Babysitting, limousine services, complimentary shoeshine (Tower only), laundry service.

Facilities: Five restaurants and bars, business center, beauty salon, fitness center, squash court, shopping arcade.

RATES: HK$920–HK$1,100 ($119–$143) single; HK$980–HK$1,170 ($127–$152) double; from HK$1,320 ($171) in the Tower. AE, CB, DC, MC, V. MTR: Tsimshatsui.

- **Windsor Hotel,** 39-43A Kimberley Rd., Tsimshatsui (tel. 7395665). 167 rms. A/C MINI-BAR TV TEL

Although it's about a 15-minute walk from the Star Ferry, this new hotel is pleasant and modern, with a spotless white interior, marbled lobby, and pastel-colored rooms. Typical of the many new, medium-range hotels mushrooming throughout the colony, it caters to both groups and individuals, with Westerners accounting for 30% of its guests. It has a shuttle bus to and from the airport.

Services: Limousine service, babysitting, laundry service, airport shuttle bus.

Facilities: Two restaurants, business center.

RATES: HK$900–HK$1,100 ($117–$143) single/double. AE, DC, MC, V. MTR: Tsimshatsui.

WANCHAI/CAUSEWAY BAY

• **China Harbour View,** 189 Gloucester Rd., Wanchai (tel. 8382222). 325 rms. A/C MINI-BAR TV TEL

Opened in 1988, this hotel looks like it went up in a hurry to cash in on Hong Kong's rush of tourists. The workmanship leaves something to be desired, but it's a reasonably priced hotel in Wanchai. Rooms offer all the basics, including a safe and hairdryer, and the best rooms are those with views of the harbor. Since harbor-view rooms are the same price no matter which floor you're on, ask for one higher up.

Services: Limousine service, babysitting, laundry service, free shuttle bus to Central.

Facilities: Two restaurants, one lounge, business center.

RATES: HK$780–HK$1,320 ($101–$171) single; HK$840–HK$1,440 ($109–$187) double. AE, MC, V. MTR: About halfway between Wanchai and Causeway Bay.

• **Lee Gardens,** Hysan Ave., Causeway Bay (tel. 8953311). 800 rms. A/C MINI-BAR TV TEL

Located inland without harbor views, this hotel caters mostly to group tours from Japan, Taiwan, and China. The prices of its rooms are based on size, decor, and floor number rather than view. Decorated on a South Pacific theme with bamboo furniture and soothing colors of beige and bisque, the rooms are pleasant and bright.

Services: House doctor, babysitting, free shuttle bus to Central, limousine service.

Facilities: Eight restaurants and bars serving Chinese, Western, Korean, and Japanese food; business center; shopping arcade; beauty salon.

RATES: HK$960–HK$1,400 ($125–$182) single or double occupancy. AE, CB, DC, MC, V. MTR: Causeway Bay.

• **Hotel New Harbour,** 41-49 Hennessy Rd., Wanchai (tel. 8611166). 173 rms. A/C FRIDGE TV TEL

An older hotel that has been completely renovated, it caters largely to tour groups from China. In fact, since it's affiliated with the China Travel Service, the hotel can help with visa applications as well as accommodation arrangements for China. Although located on a busy street in the heart of Wanchai, rooms are quiet and comfortable. Rates are based on room size and height, with deluxe rooms on the 18th floor, some of which offer glimpses of the harbor.

Services: 24-hour room service, limousine service, babysitting, house doctor, secretarial service.

Facilities: One coffeeshop, one Chinese/Western restaurant.

RATES: HK$630–HK$930 ($82–$121) single; HK$690–HK$1,020 ($90–$132) double. AE, DC, MC, V. MTR: Wanchai.

- **New Hong Kong Cathay Hotel,** 17 Tung Lo Wan Rd., Causeway Bay (tel. 5778211). 229 rms. A/C FRIDGE TV TEL

Built in 1967 and finally undergoing a much-needed renovation in 1989, this hotel was not a member of HKHA at last check. However, it offers large, bright rooms, modestly furnished with the basics. The singles all face toward the back, a rather uninspiring view, so you may want to spring for a twin. By far the best rooms are the deluxe twins on the 10th floor—they come with large balconies that are great for looking out on the city. When I checked this hotel it was still in the midst of renovation—be aware that prices may rise once the inconvenience of jackhammers is eliminated.

Facilities: One Chinese restaurant.

RATES: HK$620 ($81) single; HK$700–HK$840 ($91–$109) twin. AE, DC, MC, V. MTR: Causeway Bay.

- **Ramada Inn Hong Kong,** 61-73 Lockhart Rd., Wanchai (tel. 8611000). 340 rms. A/C MINI-BAR TV TEL

One of three Ramada properties to open in Hong Kong in recent years, this business hotel offers small but adequate rooms that feature safes and free in-house movies. There are two types of rooms, with only 16 available in the cheaper category.

Services: Babysitting, laundry service, complimentary newspaper, limousine service.

Facilities: One restaurant, one bar, rooftop swimming pool, sauna.

RATES: HK$900–HK$980 ($117–$127) single or double occupancy. AE, DC, MC, V. MTR: Wanchai.

---

4. The Budget Category

While the majority of budget hotels listed in this section are members of the Hong Kong Hotel Association (HKHA) or the Hong Kong Tourist Association (HKTA), a few of them are not. In any case, it's wise to see a room before committing yourself, since some rooms may be better than others in terms of traffic noise, view, condition, and size. For the most part, however, you shouldn't have any problems with these recommendations and the rooms should be clean—but don't expect luxury. A $60 twin in Hong Kong isn't going to be any more luxurious than a $30 motel room in Topeka, Kansas.

KOWLOON

- **Bangkok Royal,** 2-12 Pilkem St., Kowloon (tel. 3679181 or 7359181). 70 rms, all with bath. A/C TV TEL

Located off Nathan Road just north of Kowloon Park, the Bangkok Royal has renovated many of its rooms and is one of the more expensive hotels in this category. A member of HKHA, it's an older hotel (and still looks it despite renovation) and has a popular Thai restaurant, not surprising considering its name. A good choice.

RATES: HK$420–HK$600 ($55–$78) single; HK$550–HK$740 ($71–$96) twin. AE, DC, MC, V. MTR: Jordan.

• **Booth Lodge,** 11 Sing Sing Lane, Yaumatei, Kowloon (tel. 7719266). 33 rms, all with bath. A/C FRIDGE TV TEL

About a 30-minute hike to the Star Ferry but close to the Jade Market and the Temple Street night market, Booth Lodge is located on the seventh floor of the Salvation Army building and is a member of the Hong Kong Tourist Association. Its rooms are all doubles and twins, and though they have as much personality as a college dormitory, they're perfectly adequate.

RATES: HK$380–HK$480 ($49–$62) double or twin. MTR: Yaumatei.

• **Caritas Bianchi Lodge,** 4 Cliff Rd., Yaumatei, Kowloon (tel. 3881111). 90 rms, all with bath. A/C FRIDGE TV TEL

Just down the street from Booth Lodge, this HKTA member is another good choice in this price category. Most of its rooms face toward the back of the hotel with a view of a cliff and a small park, certainly a more pleasant view than most hotels can boast. Try to get a room on a higher floor.

RATES (INCLUDING CONTINENTAL BREAKFAST): HK$330 ($43) single; HK$450 ($58) double or twin; HK$540 ($70) triple. MTR: Yaumatei.

• **Fuji Hotel,** 140-142 Austin Rd., Tsimshatsui (tel. 3678111). 60 rms, all with bath. TV TEL

This hotel is rather run-down and is not a member of HKTA, but may be worth a try if other hotels are full. It has a young staff and caters mainly to a younger Asian crowd. Only those rooms facing the front street have a window, and although they're brighter, they are also much noisier. This hotel has a variety of different rooms, so if you don't like the one you're shown, ask to see another one.

RATES (INCLUDING CONTINENTAL BREAKFAST): HK$410 ($53) single; HK$440 ($57) double; HK$470 ($61) twin. MTR: Jordan.

• **International Hotel,** 33 Cameron Rd., Tsimshatsui (tel. 3662281). 89 rms, all with bath. A/C TV TEL

A member of HKHA, this hotel is about 40 years old and looks it. However, it has one of the best locations in this category, right in the heart of Tsimshatsui about a 15-minute walk from the Star Ferry. Only international guests are accepted at the International. Some of the double rooms have balconies, although the view is nothing to write home about; rooms that face toward the back of the hotel have glazed windows. The one restaurant serves Swatow Chinese dishes and Western fare.

RATES: HK$450–HK$810 ($58–$105) single; HK$600–

HK$1,050 ($78–$136) twin. MC, V. MTR: Tsimshatsui.

- **Jade Hotel,** 23 Cameron Rd., Tsimshatsui (tel. 3697491). 62 rms.

Right down the street from the International is the Jade Hotel. Although not a member of HKHA and manned by a staff that's sometimes surly, it's worth a try if other hotels are full. It's a bit old and shabby, but prices are reasonable and are slightly lower off-season. Insist on seeing a room beforehand.

RATES: HK$360–HK$480 ($47–$62) single; HK$480–HK$600 ($62–$78) double or twin. MTR: Tsimshatsui.

- **King's Hotel,** 473 Nathan Rd., Kowloon (tel. 7801281). 72 rms, all with bath. `FRIDGE` `TV` `TEL`

Just a basic hotel with no frills, it's a member of HKHA and caters primarily to Asians, including mainland Chinese. It has a good Thai restaurant.

RATES: HK$400–HK$430 ($52–$56) single; HK$480–HK$510 ($62–$66) twin. MTR: Yaumatei.

- **Shamrock Hotel,** 223 Nathan Rd., Kowloon (tel. 3662271). 150 rms, all with bath. `A/C` `TV` `TEL`

A pioneer member of HKHA, the Shamrock was built in the early 1950s and caters mainly to visitors from Asia. Guest rooms are rather small, but high ceilings give them a bit more of spacious feeling. A restaurant on the 10th floor serves Western, Chinese, and Malaysian dishes. The most remarkable thing about this hotel is its lobby—although small, the ceiling is covered with about two dozen chandeliers and lights of all different designs. I don't think this place has changed much in the past 30 years.

RATES: From HK$450 ($58) single; HK$540–HK$580 ($70–$75) twin; HK$660 ($86) double. AE, DC, MC, V. MTR: Jordan.

The Ys

- **YMCA,** Salisbury Rd., Tsimshatsui (tel. 3692211). 135 rms, all with bath. `A/C` `FRIDGE` `TV` `TEL`

The overwhelming number-one choice in budget accommodation has always been the YMCA on Salisbury Road, which has the good fortune to be on the waterfront right beside the Peninsula. For years there was a fear that it might be torn down in the face of land-hungry developers, but instead the YMCA is expanding—in the latter half of 1991 an additional 263 rooms and a sports facility will make their debut. Until then the Y is operating with 135 twin rooms only, as well as a popular and inexpensive cafeteria called the Salisbury. The YMCA welcomes families, men, and women, but it's so popular you should make reservations at least three months in advance.

RATES: HK$470 ($61) twin. MTR: Tsimshatsui.

- **YMCA International House,** 23 Waterloo Rd., Kowloon (tel. 7719111). 286 rms, all with bath. `A/C`

This modern facility accepts both males and females in its single and twin rooms. It has a fitness center.

RATES: HK$370 ($48) single; HK$400 ($52) double. MTR: Yaumatei.

• **YWCA Guest House,** 5 Man Fuk Rd., Kowloon (tel. 7139211). 164 rms, some with bath. `A/C`

Inconveniently located but with reasonable prices, this Y accepts both men and women. To reach it, take bus 3, 7, or 8 from the Star Ferry. Singles come with or without private bathroom; all the twins have a bathroom. Its restaurant serves Western and Chinese dishes.

RATES: HK$230 ($30) single without bath, HK$430 ($56) with bath; HK$430 ($56) twin.

WANCHAI/CAUSEWAY BAY

• **Caravelle Hotel,** 84 Morrison Hills Rd., Happy Valley (tel. 5754455). 102 rms, all with bath. `A/C` `TV` `TEL`

Located between Wanchai and Causeway Bay to the south, this is where you'll want to stay if you've come to Hong Kong primarily for the horse races. It's situated right across the street from Happy Valley racetrack and its front rooms even have views of the racecourse. To reach it, board one of the trams bound for Happy Valley. It's a small hotel with only 10 rooms on each floor, and though corridors are dimly lit, there's an attendant on each floor. The rooms are bright, though the furniture looks as old as the hotel. Rates are the same whether your room faces the front or the back of the hotel.

RATES: HK$540 ($70) single; HK$600 ($78) double or twin. AE, DC, MC, V.

• **Harbour Hotel,** 116-122 Gloucester Rd., Wanchai (tel. 5748211). 200 rms, all with bath. `A/C` `TV` `TEL`

This older, renovated hotel sits slightly back from the waterfront and offers some harbor-view rooms at a reasonable price. Popular with groups of visiting businessmen from mainland China, it has a coffeeshop, Chinese restaurant, and sauna. The cheapest rooms are windowless and are the same rate whether there are one or two of you; next up the scale are those that face a quiet back street. The largest rooms are deluxe twins with refrigerators that have partial harbor views, and since they're all the same price, ask for one on a higher floor where the view is better.

RATES: HK$510–HK$800 ($66–$104) single; HK$510–HK$1,020 ($66–$132) twins. AE, DC, MC, V. MTR: Wanchai.

The Y

• **Harbour View International House,** 4 Harbour Rd., Wanchai (tel. 5201111). 320 rms, all with bath. `A/C` `FRIDGE` `TV` `TEL`

Opened in 1986, this modern YMCA occupies a prime spot on the waterfront, right next to the Hong Kong Arts Center. Rooms, all twins or doubles, are simple but functional, and facilities include a coffeeshop, one restaurant with a view of the harbor, room service, laundry service, and Telex. Best yet, more than half the rooms face the harbor, making this one of the cheapest places in the colony with great views. Rooms facing inland are cheaper.

RATES: HK$520–HK$660 ($67–$86) double or twin. AE, DC, MC, V. MTR: Wanchai.

5. Rock-Bottom Choices

CHUNGKING MANSION

Of Hong Kong's rock-bottom establishments, none is more notorious than Chungking Mansion. Although it occupies a prime spot at 40 Nathan Road, between the Holiday Inn Golden Mile and the Sheraton in Tsimshatsui, Chungking Mansion is easy to overlook; there's no big sign heralding its existence. In fact, its ground floor is one huge maze of inexpensive shops, many of them owned by Indians living in Hong Kong.

But above all those shops are five towering concrete blocks, each served by its own tiny elevator and known collectively as Chungking Mansion. Inside Chungking Mansion are hundreds of little businesses, apartments, guesthouses, and eateries. Some of the guesthouses are passable; many are not.

I stayed in Chungking Mansion on my first trip to Hong Kong in 1983, living in a neon-colored cell that contained two sagging beds, a night table, and a closet. I shared my room with another woman and we paid about $5 (U.S.) each. In the shared bathroom down the hall lived the biggest spider I have ever seen, a hairy thing that nevertheless behaved itself quite well whenever I was there—it never moved an inch the whole time I took a shower.

Chungking Mansion has changed a lot since then. Ten years ago there wasn't much choice among the guesthouses within Chungking Mansion, and most of them were on the borderline of squalor. Today there are literally dozens of new ones, and many of the old ones have cleaned up their act in their bid for the tourist's dollar. I myself counted about 70 guesthouses here, though a security guard estimated that there were as many as 200 spread throughout the complex, many of them small affairs with only a handful of rooms. The new ones are spanking clean, and during my last visit I noticed something I had never seen in Chungking Mansion before—respectable-looking middle-aged tourists.

Chungking is still not the kind of place you'd recommend to your grandmother or to those uninitiated in the seamier side of travel. The views from many room windows are more insightful than some guests might wish for—the backside of the building and mountains of trash down below. Even worse are the ancient-looking elevators filled to capacity with human cargo; you might want to stick to the stairs. Still, for the budget traveler, Chungking Mansion is a viable alternative to Hong Kong's high-priced hotels. And you can't beat it for location.

Chungking Mansion is divided into five separate blocks, from A Block to E Block. For the less daring, A Block is the best, since its elevator is nearest the front entrance to the building. The other elevators are farther back in the shopping arcade, which can be a little disconcerting at night when the shops are all closed and the corridors are deserted. Below is a list of what I consider to be some of Chungking's better guesthouses. If these are full or you want to save money, check the guesthouses toward the back of the building in Blocks C, D, and E.

• **Chungking House,** A Block, 4th and 5th floors, Chungking Mansion, 40 Nathan Rd., Tsimshatsui (tel. 3665362). 85 rms, all with bath. A/C TV TEL

This is the best-known guesthouse in Chungking Mansion, due primarily to its years of membership in the HKTA. With its front desk and lobby, it's more like a hotel than a guesthouse. Rooms are larger too, though wood paneling makes the place a bit dreary and the staff tends to be unconcerned and gruff. However, it's often fully booked.

RATES: HK$180–HK$240 ($23–$31) single; HK$240–HK$360 ($31–$47) double. No credit cards accepted. MTR: Tsimshatsui.

• **Peking Guest House,** A Block, 12th floor, Chungking Mansion, 40 Nathan Rd., Tsimshatsui (tel. 7238320). 6 rms with bath, 3 without bath. A/C TV

Opened in 1988, this is my own personal favorite. It's newer, brighter, cleaner, and more cheerful than most of the older establishments and the owners are friendly. All its rooms have windows, and four rooms even face Nathan Road (although noisier, it's a much more uplifting view than the back side of Chungking).

RATES: HK$100 ($13) single without bath, HK$120 ($15.50) with bath; HK$165 ($21.50) double without bath, HK$175–HK$260 ($22.75–$33.75) with bath. MTR: Tsimshatsui.

• **Welcome Guest House,** A Block, 7th floor, Chungking Mansion, 40 Nathan Rd., Tsimshatsui (tel. 7217793). 35 rms, some with bath. A/C

This is another good choice in accommodation. Managed by a friendly young couple who maintain a variety of rooms spread throughout A Block, it offers laundry service and help in arranging visas for China. Many rooms face Nathan Road.

RATES: HK$77–HK$100 ($10–$13) single/double without bath; HK$120–HK$130 ($15.50–$17) single with bath; HK$155 ($20.25) double with bath; from HK$200 ($26) family room. No credit cards accepted. MTR: Tsimshatsui.

• **Park Guest House,** A Block, 15th floor, Chungking Mansion, 40 Nathan Rd., Tsimshatsui (tel. 3681689 or 3677889). 18 rms with bath, 12 without bath. A/C TV

The owners here are oldtimers in Chungking and have been in business more than 20 years. Their rooms are clean and many have been renovated; some face Nathan Road.

RATES: HK$77 ($10) single without bathroom, HK$170 ($22) with bath; HK$170–HK$290 ($22–$37.75) double with bath. No credit cards accepted. MTR: Tsimshatsui.

- **New International Guest House,** A Block, 11th floor, Chungking Mansion, 40 Nathan Rd., Tsimshatsui (tel. 3667936). 12 rms without bath, 3 with bath. `TV`

    This guesthouse is managed by young Elizabeth Kam, daughter of the owners of Park Guest House. She grew up in Chungking Mansion. Rooms are small, but all have windows and color TV.

    RATES: HK$75 ($9.75) single; double HK$90–HK$120 ($11.75–$15.50). MTR: Tsimshatsui.

- **New Asia Guest House,** A Block, 8th floor, Chungking Mansion, 40 Nathan Rd., Tsimshatsui (tel. 7240426).

    There are a variety of rooms here, most with private bath and air conditioning. Rooms are old but fairly clean, and the owners are friendly. Some rooms do not have windows; the others face the back of Chungking.

    RATES: HK$130–HK$220 ($17–$28.50) single or double occupancy. No credit cards accepted. MTR: Tsimshatsui.

- **New Washington Guest House,** B Block, 13th floor, Chungking Mansion, 40 Nathan Rd., Tsimshatsui (tel. 3665798). 10 rms, none with bath.

    In operation more than 20 years, it offers simple and clean cell-like rooms, some windowless. But there's not a lot of privacy, since you can hear everything in neighboring rooms and down the hall.

    RATES: HK$100 ($13) with fan; HK$130 ($17) with air conditioning. No credit cards accepted. MTR: Tsimshatsui.

- **Capital Guest House,** Block A, 13th floor, Chungking Mansion, 40 Nathan Rd., Tsimshatsui (tel. 3663455). 11 rms, some with bath. `A/C`

    Not quite up to the standards of the above establishments, it's nonetheless worth a try if the other places are all full. Be sure to take a look at what's available, since some rooms are brighter than others.

    RATES: HK$90–HK$260 ($11.75–$33.75). No credit cards accepted. MTR: Tsimshatsui.

- **Traveller's Hostel,** Block A, 16th floor, Chungking Mansion, 40 Nathan Rd., Tsimshatsui (tel. 3682505). 3 dormitory rms with 6, 8, and 10 bunk beds, 1 private room with 2 bunk beds.

    Popular with the backpacking crowd, this hostelry has suffered somewhat from management neglect in recent years. It could be cleaner, but working in its favor is the fact that it's high up and has lots of windows. In addition, it's a good place to stay if you want to meet other travelers, and there's even a travel service here that specializes in arranging trips to China. Many backpackers spend their first nights in Hong Kong here, waiting to get into one of the better guesthouses in Chungking Mansion.

    RATES: HK$33 ($4.30) dormitory bed; HK$90 ($12.75) double. No credit cards. MTR: Tsimshatsui.

OTHER ROCK-BOTTOM RECOMMENDATIONS

- **Great Wall Hotel,** 14th floor, 300 Nathan Rd., Kowloon (tel. 3887675). All rms with bath. `A/C` `TV`

If staying in Chungking Mansion doesn't appeal to your sense of adventure, you might try this guesthouse located on the corner of Nathan Road and Jordan Road near the Jordan MTR station. Its rooms are old but clean and the premises are orderly. The woman running the place doesn't understand English but she does understand the basics of "single" and "double."

RATES: HK$250 ($32.50) single; HK$280 ($36.25) double. No credit cards. MTR: Jordan.

• **International Youth Accommodation Centre,** 6th floor, 21A Lock Rd., Tsimshatsui (tel. 3663419). 26 bunk beds.
Located right behind the Hyatt Regency in the heart of Tsimshatsui, this place is not for the squeamish. It's a chaotic but mellow place with backpacks, belongings, and unidentifiable objects strewn all over the place. It could definitely be a lot cleaner, but people who have stayed here swear that it has the best atmosphere in town. Of course, it should be mentioned that these are long-term travelers, mostly Europeans, who have been roughing it for who knows how many years.

RATES: HK$33 ($4.30) for a bunk bed. No credit cards accepted. MTR: Tsimshatsui.

---

6. Youth Hostels and Campsites

There are a number of youth hostels and camping sites in Hong Kong, including its islands and territories, and they offer the cheapest rates around.

YOUTH HOSTELS

The most conveniently located youth hostel is **Ma Wui Hall,** located on the top of Mount Davis on Hong Kong Island (tel. 8175715). It charges HK$18 ($2.40) for members and HK$33 ($4.30) for nonmembers. Seven other youth hostels are spread on some of the outlying islands and in the New Territories, with prices ranging from HK$11 to HK$18 ($1.45 to $2.40). Nonmembers pay HK$15 ($1.95) more. For more information on Hong Kong's youth hostels, contact the **Hong Kong Youth Hostels Association,** 1408A Watson's Estate, Causeway Bay (tel. 5700985 or 5706222). You may also purchase a youth hostel card here for HK$90 ($11.75).

CAMPSITES

There are camping facilities on some of the outlying islands, ranging in price from free to about HK$33 ($4.30). You must bring your own tent, but some of the camps provide the sheets and blankets. The more primitive campsites lack water or latrine facilities— but they're free. For more information on campsites, contact the HKTA (tel. 7225555).

WHERE TO DINE IN HONG KONG

Dining ranks as one of *the* things to do while in Hong Kong. Not only is the food excellent, but prices are reasonable and the range of culinary possibilities is nothing short of staggering. With an estimated 7,000 restaurants, Hong Kong has what is probably the greatest concentration of Chinese restaurants in the world, as well as a wide range of Japanese, Indian, Thai, Vietnamese, Italian, French, and other international establishments. I'm convinced that you can eat as well in Hong Kong as in any other city in the world. And no matter where you eat or how much you spend, it's sure to be an adventure of the senses.

Little wonder that a common greeting among Chinese in Hong Kong translates literally as "Have you eaten?" In Hong Kong, eating is the most important order of the day.

1. An Introduction to Chinese Food

Traditionally speaking, Chinese restaurants tend to be noisy and crowded affairs, the patrons much more interested in food than decor. They can range from simple diners where the only adornment is likely to be Formica-topped tables, to very elaborate affairs with Chinese lanterns, splashes of red and gold, and painted screens. In addition, the past few years have witnessed the explosion of a new kind of Chinese restaurant—trendy, chic, and sparsely decorated, many in art deco.

In any case, Chinese restaurants are places for social gatherings. After all, apartments in Hong Kong are often too small to entertain friends and family—so the whole gang simply heads for their favorite restaurant.

Thus Chinese dining is usually in large groups, and the basic rule is to order one dish per person, plus one more, with all dishes placed in the center of the table and shared by everyone. The more of you there are, therefore, the more dishes ordered and the more fun you'll have. Dishes usually come in two or three different sizes, so ask your waiter which size is sufficient for your group.

You shouldn't have any problems ordering, because most Chinese restaurants have English menus. If you want to be correct about it, a well-balanced meal should contain the five basic tastes of Chinese cuisine—acid, hot, bitter, sweet, and salty. The texture should vary as well, ranging from crisp and tender to dry and saucy. The proper order is to begin with a cold dish, followed by dishes of fish or seafood, meat (pork, beef, or poultry), vegetables, soup, and noodles or rice. Some dishes are steamed, while others may be fried, boiled, or roasted. Many of the dishes are accompanied by sauces, the most common being soy sauce, chili sauce, and hot mustard.

The beginning of your meal is heralded by a round of hot towels, a wonderful custom you'll soon grow addicted to and wish would be imported to restaurants in the United States. Your eating utensils, of course, will be chopsticks, which have been around for 3,000 years and are perfect for picking up bite-size morsels. If you're eating rice, the correct way is to pick up the bowl and scoop the rice directly into your mouth with your chopsticks.

CHINESE TEAS AND WINES

Tea is often provided whether or not you ask for it, and for which there may be a small charge. Grown in China for more than 2,000 years, tea is thought to help clear the palate and aid in digestion. There are three main types: green or unfermented tea; black *bo lay* fermented tea; and *oolong,* or semi-fermented tea. These three teas can be further subdivided into a wide variety of specific teas, with taste varying according to the region, climate, and soil. At any rate, if you want more tea, simply cock the lid half open on top of the tea pot—someone will come around to refill it.

If you want something a bit stronger than tea, there are also **Chinese wines,** though they aren't really wines in the Western sense of the word. Rather, they are spirits distilled from rice, millet, and other grains, as well as from herbs and flowers. Popular Chinese wines include *siu hing,* a mild rice wine that resembles a medium-dry sherry, goes well with all kinds of Chinese foods, and is best served warm; *go leung* and *mao toi,* fiery drinks made from millet with a 70% alcoholic content; and *ng ka pay,* a sweet herbal wine favored for its medicinal qualities. As for **beer,** there's Tsingtao from mainland China, begun years ago by Germans and made from sparkling mineral water. One thing to keep in mind, however, is that excess drinking is very much frowned upon by the Chinese, who often don't drink anything stronger than tea in restaurants. In fact, one waiter told me that Westerners spend much more in restaurants than Chinese, simply because Westerners drink alcoholic beverages.

REGIONAL CHINESE FOODS

Chinese cooking has developed through several thousands of years, dictated often by a population too numerous to feed. Famine meant that nothing could be wasted, and lack of fuel meant that food had to be chopped into small pieces and quickly stir-fried. Foods had to be as fresh as possible to avoid spoiling. There are various types of regional Chinese cuisine, and the most common styles in Hong Kong are those from Canton, Beijing (or Peking), Shanghai, Sichuan (Szechuan), and Swatow (Chiu Chow).

Of course there are many other dishes and styles of cuisine in addition to the ones outlined below. It's said that the Chinese will eat anything that swims, flies, or crawls, and though that may not be entirely true, if you're adventurous enough you may want to try such delicacies as snake soup, pig's brain, bird's-nest soup (derived from the saliva of swallows), or eel heads simmered with Chinese herbs.

If you want to know more about the great variety of Chinese food available, there's an excellent booklet called "Visitor's Guide to Chinese Food in Hong Kong," available at HKTA offices.

Cantonese Food

The majority of Chinese restaurants in Hong Kong are Cantonese, not surprising since most Hong Kong Chinese are originally from the area of Canton in China. It's also the most common style of Chinese cooking around the world and is probably the one you're most familiar with.

Cantonese food is either steamed or fried and is known for its fresh, delicate flavors. Little oil or spices are used in the belief that the natural flavors of the various ingredients should prevail, and the Cantonese are sticklers for freshness. If you're concerned about cholesterol, therefore, Cantonese food is the best. On the other hand, those with burned-out taste buds may find it rather bland.

Since the Cantonese eat so much seafood, the best thing you can have in a Cantonese restaurant is fish. I love steamed whole fish prepared with fresh ginger and spring onions, but equally good are slices of garoupa (a local fish), pomfret, red mullet, sole, and bream. Keep in mind that it's considered bad luck to turn a fish over on your plate (it represents a boat capsizing), so the proper thing to do is to eat the top part of the fish, lift the backbone in the air and then extract the bottom layer of meat with your chopsticks. Other popular seafood selections include shrimp and prawns, abalone, squid, scallops, crab, and sea cucumber. Shark's-fin soup is an expensive delicacy.

More Cantonese specialties include roasted goose, duck, and pigeon; pan-fried lemon chicken; stir-fried minced quail and bamboo shoots rolled in lettuce and eaten with the fingers; *congee* (thick rice porridge); and sweet-and-sour pork.

DIM SUM Another popular Cantonese dish is *dim sum,* which means "light snack" but whose Chinese characters literally translate as "to touch the heart." Dating back to the 10th century, dim sum is eaten for breakfast and lunch and with afternoon tea. It consists primarily of finely chopped meat, seafood, and vegetables wrapped in thin dough and then either steamed, fried, boiled, or braised. These can range from steamed dumplings to meatballs, fried spring rolls, and spareribs.

Many Cantonese restaurants offer dim sum from about 7:30 am until 4 pm, served from trolleys wheeled between the tables. The trolleys are piled high with steaming bamboo baskets, so ask the server to let you have a peek inside. If you like what you see, simply nod your head. There are nearly 100 different kinds of dim sum, but some of my favorites are *shiu mai* (steamed minced pork and shrimp dumpling), *har gau* (steamed shrimp dumpling), *au yuk* (steamed minced beef balls), *fun gwor* (steamed rice-flour dumpling filled with pork, shrimp, and bamboo shoots), and *tsuen guen* (deep-fried spring roll filled with shredded pork, chicken, mushrooms, bamboo shoots, and bean sprouts). A serving of dim sum usually comes two to four pieces on a plate and averages about HK$6 (80¢) to HK$12 ($1.55). Your bill is figured at the end of the meal by the number of plates on your table or by a card that was stamped each time you ordered a dish.

Since I can usually manage only two to three dishes, dim sum is one of the cheapest meals I eat in Hong Kong. I often have it for breakfast with lots of tea. But it's more than just the price that draws me to traditional dim sum restaurants—they are noisy, seemingly chaotic, and the perfect place to read a newspaper or gossip. No one should go to Hong Kong without visiting a dim sum restaurant at least once—for a list of dim sum restaurants, refer to the "Specialty Dining" section at the end of this chapter.

Pekinese Food

Many Pekinese dishes originated in the imperial courts of emperors and empresses and were served in elaborate court banquets. Its theatrical flamboyance is still evident today in the making of Pekinese noodles and the smashing of the clay around "beggar's chicken." Because of its northern source, the food of Peking (or Beijing) tends to be rather substantial to keep the body warm, and it uses a liberal amount of peppers, garlic, ginger, leeks, and coriander. Noodles and dumplings are more common than rice, the food is richer than Cantonese food, and roasting is the preferred method of cooking.

Most famous among Peking-style dishes is **Peking duck**

(called Beijing duck on some menus), but unfortunately a minimum of six persons is usually required for this elaborate dish. The most prized part is the crisp skin, which comes from air-drying the bird and then coating it with a mixture of syrup and soy sauce before roasting. It's served by wrapping the crisp skin and meat in thin pancakes together with spring onion, radish, and sweet plum sauce.

Another popular dish prepared with a lot of fanfare is **beggar's chicken,** a whole chicken stuffed with mushrooms, pickled Chinese cabbage, herbs, and onions, sealed in clay and baked all day. The guest of honor usually breaks open the hard clay with a mallet, to reveal a tender feast more fit for a king than a beggar.

For do-it-yourself dining, try the **Mongolian hotpot,** where diners gather around a common pot in a scene reminiscent of campfires on the Mongolian steppes. One version calls for wafer-thin slices of meat, usually mutton, to be dipped in a clear stock and then eaten with a spicy sauce. Another variety calls for a sizzling griddle, over which thin-sliced meat, cabbage, bean sprouts, onions, and other vegetables are barbecued in a matter of seconds.

Shanghainese Food

A big, bustling city, Shanghai does not really have a cuisine of its own. Rather, it incorporates the food of several surrounding regions and cities, making it the most diverse cuisine in China. Because of the cold winters in Shanghai, its food is heavier, richer, sweeter, and oilier than either Cantonese or Pekinese food. In addition, because of hot summers which can spoil food quickly, specialties include pickled or preserved vegetables, fish, shrimp, and mushrooms. Some dishes are rather heavy on the garlic, and portions tend to be enormous. Dishes are often stewed, braised, or fried.

The most popular Shanghainese dish in Hong Kong is freshwater hairy crab, flown in from Shanghai in autumn, steamed, and eaten with the hands. Other Shanghainese dishes include "yellow fish," braised eel with huge chunks of garlic, "drunken chicken" (chicken marinated in Chinese wine), sautéed shrimp in spicy tomato sauce over crispy rice, and sautéed shredded beef and green pepper. As for the famous hundred-year-old egg, it's actually only several months old, with a limey, pickled-ginger taste.

Szechuan Food

This is my favorite Chinese cuisine, as it's the spiciest, hottest, and most fiery style of cooking. The fact that it shares a spiciness with Thailand, India, and Malaysia is no coincidence, since this huge province shares a border with Burma and Tibet.

The culprit is the Szechuan chili, fried to increase its explosiveness. Seasoning is then done with chili-bean paste, peppercorns, garlic, ginger, coriander, and other spices. Foods are simmered and smoked rather than stir-fried. The most famous Szechuan dish is smoked duck, which is seasoned with peppercorns, ginger, cinnamon, and coriander; marinated in rice wine; then steamed and then smoked over a charcoal fire of camphor wood and tea leaves.

Other specialties include pan-fried prawns in spicy sauce, sour-and-peppery soup, sautéed diced chicken in chili-bean sauce, and dry-fried spicy string beans. Most Szechuan menus indicate which dishes are hot.

Chiu Chow Food

A few years ago Szechuan restaurants were opening like crazy, but now the new trend appears to be Chiu Chow restaurants. The name refers to the people, dialect, and food of the area of Swatow in southeast Canton. Chiu Chow chefs pride themselves on their talents for vegetable carvings—those incredible birds, flowers, and other adornments that are a part of every Chiu Chow banquet.

Influenced by Cantonese cooking, Chiu Chow food is rich in protein, light and tasty, and sauces are liberally applied. A meal begins with a cup of *kwun yum* tea, popularly called Iron Buddha and probably the world's strongest and bitterest tea. It's supposed to cleanse the system and stimulate the taste buds. Drink some of this stuff and you'll be humming for hours.

Two Chui Chow delicacies are shark's fin and birds' nests, both of which are very expensive. Other favorites include steamed lobster, deep-fried shrimp balls, sautéed slices of whelk, fried goose blood, goose doused in soy sauce, stuffed eel wrapped in pickled cabbage, and crispy fried *chuenjew* leaves, which literally melt in the mouth.

---

2. Dining Hints and Warnings

You're safe eating anywhere in Hong Kong, even at roadside food stalls, but residents warn foreigners never to eat local oysters —there have been too many instances of oyster poisoning. *Warning:* Eat oysters *only* if they're imported from, say, Australia. The good restaurants will clearly stipulate on the menu that their oysters are imported.

Another thing you should watch in eating Chinese food is your reaction to monosodium glutamate (MSG), used to enhance the flavor in Chinese cooking. Some people react strongly to this spice, reporting bouts of nausea and headaches and a feeling of being bloated. Fortunately, in the past couple of years there has been an increased awareness in Hong Kong of the detrimental side effects of MSG, with the result that most Chinese upper- and medium-range restaurants have stopped using it altogether.

In addition to a wide range of Chinese restaurants recommended in the dining sections below, I've also included a good selection of Asian and Western restaurants that could easily stand on their own anywhere in the world. By far Hong Kong's best and most exclusive restaurants, both Chinese and Western, are in the hotels. That's not surprising when you realize that first-class hotels are used to catering to well-traveled visitors who demand high quality in service, cuisine, and decor.

Keep in mind, however, that Western restaurants tend to be more expensive than Chinese ones, and that wine is especially expensive. All the estimated meal prices for the restaurants below *do not* include wine, since you could easily spend a fortune on drinks alone. To keep costs down, stick with beer: the two most popular brands are San Miguel (Filipino) and Tsingtao (Chinese). And talking about beer, there are many bars and pubs in Chapter IX, "Hong Kong After Dark," that serve food. In any case, keep in mind that in addition to all the prices given for food and drink, a 10% service charge will be added to your bill. There is no tax, however.

One good way to save money is to eat your big meal at lunch. Many restaurants offer a lunchtime special menu, at a price much lower than evening meals. These fixed-price menus often include an appetizer, main entrée, and side dishes, and are available in many Asian and Western restaurants in all price categories. Thus if you feel like splurging, lunch in an expensive restaurant may be the way to go. Don't neglect the listings of restaurants in the expensive bracket, therefore, just because you assume they're out of your price range. You can eat lunch at Gaddi's, for example, one of Hong Kong's most famous restaurants, for less than $21 per person. Buffets are also ways to economize, especially if you have a hearty appetite or like a variety of foods. Refer to the "Specialty Dining" section at the end of this chapter for more information on buffet dining.

For the cheapest meal in Hong Kong, try a *dai pai dong,* a roadside food stall. These are found virtually everywhere in Hong Kong and offer everything from stir-fried vegetables to congee. You can find them on many side streets in Wanchai, Causeway Bay, and the Western District, as well as at night markets, including Temple Street in Yaumatei and Poor Man's Nightclub near the Macau Ferry Pier on Hong Kong Island.

When planning your day's itinerary, keep in mind that the usual lunch hour in Hong Kong is from 1 to 2 pm, when thousands of office workers pour out of buildings and into the city's more popular restaurants. Try to eat before or after the lunch rush hour, therefore, unless you plan on eating at an expensive restaurant and make a reservation.

Reservations are always recommended for upper-bracket restaurants, as well as for medium-range establishments on weekend nights. In addition, reservations are more readily accepted in Western-style restaurants than in Chinese locales. I hardly ever make reservations, but the few exceptions where reservations are absolutely necessary are noted in the restaurant listings below.

---

3. Restaurants at a Glance

Descriptions of the various restaurants along with addresses, prices, and pertinent information are given in the sections that follow. Below, however, is a list of most of the restaurants covered later, but here they are divided into various areas for easy reference. You may, for example, find yourself in Tsimshatsui with an appetite for Szechuan food but not a desire to read through the entire restaurant section to find a Szechuan restaurant in Tsimshatsui. For specialty dining (floating restaurants, dimsum, and buffets), see pages 112–116.

Name of Restaurant	Price Bracket	Type of Cuisine
KOWLOON—TSIMSHATSUI		
Asian Food		
Lai Ching Heen (p.80)	E	Cantonese
Golden Unicorn (p.81)	E	Cantonese
The Chinese (p.85)	M	Cantonese
Full Moon (p.86)	M	Cantonese
Fook Lam Moon (p.86)	M	Cantonese
Tsui Hang Village (p.86)	M	Cantonese
Can Do (p.91)	B	Cantonese/Western
Jade Garden (p.92)	B	Cantonese
Spring Deer (p.87)	M	Pekinese
Lotus Pond (p.87)	M	Szechuan
Fung Lum Restaurant (p.91)	B	Szechuan
Great Shanghai (p.87)	M	Shanghainese
Wu Kong (p.88)	M	Shanghainese
Golden Island Bird's Nest Restaurant (p.92)	B	Chiu Chow
Unkai (p.81)	E	Japanese
Golden Elephant Thai (p.88)	M	Thai
Bangkok Royal Thai (p.92)	B	Thai
Golden Bull (p.89)	M	Vietnamese
New Delhi (p.93)	B	Indian
Sheri Punjab Club Mess (p.93)	B	Indian
Western Food		
Gaddi's (p.82)	E	French
Verandah Grill (p.82)	E	Steaks/Seafood
Plume (p.84)	E	European nouvelle
Hugo's (p.84)	E	Steaks/Continental
Au Trou Normand (p.85)	E	French
Capriccio (p.85)	E	Italian
The Bostonian (p.89)	M	American
Harbour Side (p.89)	M	Continental
Jimmy's Kitchen (p.90)	M	Steaks/European
Lindy's (p.90)	M	American
Palm Steak House (p.90)	M	Portuguese/steaks
The Pizzeria (p.91)	M	Italian
Beverly Hills Deli (p.93)	B	Sandwiches/deli
The Salisbury (p.94)	B	Western/Asian
Spaghetti House (p.94)	B	Pizza/pasta
KOWLOON—EAST TSIMSHATSUI		
Asian Food		
Shang Palace (p.81)	E	Cantonese
Full Moon (p.86)	M	Cantonese

Name of Restaurant	Price Bracket	Type of Cuisine
City Chiuchow Restaurant (p.88)	M	Chiu Chow

Western Food

Margaux (p.84)	E	French/Continental

CENTRAL DISTRICT

Asian Food

The Bloom (p.94)	E	Cantonese
Eagle's Nest (p.95)	E	Cantonese
Man Wah (p.95)	E	Cantonese
Luk Yu Tea House (p.98)	M	Cantonese
United (p.99)	M	Cantonese
City Hall Restaurant (p.102)	B	Cantonese
Yung Kee (p.102)	B	Cantonese
Hunan Garden (p.99)	M	Hunanese
Shanghai Garden (p.100)	M	Shanghainese
Sichuan Garden (p.100)	M	Szechuan
Benkay (p.95)	E	Japanese
The Ashoka (p.100)	M	Indian
Vietnam Restaurant (p.101)	M	Vietnamese

Western Food

Bentley's (p.96)	E	Oysters/seafood
Café de Paris (p.96)	E	French
Mandarin Grill (p.96)	E	Continental
Ninety-Seven (p.98)	E	Continental
Pierrot (p.98)	E	French
Jimmy's Kitchen (p.101)	M	European
La Taverna (p.101)	M	Italian
Le Tire Bouchon (p.102)	M	French
Seasons (p.102)	M	Italian/Continental
Beverly Hills Deli (p.103)	B	Sandwiches/deli
Spaghetti House (p.103)	B	Pizza/pasta

WANCHAI

Asian Food

Sze Chuen Lau (p.107)	M	Szechuan
Golden Poppy (p.107)	M	Thai
American Restaurant (p.108)	B	Pekinese
SMI Curry Restaurant (p.109)	B	South Asian
Wishful Cottage (p.110)	B	Vegetarian

Western Food

Landau's (p.104)	E	European
Rigoletto (p.106)	E	Italian
Spaghetti House (p.110)	B	Pizza/pasta

CAUSEWAY BAY

Asian Food

Sunning Unicorn (p.104)	E	Cantonese
Riverside (p.107)	M	Cantonese

Name of Restaurant	Price Bracket	Type of Cuisine
Harbour City Chiuchow Restaurant (p.106)	M	Chiu Chow
Red Pepper (p.106)	M	Szechuan
Cleveland Szechuan Restaurant (p.109)	B	Szechuan
Vegi Food Kitchen (p.107)	M	Vegetarian
Sogo Department Store (p.109)	B	Japanese/Chinese
Western Food		
Excelsior Grill (p.104)	E	European
Bologna Ristorante Italiano (p.108)	M	Italian
Spaghetti House (p.110)	B	Pizza/pasta
HAPPY VALLEY		
Amigo Restaurant (p.110)	E	French
Pep N' Chili (p.111)	M	Szechuan
VICTORIA PEAK		
Peak Tower Restaurant (p.111)	M	European
Peak Café (p.111)	B	Snacks/sand-wiches/rice
STANLEY		
Stanley's Restaurant (p.111)	E	French

4. Restaurants in Kowloon

Since this is Hong Kong's main tourist area, you won't have any problems finding a place to eat here. Rather, with so many choices, your problem will be in making your selection. Remember that the estimated prices for meals given below do not include wines of drinks.

EXPENSIVE

Asian Food

• **Lai Ching Heen,** Regent Hotel, Salisbury Rd., Tsimshatsui (tel. 7211211). *Prices:* Average dinner HK$400 ($52); average lunch HK$300 ($39). AE, DC, MC, V.

One of Hong Kong's top Cantonese restaurants, Lai Ching Heen emphasizes the beauty of stark simplicity. Bonsai trees and a color scheme of rose and pale gray offset beautiful jade table settings and ivory and silver chopsticks, and large windows treat diners to a view of famous Victoria Harbour. Dishes are traditional Cantonese, as well as imaginative creations of the executive chef that border on Chinese nouvelle cuisine. The menu changes with each lunar month but always includes seafood, seasonal vegetables, and a wide selection of desserts.

Open: Daily noon–3pm and 6–11:30 pm. *Reservations:* Recommended. *MTR:* Tsimshatsui. CANTONESE

▪ **Shang Palace,** Shangri-La Hotel, 64 Mody Rd., East Tsimshatsui (tel. 7212111). *Prices:* Dishes for 2–4 people average HK$50–HK$100 ($6.50–$13); dinners average HK$270 ($35) per person; fixed-price lunches HK$129 ($16.50) for two people. AE, CB, DC, MC, V.

This is one of the most elaborately decorated Chinese restaurants in Hong Kong, evident even in the entryway with its rows of red columns, which are cleverly multiplied by the use of mirrors to give the illusion of a long corridor. The walls of the restaurant itself are of red lacquerware carved in designs, and Chinese lanterns hang from the ceiling. All in all, it fits all expectations of how an authentic Chinese restaurant should look.

The dinner menu is quite extensive, with a large variety of seafood, chicken, duck, pigeon, beef, and pork cooked Cantonese style. Specialties include shark's-fin soup, barbecued pork, Peking duck, steamed shrimp in lotus leaf, braised vegetables, and pan-fried minced pigeon with lettuce. If money is no object, you might consider bamboo fungus with crabmeat or bird's nest, with dishes running HK$200 ($26) or more.

More economical is lunch. Although the lunch menu changes every two weeks, it always includes more than a dozen varieties of dim sum, as well as a great fixed-price menu for two people.

Open: Daily noon–3pm (from 11am Sun and hols) and 6:30–11pm. *Reservations:* Imperative. *MTR:* Tsimshatsui. CANTONESE

▪ **Golden Unicorn Restaurant,** Omni Hongkong Hotel, 3 Canton Rd., Tsimshatsui (tel. 7226565). *Prices:* Fixed-price menu HK$218 ($28.25); average meal HK$550 ($71.50). AE, DC, MC, V.

Opened in 1986, this sixth-floor restaurant was one of the forerunners in the recent trend to present Chinese food in a more modern and formal setting. Serving Cantonese food with a Western flair, this restaurant uses Wedgwood china and Christofle silverware in its presentation of such specialties as drunken prawn, deep-fried chicken, duck, pork, and seafood selections. If you're by yourself you'll probably want to order the fixed-price menu, which changes monthly and allows you to sample several dishes.

Open: Daily noon–midnight. *Reservations:* Recommended. *MTR:* Tsimshatsui. CANTONESE

▪ **Unkai,** Sheraton Hotel, 20 Nathan Rd., Tsimshatsui (tel. 3691111). *Prices:* Average dinner HK$400 ($52); fixed-price lunch menus from HK$75 ($9.75). AE, CB, DC, MC, V.

The Hong Kong branch of a well-known group of restaurants in Japan, Unkai may well be the best Japanese restaurant in town. True to Japanese form, the elegance of the restaurant is subtly understated, an aesthetic form that is also carried into the presentation of its food. Foremost, of course, are the kaiseki courses, which start at HK$300 ($39) and are the epitome of Japanese cuisine, with artfully arranged dishes that change according to the seasons. There's also teppanyaki (Japanese-style steaks cooked on a hot grill), tempura (meat and vegetables coated in batter and then deep-fried), shabu-shabu (thinly sliced beef cooked in a broth with vegetables at your table), and sushi (raw fish).

If you come for lunch, you have a selection of fixed-price menus, including a sushi course for HK$100 ($13), a tempura course for HK$75 ($9.75), and an obento lunch box. The obento is especially charming, a small lacquered chest with dishes of food in each of the drawers.

Open: Daily noon–2:30pm and 6:30–10:30pm. *Reservations:* Recommended. *MTR:* Tsimshatsui. JAPANESE

Western Food

- **Gaddi's,** Peninsula Hotel, Salisbury Rd., Tsimshatsui (tel. 3666251, ext. 3989). *Prices:* Average dinner from HK$650 ($84.50); fixed-price lunch HK$160 ($20.75). AE, CB, DC, MC, V.

Named after a former general manager of the Peninsula, Gaddi's has had a reputation for being the best European restaurant in town ever since it opened in 1953. Although that is now being challenged by some pretty stiff competition from other hotels, the service is still excellent, the waiters are all professionals, the food is always beyond reproof, and it's still a legend in the Orient.

The atmosphere is that of an elegant European dining room blended with the best of Asia, with two crystal-and-silver chandeliers from Paris, a pure-wool Tai Ping carpet in royal blue, and a Chinese coromandel screen dating from 1670. As for the food, it's French haute cuisine at its finest and the soufflés are sublime. The menu changes every six months, but always includes steak and seafood. Its wine selection is among the best and most extensive in Hong Kong, with a collection of rare vintages—but who could blame you if you get carried away and splurge on champagne. There's live music at night and a small dance floor. Needless to say, jacket and tie are required for dinner.

Lunches, especially the Squire fixed-price menu, are very affordable, making this the top choice in a splurge for the money-conscious.

Open: Daily noon–3pm and 7–11pm. *Reservations:* Recommended for lunch, a necessity for dinner. *MTR:* Tsimshatsui. FRENCH

- **Verandah Grill,** Peninsula Hotel, Salisbury Rd., Tsimshatsui (tel. 3666251, ext. 3971). *Prices:* Entrées from HK$150 ($19.50); average dinner HK$270 ($35); fixed-price lunch menu HK$130 ($17). AE, CB, DC, MC, V.

If you find Gaddi's too stuffy and pretentious, the Peninsula's other restaurant may be more to your liking. Visible from Salisbury Road as the restaurant with the light-blue-and-green canopy, the Verandah Grill is an airy, bright, and cheerful place that does give the illusion of being a veranda. Its big windows wrap themselves around the U-shaped front façade of the hotel, offering a view that unfortunately has been spoiled somewhat by that monstrosity across the street, the Space Museum. However, the food is so good and the

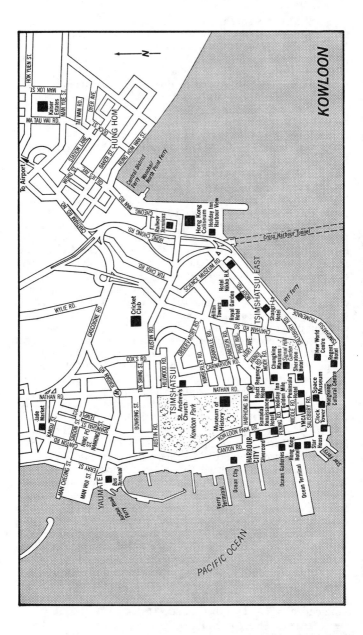

service so attentive that you'll soon forget to look any farther than your own table.

Grilled foods are the specialty here, with selections of steak, seafood, and veal. If you want to splurge, you can order fresh beluga caviar or lobster soup, but be sure to save room for dessert. The wine list seems endless, with a great choice of American vintages. If you have an extra thousand Hong Kong dollars, you could easily spend it here, but otherwise the light luncheon fixed-price menu is a good choice, which includes a salad or soup, entrée, dessert, and coffee or tea. You might also want to start your day in style by coming for breakfast. Dress is casual during the day, but jacket and tie are required for dinner.

Open: Daily 7–11am, noon–3pm, and 7–11pm. *Reservations:* Highly recommended for lunch or dinner. *MTR:* Tsimshatsui. GRILLED STEAKS AND SEAFOOD

• **Plume,** Regent Hotel, Salisbury Rd., Tsimshatsui (tel. 7211211). *Prices:* Entrées average HK$180 ($23.50), but expect to pay at least HK$500 ($65) per person for dinner. AE, DC, MC, V.

Giving Gaddi's a run for its money is the Plume in the upstart Regent. In fact, some people consider the Plume to be the best European restaurant in Hong Kong. Certainly it feels like a great restaurant, sitting right over the water with a grand view of Hong Kong Island and serving very interesting nouvelle cuisine.

It's open only for dinner, which begins with a complimentary glass of champagne Mir (champagne with a hint of blackberry liqueur), Indian bread, and goose-liver pâté. The menu, which contains only original creations that mix the best of the East and the West, changes every day but always includes the house specialty: a delicate cream of artichoke with beluga. In any case, the food is so imaginative and full of surprises that epicures will want to set up camp—assuming, of course, that they remembered to pack a coat and tie or cocktail dress, the required uniform here.

Open: Daily 7–11pm. *Reservations:* Recommended. *MTR:* Tsimshatsui. EUROPEAN NOUVELLE CUISINE

• **Hugo's,** Hyatt Regency, 67 Nathan Rd., Tsimshatsui (tel. 3662321). *Prices:* Average dinner HK$300–HK$400 ($39–$52); lunch fixed-price menu HK$143 ($18.75). AE, DC, MC, V.

This was the first Hugo's that Hyatt opened in Asia and now there's a Hugo's in all their upper bracket hotels. Its decor is very masculine, with swords on the walls, huge leather-bound menus, and big green water glasses. Popular with the locals and visiting business travelers, it's a lively place, and in the evenings Filipino musicians serenade the diners. The specialty is U.S. prime rib of beef, with seafood flown in from around the world. The menu changes twice a year, but if lobster bisque is on the menu, you can't go wrong ordering it. The desserts are always spectacular, and the wine list is extensive. A jacket and tie are required.

Open: Daily noon–2:30pm and 7–11pm. *Reservations:* Recommended. *MTR:* Tsimshatsui. CONTINENTAL

• **Margaux,** Shangri-La Hotel, 64 Mody Rd., East Tsimshatsui (tel. 7212111). *Prices:* Average dinner HK$450 ($58.50), fixed-price dinner menu HK$380 ($49.25); fixed-price lunch menu HK$108 ($14). AE, CB, DC, MC, V.

Tastefully decorated with teakwood and Viennese chandeliers and offering an inspiring view of the harbor, the Margaux serves Continental food with an emphasis on French nouvelle cuisine. Its menu changes often, though it always includes beef, veal, and seafood dishes that are dependably good. Its sommeliers are female, which is still rather rare in Asia, and its wine cellars lean toward the French vintages. Château Margaux is widely featured, so it may be hard to resist uncorking a bottle here. Dinner, by candlelight, requires a coat and tie. Lunch is considerably more casual, but jeans are frowned upon. Sunday features a popular brunch.

Open: Daily noon–3pm and 7–11:30pm. *Reservations:* Recommended for lunch, necessary for dinner. *MTR:* Tsimshatsui. FRENCH/CONTINENTAL

- **Capriccio,** Ramada Renaissance, 8 Peking Rd., Tsimshatsui (tel. 3113311). *Prices:* Entrées average HK$150–HK$200 ($19.50–$26); dinners average HK$500 ($65). AE, DC, MC, V.

Whereas most hotels feature French or Continental cuisine in their top restaurant, the Ramada Renaissance has chosen to premier northern Italian cuisine from Tuscany. This is easily the most exclusive Italian restaurant in all of Hong Kong, elegant with exquisite flower arrangements, innovative lighting, and an interior design of yellow and gray. All the pasta is homemade, and though the menu changes often, popular demand may dictate that it always offer lobster with eggplant, tomato, and pesto. Future plans for this new restaurant call for a daily business lunch. Coat and tie required.

Open: Daily noon–3pm and 7–11pm. *Reservations:* Recommended. *MTR:* Tsimshatsui. ITALIAN

- **Au Trou Normand,** 6 Carnarvon Rd., Tsimshatsui (tel. 3668754). *Prices:* Average dinner HK$270 ($35); fixed-price lunch menu HK$88 ($11.50). AE, DC, MC, V.

If you absolutely refuse to dine in a hotel or don't own a jacket and tie, then this cheerful, small restaurant—a mainstay in Hong Kong since it opened in 1964—decorated in the style of a farmhouse in Normandy may be for you. Its prices are slightly lower than the hotel restaurants listed above. French owner Bernard Vigneau is always present, a plus for any restaurant. The menu includes such dishes as pork and duck liver, grilled steaks, sautéed frogs' legs, an excellent cheese board, and superb chocolate mousse. A good buy is the fixed-price lunch, which includes a buffet appetizer table, choice of entrée, dessert, and a glass of wine.

Open: Daily noon–3pm and 7–11pm. *Reservations:* Recommended. *MTR:* Tsimshatsui. FRENCH

MODERATE
Asian Food

- **The Chinese,** Hyatt Regency, 67 Nathan Rd., Tsimshatsui (tel. 3662321). *Prices:* Average dinner HK$160 ($20.75); dim sum lunch HK$60 ($7.80). AE, DC, MC, V.

Decorated in stark black and white with a blend of art deco and modern Chinese decor, the Chinese is one of Hong Kong's most refined Cantonese restaurants. The dining room, small and intimate, features walls lined with wooden booths, reminiscent of Chinese tea houses of the 1920s. The specialty of the restaurant is its seasonal menu in which beef, pork, pigeon, chicken, duck, shellfish, fish, abalone, and vegetables are prepared in innovative ways. If available, deep-fried crispy chicken, minced pigeon with butter lettuce, drunken shrimp, and fried lobster balls are all equally delicious. Another great deal is the special dim sum lunch.

Open: Daily noon–3pm and 6:30–11pm. *MTR:* Tsimshatsui. CANTONESE

• **Full Moon,** 102 Barnton Court, Harbour City, Tsimshatsui (tel. 7309131); and Empire Center, 68 Mody Rd., East Tsimshatsui (tel. 7392868). *Prices:* Meals average HK$100–HK$150 ($13–$19.50); dim sum HK$13 ($1.70) a plate. Cash only.

This Cantonese restaurant has two locations. One is across the street from the Silvercord building just off Canton Road in a small courtyard nestled in Harbour City in Tsimshatsui, and with pink tablecloths and modern decor it's one of Hong Kong's trendier Chinese restaurants. Slightly newer is its companion restaurant in East Tsimshatsui, in the lower ground floor of the Empire Center. Both offer more than 100 items on their Cantonese menus, including barbecued Beijing duck. Although not on the menu, one of its specialties is "drunken prawns," which are supposedly drowned in Chinese yellow wine and then cooked in a soup, at HK$110 ($14.25) for two persons.

Open: Daily 11:30am–3pm (from 10am Sun and hols) and 5:30pm–midnight. *MTR:* Tsimshatsui for both. CANTONESE

• **Fook Lam Moon,** 31-35A Mody Rd., Tsimshatsui (tel. 3660286). *Prices:* Average meal HK$100 ($13); dim sum averages HK$12 ($1.55). Cash only.

The entrance to this restaurant is around the corner on Hart Avenue, and upon entering you immediately feel like you've stepped back a couple decades to a Hong Kong that has all but vanished. Even the waiters seem to be left over from the old Hong Kong— indifferent, slow, and seemingly bored (Chinese waiters in Hong Kong used to be notorious for their indifference, but their breed is being replaced by a corps of ambitious youths as Chinese restaurants modernize into trendy establishments). In any case, it offers the usual bird's nest, abalone, seafood, chicken, frog, pork, pigeon, and beef selections. Shark's fin, however, is the obvious specialty, with 19 different renditions listed on the menu. If you feel like splurging, prices for half a bowl of shark's fin begin at HK$125 ($16.25). Other specialties are lemon chicken and crispy chicken.

Open: Daily 11:30am–11:30pm. *MTR:* Tsimshatsui. CANTONESE

• **Tsui Hang Village Restaurant,** 15th floor of Keewan Tower, Park Lane Square, 132-134 Nathan Rd., Tsimshatsui (tel.

3686363). *Prices:* Average meal HK$150–HK$200 ($19.50–$26); dim sum HK$8–HK$16 ($1.05–$2.10). AE, MC, V.

Located near the Miramar Hotel, this Cantonese restaurant offers a good view of Kowloon Park and beyond. Named after the home village of Dr. Sun Yat-sen, it features a white jade statue of the Goddess of Mercy and specializes in its own nouvelle Cantonese original creations. Its award-winning dish is its shark's fin with bamboo-pitch, asparagus, and crab claw, which is priced at HK$150 ($19.50). Other dishes you might consider trying are fresh lobster, deep-fried minced shrimp balls with crisp almond, sautéed minced pigeon with lettuce, barbecued Peking duck, roast goose, wonton noodles, or fried milk fritters.

Open: Daily 11am–midnight (from 10am Sun). *MTR:* Tsimshatsui. CANTONESE

- **Spring Deer Restaurant,** 42 Mody Rd., Tsimshatsui (tel. 3664012). *Prices:* Average meal HK$120–HK$150 ($15.50–$19.50). V.

An old standby favorite in Hong Kong, this long-established restaurant offers excellent Pekinese food at reasonable prices. Spring Deer is cheerful and very accessible to foreigners, but don't expect anything fancy; in fact, your tablecloth is likely to have holes in it, but it will be clean—and the place is often packed with loyal fans. This is one of the best places to come if you want to try its specialty —Peking duck. Since you'll probably have to wait 40 minutes for the duck if you order it during peak time (7:30 to 9:30pm), it's best to arrive either before or after the rush. Chicken dishes are also well liked, including the deep-fried chicken in soy sauce, and the handmade noodles are excellent. Most dishes come in small, medium, and large sizes.

Open: Daily noon–3pm and 6–11pm. *MTR:* Tsimshatsui. PE-KINESE

- **Lotus Pond,** 15 Harbour City, Canton Rd., Tsimshatsui (tel. 7308688). *Prices:* Average meal HK$100–HK$200 ($13–$26); dim sum from HK$6 (80¢). AE, V.

This smartly decorated Szechuan restaurant is located on Canton Road across from its junction with Haiphong Road. It lists more than 100 dishes on its menu, including such specialties as fried prawns in chili sauce, fried chicken Szechuan style, smoked duck, and shark's-fin soup. Although it's a Szechuan restaurant, it also serves its own style of dim sum.

Open: Daily 11am–3pm and 5:30–11:30pm. *MTR:* Tsimshatsui. SZECHUAN

- **Great Shanghai,** 26 Prat Ave., Tsimshatsui (tel. 3662693). *Prices:* Average meal HK$100 ($13). AE, DC, MC, V.

Established in 1958, this is a well-known restaurant in Tsimshatsui serving Shanghainese food. An old-fashioned big dining hall with bright lights, white tablecloths, and plenty of waiters in white shirts and black bow ties, it has a gigantic menu with more than 300 items, including Szechuan dishes (having no cuisine of its own, Shanghai has borrowed heavily from neighboring provinces).

Try the prawns in chili sauce, diced chicken with cashews, cold chicken in wine sauce, hot-and-sour soup, or Peking duck. The house specialty is beggar's chicken, but it's available only at night and it's necessary to call in your order by mid-afternoon. My own particular favorite is braised eel, which is cooked in an oily garlic sauce, but all eel dishes here are good.

Open: Daily 11am–11pm. *MTR:* Tsimshatsui. SHANG-HAINESE

■ **Wu Kong,** 27 Nathan Rd. (entrance on Peking Rd.), Tsimshatsui (tel. 3667244). *Prices:* Average meal HK$100–HK$150 ($13–$19.50). Cash only.

Another popular restaurant, Wu Kong is often packed with locals during mealtimes. More upscale than most Shanghainese restaurants with its soothing green-and-white color scheme, it serves a variety of shark's-fin dishes, as well as the usual pigeon in wine sauce, sautéed fresh prawn, braised shredded eels, and other dishes common to Shanghai.

Open: Daily 11:30am–midnight. *MTR:* Tsimshatsui. SHANGHAINESE

■ **City Chiuchow Restaurant,** East Ocean Centre, 98 Granville Rd., East Tsimshatsui (tel. 7236226). *Prices:* Average meal HK$100 ($13). AE, DC, MC, V.

Riding the crest of the wave of a new-found popularity for Chiu Chow food, this spacious restaurant overlooks the gardens that lead down to a major promenade in East Tsimshatsui. Decorated in colors Chinese adore—gold and red—it seats 500 and features a big tank with fish swimming happily about, unaware of their impending fate.

Famous dishes here include Chiu Chow shark's-fin soup, much thicker and stronger tasting than the Cantonese version; double-boiled shark's-fin-and-chicken soup, not as strong but equally popular; sliced soy goose; fried chicken with a black spicy sauce; and seafood dishes, including lobster. I particularly recommend the cold sliced lobster in a special honey sauce—it's not on the menu but it's available year round. It also serves dim sum. And don't forget to try the Iron Buddha tea, Chiuchow's special tea, which is so strong it will knock your socks off—and may keep you awake all night.

Open: Fri–Sun 11am–midnight, Mon–Thurs 11am–3pm and 5pm–midnight. *MTR:* Tsimshatsui. CHIU CHOW

■ **Golden Elephant Thai Restaurant,** 3 Barnton Court, Harbour City, Tsimshatsui (tel. 7350733). *Prices:* Average meal HK$150 ($19.50); lunch buffet HK$75 ($9.75). AE, DC, MC, V.

Thai food is very popular in Hong Kong these days, and one of the first Thai restaurants to open its doors was this restaurant just off Canton Road across from the Silvercord building. Affiliated with Thai Airways, it serves both spicy and mild foods that are toned down for the Chinese tongue, so if you want something authentically hot, be sure to tell the waitress. The lunch buffet is a good bargain, but if you opt for an à la carte meal, you might want to start out with such appetizers as Thai crispy rice served with minced pork and shrimp sauce, Thai shrimp crackers, or the spicy beef salad. Main courses include such delectables as boiled beef with satay sauce, fried diced chicken with red chili and hot basil leaf, Thai fish cake, steamed fish with plum sauce and ginger, and grilled chicken.

Open: Daily noon–3pm and 6–11pm. *MTR:* Tsimshatsui. THAI

• **Golden Bull,** New World Center, 20 Salisbury Rd., Tsimshatsui (tel. 3694617); and Ocean Centre, Harbour City, Tsimshatsui (tel. 7304866). *Prices:* Average meal HK$100 ($13). AE, DC, MC, V.

Serving Vietnamese food, the Golden Bull has two locations, both in shopping arcades. If you're not familiar with this cuisine, you might want to opt for the Golden Bull Platter for HK$95 ($12.25) which gives you a variety of dishes. Otherwise, typical Vietnamese items include crisp spring rolls wrapped in lettuce and dipped in a tangy sauce, hot-and-sour prawns, roast pig, various noodle dishes, barbecued prawns on sugarcane, barbecued chicken, and seafood.

Open: Daily noon–11:30pm for both. *MTR:* Tsimshatsui for both. VIETNAMESE

Western Food

• **The Bostonian,** Ramada Renaissance Hotel, 8 Peking Rd., Tsimshatsui (tel. 3113311). *Prices:* Entrées HK$120–HK$140 ($15.50–$18.25) for most; executive lunch HK$140 ($18.25). AE, DC, MC, V.

It's hard to think of a more fun-oriented restaurant than the Bostonian. All its tables feature paper tablecloths and plenty of crayons so you can scribble to your heart's content. The menu makes wisecracks, such as "All foods are made in the kitchen where we can hide our shame (we still can't break open an egg with one hand)" and "For an explanation of any item on our menu, ask any employee. If he doesn't know, he'll make up something." Needless to say, the atmosphere is laid-back and casual, and the restaurant looks as though it were imported intact from the U.S. East Coast.

It has an eclectic menu, with marinated shiitake mushrooms, quesadillas, Cajun popcorn, buffalo chicken wings with plum sauce and bleu cheese dip, and fried alligator fritters listed in its "Starters and Other Leftovers" column. For main courses it features Kansas beef, blackened catfish with Cajun spices, sautéed soft-shell crab with a spicy succotash, grilled salmon steak, grilled swordfish, and other seafood dishes. It also has a raw bar, where you can order crawdaddies, oysters, and other delicacies by the piece. There is a huge selection of American wines, with more than 300 vintages. Clearly, you could spend a small fortune here.

Open: Daily noon–1am. *MTR:* Tsimshatsui. AMERICAN

• **Harbour Side,** Regent Hotel, Salisbury Rd., Tsimshatsui (tel. 7211211). *Prices:* Entrées HK$50–HK$100 ($6.50–$13). AE, DC, MC, V.

Although located in the elegant Regent hotel, this is an informal dining hall with a view of the harbor. Rather plain and bare with a brick floor and wooden chairs, it serves hamburgers, seafood, chicken and shrimp curry, and other dishes listed on a menu that changes daily. If you want to come just for the view, a cup of coffee is HK$20 ($2.60) and cocktails average HK$38 ($4.95).

Open: Daily 6am–midnight. *MTR:* Tsimshatsui. CONTINENTAL

• **Jimmy's Kitchen,** 29-39 Ashley Rd., Tsimshatsui (tel. 3684027). *Prices:* Average meal from HK$170 ($22). AE, DC, MC, V.

This is the Kowloon version of Central District's Jimmy's Kitchen, which originated in Shanghai and opened in Central more than 60 years ago. It serves dependably good European food, including seafood, steaks, chicken, imported oysters, and curries. And don't forget to check the blackboards for the daily specials.

Open: Daily noon–11pm. *MTR:* Tsimshatsui. EUROPEAN

• **Lindy's,** 1st floor, 57 Peking Rd., Tsimshatsui (tel. 3671683). *Prices:* Average dinner HK$100–HK$150 ($13–$19.50); fixed-price dinner from HK$105 ($13.75); average lunch HK$50–HK$100 ($6.50–$13); American breakfast HK$37 ($4.80). AE, DC, MC, V.

Open since 1965, Lindy's caters primarily to tourists staying in neighboring hotels. Decorated like an American steakhouse with lots of tables along the windows where you can observe the action in Tsimshatsui, this upstairs restaurant serves breakfast until 11am, one of the main reasons for its popularity. The lunch menu lists soups, salads, sandwiches, hamburgers, steaks, seafood, spareribs, lasagne, and lobster. Dinner is more of the same but with higher prices; the steaks are especially good here. If you're starving for raw vegetables, you can forage along the salad bar for your main dish for HK$60 ($7.80). There are also fixed-price dinners starting at HK$105 ($13.75) that include a trip through the salad bar.

Open: Daily 8am–11pm. *MTR:* Tsimshatsui. AMERICAN/ CONTINENTAL

• **Palm Steak House,** 38 Lock Rd., Tsimshatsui (tel. 7211271). *Prices:* Average dinner HK$90–HK$200 ($11.75–$26); fixed-price lunches from HK$50 ($6.50). AE, DC, MC, V.

This basement establishment is actually two restaurants in one: a steakhouse and a Portuguese restaurant. Steaks are served in a cavernlike room where the walls are literally covered with graffiti and signatures. Pictures of celebrities line the walls, and as nothing is sacred anymore, even these are written on. A very good U.S. prime rib served with potatoes is priced at HK$150 ($19.50). Other dishes include rock oysters from Long Island, smoked Scottish salmon, southern fried chicken, and lobster, and there's a minimum charge of HK$100 ($13) per person at night. Lunch specials range from HK$65 to HK$90 ($8.45 to $11.75) and include soup, main course, salad bar, and coffee.

Another dining room serves Portuguese specialties and other

fare, including boned half chicken in its own secret sauce, braised chicken Portuguese style, baked cod, and curry crab. It offers a fixed-price lunch for HK$50 ($6.50), and the minimum dinner charge here is HK$65 ($8.45) per person.

Open: Daily noon–3pm and 5:30pm–midnight. *MTR:* Tsimshatsui. STEAKS/CONTINENTAL/PORTUGUESE

- **The Pizzeria,** Kowloon Hotel, 19-21 Nathan Rd., Tsimshatsui (tel. 3698698). *Prices:* Entrées HK$90–HK$110 ($11.75–$14.25); pizza from HK$45 ($5.85); lunch pasta buffet HK$63 ($8.20). AE, CB, DC, MC, V.

Located on the second floor of the Kowloon Hotel, this informal dining hall with large windows specializes in pasta. Its à la carte menu lists green lasagne with Bel Paese cheese, tortellini with bacon and truffles in a herb-cream sauce, ravioli with snails, and spaghetti. The best deal is the lunchtime pasta bar for HK$63 ($8.20); you can add a trip through the salad bar for an extra HK$39 ($5.05). There are also nine different kinds of pizza.

Open: Daily 11:45am–2:30pm and 6–10:45pm. *MTR:* Tsimshatsui. ITALIAN

BUDGET

In addition to the restaurants listed below, be sure to check the buffet spreads and dim-sum restaurants at the end of this chapter in the "Specialty Dining" section, since they're good choices for budget-conscious diners.

Asian Food

- **Can Do,** 37 Cameron Rd., Tsimshatsui (tel. 7218183). *Prices:* Meals average HK$20–HK$50 ($2.60–$6.50); American breakfast HK$25 ($3.25). Cash only.

Nothing fancy about this place. In fact, it looks like an American diner or truck-stop restaurant, except that here both tables and customers are so packed in that there's hardly room to walk. More than likely you'll share your table with other diners and you'll be expected to clear out when you've finished eating. People come here to chow down, not socialize. Popular with both locals and tourists, it advertises "bloody good cheap Chinese and Western food at fair dinkum prices" and lives up to its claim by serving a daily special for only HK$20 ($2.60). Its English menu lists Cantonese dishes such as sweet-and-sour pork, chicken with cashews, beef in oyster sauce, and mixed vegetables in curry sauce, as well as such Western fare as fish and chips, sandwiches, and spaghetti.

Open: Daily 7am–1am. *MTR:* Tsimshatsui. CANTONESE/WESTERN

- **Fung Lum Restaurant,** 23 Granville Rd., Tsimshatsui (tel. 3678919). *Prices:* Small dishes HK$35–HK$60 ($4.55–$7.80); large dishes about HK$80 ($10.50). Cash only.

Rather bare-looking but very popular, this Szechuan restaurant has been here more than a quarter of a century, surviving so far the onslaught of clothing stores that have slowly transformed this street

from one of dining to one of shopping. It seats only about 80 people, so try to get here ahead of dining rush hours. Specialties include
Szechuan chicken, shrimp with chili-and-garlic sauce, sliced pork in
garlic-and-chili sauce, beef filet with pepper and hot garlic sauce,
scallops in garlic-and-onion sauce, and frogs' legs with chili. Spicy
dishes are indicated on the menu.

Open: Daily noon–11pm. *MTR:* Tsimshatsui. SZECHUAN

• **Golden Island Bird's Nest Restaurant,** 2nd floor of Star
House, 3 Salisbury Rd., Tsimshatsui (tel. 7226228); and Hanoi
Rd., Tsimshatsui (tel. 3695211). *Prices:* Most dishes average
HK$40–HK$65 ($5.20–$8.45). AE, DC, MC, V.

This Chiu Chow restaurant has two locations, one at the junction of Carnarvon Road and Hanoi Road and the other in the Star
House in front of the Star Ferry terminus. As the prices for dishes
above indicate, you can eat quite cheaply here if you order only one
dish per person, but you'll pay more if you consume such exotic fare
as bird's nest, shark's fin, abalone, whelk, or lobster. As is evident
from its name, the house specialty is bird's nest, prepared 14 different ways. The menu also includes minced pigeon with ham and
roast goose, as well as dishes that use frogs, mutton, crab, bean curd,
bamboo shoots, beef, pork, chicken, and seafood as main ingredients.

Open: Daily 11am–11:30pm (the Hanoi Road restaurant stays
open till midnight). *MTR:* Tsimshatsui for both. CHIU CHOW

• **Jade Garden Chinese Restaurant,** 4th floor of Star House, 3
Salisbury Rd., Tsimshatsui (tel. 7226888). *Prices:* Average meal
HK$80 ($10.50); dim sum HK$8–HK$12 ($1.05–$1.60). AE,
DC, MC.

Jade Garden is part of a chain of restaurants owned by the Maxim's Group, a company that has been wildly successful throughout
Hong Kong (other establishments in the group include Peking Garden, Sichuan Garden, Shanghai Garden, and Chiu Chow Garden).
Jade Garden is its Cantonese restaurant and is geared toward the
Chinese-food novice. Thus if you don't know much about Chinese
food, feel that you should try it, but still aren't very keen on the idea,
Jade Garden may be for you. Like most Cantonese restaurants, for
lunch it serves dim sum from trolleys pushed through the aisles. If
you'd rather order from the menu or come for dinner, you might
consider sautéed chicken with oyster sauce, barbecued Peking duck,
roast pigeon, or sweet-and-sour pork.

Open: Daily 11:30am–midnight. *MTR:* Tsimshatsui. CAN-
TONESE

• **Bangkok Royal Thai Restaurant,** Bangkok Royal Hotel, 2-12
Pilkem St., Kowloon (tel. 7359181). *Prices:* Average meals HK$50
($6.50); fixed-price lunch HK$27 ($3.50). AE, DC, MC, V.

This Thai restaurant is off the lobby of the Bangkok Royal Hotel and is known for its cheap prices and fairly good food. The fixed-
price lunch, served until 2:30pm, offers a couple of choices for a
soup and main dish. The menu lists typical Thai curries with coconut milk and chilis. My favorites are sour-and-spicy Thai soup with

prawns or fish, Thai-style fried rice noodles, and chicken curry with coconut milk.

Open: Daily noon–11pm. *MTR:* Jordan. THAI

• **New Delhi,** 52 Cameron Rd., Tsimshatsui (tel. 3664611). *Prices:* Entrées HK$32–HK$45 ($4.15–$5.85); fixed-price lunches from HK$38 ($4.95). v.

Serving food from northern India, this informal restaurant dishes out tandoori as well as chicken, lamb, seafood, and vegetable curries. Specialties include its chicken tandoori, shish kebab, chicken masala, and its own original creation, lamb New Delhi (cooked in a tomato-cream sauce with secret ingredients). Its HK$38 ($4.95) fixed-price lunch is served only on Monday, Wednesday, Friday, and Sunday, but a HK$57 ($7.40) vegetarian lunch is available daily.

Open: Daily noon–2:30pm and 6:30–11pm. *MTR:* Tsimshatsui. INDIAN

• **Sheri Punjab Club Mess,** 3rd floor of B Block, Chungking Mansion, 36-44 Nathan Rd., Tsimshatsui (tel. 3680859). *Prices:* Average meal HK$50 ($6.50). Cash only.

Considering the fact that many of the shops and hostels in Chungking Mansion are run by Indians, you'd expect that the complex would contain at least a few cheap Indian restaurants. Sheri Punjab Club Mess is one of the most popular, both with Indians living in Chungking and with travelers on a tight budget. A bare, clean, and simple room, it offers more than 70 items, served on plastic plates. The menu consists of things like chicken curry, mutton masala, mutton vindaloo, tandoori, and Muglai chicken, as well as a wide selection of vegetarian offerings. Dishes range from HK$15 to HK$35 ($1.95 to $4.45), but they're small and you'll probably want to order at least two plates per person. Beer is only HK$5.50 (70¢) a can.

Open: Daily 11am–3:30pm and 6–11:30pm. *MTR:* Tsimshatsui. INDIAN

Western Food

• **Beverly Hills Deli,** Level 2 of New World Centre, 20 Salisbury Rd., Tsimshatsui (tel. 3698695). *Prices:* HK$30–HK$60 ($3.90–$7.80). AE, MC, V.

If you are longing for sandwiches, hot dogs, hamburgers, and traditional deli, this place and the Beverly Hills Deli in Central (mentioned further on) offer the best such fare in town. Their lengthy menu caters to the homesick palate with Texas chili, stuffed and triple-decker sandwiches, bagels with lox and cream cheese, Cajun and fried chicken, pepper steak, roast beef, and more. There are even some vegetarian offerings and such Middle Eastern dishes as hummus, kebabs, moussaka, and Moroccan chicken. This is an informal diner that also provides take-out and delivery anywhere in Hong Kong.

Open: Daily 11am–10pm. *MTR:* Tsimshatsui. SANDWICHES/DELI

- **The Salisbury,** YMCA, Salisbury Rd., Tsimshatsui (tel. 3692211). *Prices:* Average dinner HK$42–HK$55 ($5.45–$7.15); lunch buffet from HK$38 ($4.95); breakfast buffet HK$42 ($5.45). AE, MC, V.

One of the cheapest places for a filling meal in Tsimshatsui is the YMCA's restaurant, which serves both Asian and Western food. Its à la carte menu lists soups, salads, steak, chicken, pork chops, and seafood, as well as such Asian dishes as satays, Japanese fried noodles, and Szechuan-style shrimp. There's a fixed-price dinner for HK$42 ($5.45), but the best bargain is the buffet lunch, which costs HK$38 ($4.95) on weekdays and HK$55 ($7.15) on Saturday and Sunday. Presently located on the first floor, it will move after renovations are completed in mid-1991 up to the fourth floor, from which diners will have a partial view of the harbor. Prices will be correspondingly higher.

Open: Daily 7–10:30am, noon–2:30pm, and 6–9pm. *MTR:* Tsimshatsui. WESTERN/ASIAN

- **Spaghetti House,** 3B Cameron Rd. (tel. 3688635), and Barnton Court, Harbour City (tel. 7220260), both in Tsimshatsui. *Prices:* Pizza from HK$25 ($3.25); spaghetti from HK$21 ($2.75). AE, MC, V.

These two locations are part of the Spaghetti House chain, which has a total of nine such restaurants in the entire colony. They specialize in spaghetti and pizza cooked American style, and are similar to American pizza parlors in atmosphere and decor. There are 14 different kinds of spaghetti, as well as pizzas ranging from individual to large sizes, lasagne, sandwiches, chili con carne, and fried chicken. Items can be prepared for take-out.

Open: Daily 11am–11pm. *MTR:* Tsimshatsui. ITALIAN

---

5. Restaurants in the Central District

EXPENSIVE

Asian Food

- **The Bloom,** basement of the Pedder Building, 12 Pedder St., Central (tel. 5218421). *Prices:* Average meal HK$200–HK$300 ($26–$39). AE, DC, MC, V.

In contrast to the elegant colonial-style building that houses it, the Bloom is smartly decorated in an art deco style with warm woods and flowers on the tables. Popular with business people, artists, and writers, this trendy place specializes in Cantonese food with an emphasis on fresh seafood. The presentation and preparation of some of its dishes border on nouvelle Chinese cuisine, and particularly recommended are its shark's-fin soup, flambéed drunken prawns, crispy roast Lung Kong chicken, abalone with bamboo piths, and braised noodles with shredded abalone. On Sunday it serves dim sum until 3pm. Although there is no dress code, you'll feel silly and dowdy if you're not presentable, as the people around you are apt to be dressed to the hilt. A place to see and be seen.

Open: Daily 11am–midnight (till 10pm Sun). *Reservations:* A must. *MTR:* Central. CANTONESE

• **Eagle's Nest,** Hongkong Hilton Hotel, 2 Queen's Rd., Central (tel. 5233111). *Prices:* Fixed-price meal HK$270 ($35); average à la carte meal HK$350 ($45.50); vegetarian dim sum lunch HK$60 ($7.80). AE, DC, MC, V.

With its art deco lamps, fresh flowers, and drawing-room ambience, it looks like a European restaurant—only the chopsticks betray the fact that the Eagle's Nest dishes out superb Cantonese cuisine. Perched on the top floor of the Hilton, this restaurant also offers spectacular views of Central around you and Kowloon across the harbor. A dance band serenades in the evening.

The food is traditional and a good bet for visitors trying Chinese food for the first time (no strange objects here, unless you consider abalone a strange thing to eat). Ingredients range from chicken, pigeon, duck, and beef to pork, abalone, and seafood. Vegetarian dishes are also offered. Specialties of the restaurant include vagabond chicken (beggar's chicken), fresh lobster salad, roast duck with plum sauce, double-boiled shark's fin with shredded chicken, baked stuffed sea whelk in the shell with curry sauce, steamed garoupa, and roast Peking duck.

Open: Daily noon–2pm and 7–10:30pm. *Reservations:* Recommended. *MTR:* Central. CANTONESE

• **Man Wah,** Mandarin Oriental Hotel, 5 Connaught Rd., Central (tel. 5220111). *Prices:* Average meal HK$380 ($49.25). AE, DC, MC, V.

This may well be the most elegant Chinese restaurant in all of Hong Kong. Decorated with a 600-year-old coromandel screen from the Ming Dynasty, woodcarvings, and pink tablecloths, exquisite chinaware, fresh flowers, and candles on every table set, it's about as romantic as you can get. What's more, located on the 25th floor, it offers a dazzling view of Hong Kong. Seating is for 55 diners only, however, so be sure to ask for a window seat when you make your reservation.

Although its Cantonese menu changes often, dishes might include such specialties as braised pigeon with bamboo shoots and mushrooms in oyster sauce, deep-fried scallops with minced shrimp, sautéed diced chicken with chili, roast duck Peking style (order it in advance), sweet-and-sour pork, shark's-fin soup with crab roe, or spicy pork spareribs. If available, the spicy-and-sour soup is a great choice, piquant and full of noodles, tofu, and mushrooms.

Open: Daily noon–2:30pm and 6:30–11pm. *Reservations:* Imperative. *MTR:* Central. CANTONESE

• **Benkay Japanese Restaurant,** 1st basement of the Landmark, Des Voeux Rd., Central (tel. 5213344). *Prices:* Average meals HK$250–HK$350 ($32.50–$45.50). AE, CB, DC, MC, V.

Affiliated with Japan Airlines and located among the expensive boutiques of the classy Landmark shopping complex, this Japanese restaurant uses screens and lighting to create a traditional atmosphere, complete with Japanese instrumental music in the background. Since the menu might be confusing to the novice, you might wish to order one of the fixed-price meals. Cream of the crop are its kaiseki courses which begin at HK$380 ($49.25). These change with the season and consist of many individual dishes, each artfully arranged. Other tempting dishes include a Kobe beef teppanyaki (prepared on a griddle in front of you), shabu-shabu (thin slices of beef cooked with vegetables), sushi (raw fish), tempura (deep-fried meats and vegetables), and eel.

Open: Daily noon–2:30pm and 6–10:30pm. *Reservations:* Recommended. *MTR:* Central. JAPANESE

Western Food

• **Bentley's,** Prince's Building, Chater Rd., Statue Square, Central (tel. 8680881). *Prices:* Average meal from HK$300 ($39). AE, DC, MC, V.

As part of London's famous chain of seafood restaurants, Hong Kong's own Bentley's hit the scene in 1987 and is a faithful rendition of the original Bentley's in Piccadilly. The atmosphere is cozy and chummy, and it has quickly become a favorite of business-suited expatriates working in Central. Its specialty is oysters, flown in from Scotland and Australia, and served on the half shell or on a bed of spinach, or dressed with such delicious sauces as tomato and curry or tomato, chili, and bacon. If you don't like oysters (heaven forbid), then start your meal with smoked eel filet, lobster bisque, or smoked salmon. As a main course, I highly recommend the Dover sole, lobster, and crab.

Open: Mon–Sat noon–2:30pm and 6–10:30pm. *Reservations:* A must for lunch, recommended for dinner. *MTR:* Central. OYSTERS/SEAFOOD

• **Café de Paris,** 30-32 D'Aguilar St., Central (tel. 5247521). *Prices:* Average dinner HK$270 ($35); fixed-price lunches from HK$95 ($12.25). AE, DC, MC, V.

Located in the heart of Central's nightlife district of Lan Kwai Fong, this small and intimate restaurant is decorated like a Parisian bistro with white tablecloths, candles, and fresh flowers. Its owner and chef, Maurice W. Gardett, is outgoing and gregarious, and claims to have the only true traditional French restaurant in town. "I don't compromise," he declares. "People who ask for ketchup are thrown out." The menu changes every four months but always features a pepper steak, pâté, and chateaubriand. Be sure to ask for daily specials.

Open: Mon–Sat noon–3pm and 7pm–midnight. *Reservations:* An absolute must. *MTR:* Central. FRENCH

• **Mandarin Grill,** Mandarin Oriental Hotel, 5 Connaught Rd., Central (tel. 5220111). *Prices:* Average dinner HK$400 ($52); average lunch HK$300 ($39); breakfast buffet HK$125 ($16.25). AE, DC, MC, V.

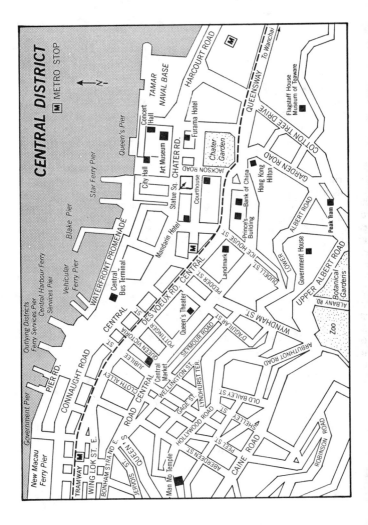

Decorated in dark green with details of gold, this is the Mandarin's most popular, all-purpose restaurant, offering everything from breakfast to steaks and seafood. But this being the Mandarin, it caters to a well-heeled clientele, and men are expected to wear jackets for lunch and dinner. Both U.S. and Kobe beef are featured, as well as veal, lamb, and a wide selection of seafood. Lobster is available in a variety of styles.

Open: Daily 7–11am, noon–3pm, and 6:30–11pm. *Reservations:* A necessity at any time. *MTR:* Central. CONTINENTAL/ GRILLED FOODS

• **Ninety-Seven,** 9 Lan Kwai Fong, Central (tel. 5260303). *Prices:* Average à la carte meal from HK$240 ($31.25); fixed-price dinner HK$320 ($41.50); fixed-price lunch HK$90 ($11.75). AE, DC, MC, V.

With a cheeky reference to Hong Kong's future, Ninety-Seven is up on the second floor (not to be confused with the cheaper eatery on the ground floor) and is a high-tech restaurant that specializes in original creations. Draped cloth on the ceiling gives it a cozy, tent-like atmosphere, while artwork of local and overseas artists adorns the walls. The fun and innovative menu changes often, with delights that might include grilled pigeon with ginger-curry sauce, sole stuffed with Japanese crab, a gratin of seafood and vegetables in chablis sauce, and vegetarian couscous. Any of the desserts are fine finales to your meal.

Open: Mon–Sat noon–3pm and 7pm–midnight. *Reservations:* A must. *MTR:* Central. EUROPEAN/ORIGINAL

• **Pierrot,** 25th floor of the Mandarin Oriental, 5 Connaught Rd., Central (tel. 5220111). *Prices:* Meals average HK$500 ($65). AE, DC, MC, V.

The Pierrot broke ground as the first hotel restaurant to introduce Hong Kong gourmets to a year-round menu of nouvelle French cuisine and has remained one of the city's favorites ever since. Its name inspired by Picasso's painting of his son in a Pierrot costume, it offers a great view of the harbor and a menu that changes twice a year. The wine list is superb and the food excellent. In any case, you can't go wrong dining here, unless you forget your jacket and tie. After dinner, you might wish to retire to the Harlequin Bar for a cocktail.

Open: Daily noon–2pm and 7–11pm. *Reservations:* A must. *MTR:* Central. FRENCH

MODERATE

Asian Food

• **Luk Yu Tea House,** 24-26 Stanley St., Central (tel. 5235464). *Prices:* Dishes from HK$40 ($5.20); average meal HK$140 ($18.25); dim sum HK$9–HK$20 ($1.15–$2.60). Cash only.

Luk Yu, first opened in 1925, is the most famous tea house remaining in Hong Kong. In fact, unless you have a time machine, you can't get closer to old Hong Kong than this wonderful Cantonese restaurant, with its ceiling fans, spittoons, individual wooden booths for couples, marble tabletops, wood paneling, and stained-glass windows. It's one of the best places to try a few Chinese teas, including bo lai, jasmine, lung ching (a green tea), and sui sin (narcissus or daffodil).

But Luk Yu is most famous for its dim sum, which is served from 7am to 5pm. The problem for foreigners, however, is that the place is always packed throughout the day with regular customers who all have their own special places to sit. In addition, if you come after 11am, dim sum is no longer served by trolley but from a menu, which is written only in Chinese. If you want to come during the day (certainly when it's at its most colorful), try to bring along a Chinese friend. Otherwise, consider going for dinner when it's not nearly as hectic. Also, at dinner there is an English menu with more than 200 items, including all the Cantonese favorites.

Open: Daily 7am–11pm. *MTR:* Central. CANTONESE

• **United,** 6th floor of the United Centre, 95 Queensway, Central (tel. 5295010). *Prices:* Average meal HK$100 ($13); dim sum about HK$10 ($1.30). Cash only.

Conveniently located in the United Centre which towers above the Admiralty MTR subway station, United is a gigantic Cantonese restaurant that caters primarily to Chinese. Popular for large banquets, wedding receptions, and private parties, it has many private rooms for the Chinese game of mah-jongg. The decor is simple but the food is good, with specialties including barbecued whole suckling pig, baked lobster in suprême soup, and deep-fried shrimp balls.

Open: Daily 7am–midnight. *MTR:* Admiralty. CANTONESE

• **Hunan Garden,** 3rd floor of the Forum, Exchange Square, Central (tel. 8682880). *Prices:* Average meal HK$150 ($19.50).

Although Hunanese food is very popular in Taiwan, this is probably the only Hunan restaurant in Hong Kong. It's puzzling, because Hunanese food is very spicy, and one would think that with the booming popularity of Thai and Szechuan food in the colony, Hunanese food would catch on. In any case, this is a great restaurant, both in decor and food. It's decorated in hot pink and green, and the motif is clearly lotus (Hunan province is famous for its lotus). The dining area is roomy, with tables spread luxuriously far apart, and there's even a view of the harbor.

But the real treat is the food. The chefs were trained in both Hunan province and Taiwan and they don't even attempt to tone down the spiciness of their authentic dishes. Start your meal with one of the soups, served in a length of bamboo. I tried the Hunan mashed-chicken soup, a clear soup base with ginger and mousse of chicken, served piping hot. If you like hot-and-spicy foods, you'll love the braised bean curd with shredded meat and chili, developed by one of Hunan province's most famous chefs. The most famous Hunanese dish, however, is probably Viceroy chicken, named after Viceroy Tso who trained the Hunanese army and invented this dish of stir-fried chicken with chili and garlic. Other good dishes include Hunan-style ham, served in pancakes, and duck tongue with a mustard sauce. As a special treat, try one of the Hunanese wines.

Open: Daily 11:30am–3pm and 6–11:30pm. *MTR:* Central.
HUNANESE

• **Shanghai Garden,** 1st floor of Hutchinson House, Murray Rd., Central (tel. 5238322). *Prices:* Average meal HK$150–HK$200 ($19.50–$26). AE, V.

Located next to the Furama Hotel, Shanghai Garden is part of the Maxim's Group of restaurants and does a good job here in presentation and cuisine. Since Shanghai does not have its own cuisine, the dishes here are from Peking, Nanking, Sichuan, Hangchow, and Wuxi, as well as a few dishes from Shanghai. The menu is extensive, including such soups as hot-and-sour shredded-meat-and-fish soup, such cold dishes as spiced duck or sautéed shredded eels in garlic sauce, and such entrées as sautéed prawn with tea leaves, quick-fried shredded eels with ginger, stewed prawns with tomato sauce and crispy rice, and fried noodles Shanghai style. Since this place does a roaring business, you should make a reservation.

Open: Daily 11:30am–3pm and 6–11pm. *Reservations:* Advised. *MTR:* Central. SHANGHAINESE

• **Sichuan Garden,** 3rd floor of Gloucester Tower, Landmark Building, Des Voeux Rd., Central (tel. 5214433). *Prices:* Small dishes from HK$45 ($5.85), medium from HK$70 ($9.10); average meal HK$100–HK$150 ($13–$19.50). AE, V.

Another Maxim's restaurant, the Sichuan Garden is in the chic Landmark Building, which explains its high prices (someone has to pay the rent). The atmosphere is bright and elegantly simple, the food excellent, and the service attentive. It's very popular and almost always crowded, especially at lunch, so if you want to play it safe, make a reservation. The hot-and-spicy dishes are indicated on the 150-item menu to help the uninitiated. Recommended are the cold prawns with four different sauces, hot-and-sour soup, fried prawns with chili sauce, shredded pork in hot garlic sauce, bean curd with minced beef in a pungent sauce, and pigeon smoked in camphor wood and tea leaves. I had the last and found it quite good, but I was unprepared for the decapitated pigeon head that accompanied the meal as decoration (at least, I assumed it wasn't for consumption).

Open: Daily 11:30am–3pm and 6–11:30pm. *Reservations:* Advised, especially at lunch. *MTR:* Central. SZECHUAN

• **The Ashoka,** 57-59 Wyndham St., Central (tel. 5249623 and 5255719). *Prices:* Average meal HK$90–HK$120 ($11.75–$15.50); fixed-price lunch HK$46 ($5.95). AE, DC, MC, V.

Within walking distance of Central up on winding Wyndham Hill, the Ashoka is just one of several Indian restaurants in the area but is probably the best known and most popular. Opened in 1973, it claims to be the oldest Indian restaurant on Hong Kong Island. In any case, it's extremely tiny and crowded, with only 60 seats, so make a reservation and be prepared to sit practically in your neighbor's lap. It's worth it, for the food is great and the prices are even greater, with the fixed-price lunch ridiculously cheap—there are two fixed-price lunches available, a vegetarian and a tandoori, both costing HK$46 ($5.95). House specialties are fish or chicken tikka, chicken bhurtha, stuffed tomato, and beef bhuna.

Open: Daily noon–3pm and 6–11pm. *Reservations:* Advised. *MTR:* Central. INDIAN

• **Vietnam Restaurant,** 3A Wyndham St., Central (tel. 5225523). *Prices:* Average meal HK$100 ($13). AE, MC, V.

Despite the fact that the Vietnam Restaurant looks like an American steakhouse with its wagon-wheel lights and beamed ceiling, it serves Vietnamese food at reasonable prices. The menu lists various congee, rice, vermicelli, curry, and seafood dishes, including prawns stewed with chopped mushrooms, crab meat, and coconut milk, and roast chicken with red bean curd sauce, both considered house specialties. The Vietnam snack combination gives a variety of appetizers.

Open: Daily 11am–11pm. *MTR:* Central. VIETNAMESE

Western Food

• **Jimmy's Kitchen,** 1 Wyndham St., Central (tel. 5265293). *Prices:* Average meal HK$170–HK$250 ($22–$32.50). AE, DC, MC, V.

First opened in 1928 and one of Hong Kong's oldest Western restaurants, Jimmy's Kitchen had several homes before moving to its present site in the 1960s. The atmosphere here reminds me of an American steakhouse, with white tablecloths, dark-wood paneling, and elevator music, but it's a favorite with foreigners living in Hong Kong and serves dependably good European food. Its daily specials are written on a blackboard, and a large à la carte menu offers seafood, steaks, salads and soups, chicken, spaghetti, and curries. You can have oysters imported from the United States, New Zealand, and Australia, and there's a large selection of seafood, including sole, scallops, and the local garoupa. It's a good place also for corned beef and cabbage, pork sausages, Stroganoff, and hearty German fare.

Open: Daily noon–11pm. *MTR:* Central. EUROPEAN

• **La Taverna,** 24-30 Ice House St., Central (tel. 5238624). *Prices:* Average dinner HK$170–HK$200 ($22–$26); fixed-price lunches from HK$70 ($9.10). AE, DC, MC, V.

First opened more than two decades ago but recently ensconced in its present home, La Taverna is Italian owned and employs an Italian chef to cook up its daily specials, as well as such favorites as homemade pasta, thinly sliced beef tenderloin in olive oil and rosemary dressing, veal, chicken, seafood, and pizza. A guitar player serenades in the evenings, while candles on all the tables bathe the restaurant in a warm, soft glow. Chianti bottles hang from the ceiling, but the wine list is actually much more extensive, with one of the largest selections of Italian wines this side of the harbor. The desserts are a sinful must.

Open: Daily 11:30am–3pm and 6:30–11pm. *MTR:* Central. ITALIAN

• **Le Tire Bouchon,** 9 Old Baily St., Central (tel. 5235459). *Prices:* Average meal HK$130–HK$150 ($17–$19.50). MC, V.

Although it's a bit of a climb up steep Old Baily Street, it's worth the hike for the authentic French cuisine (you might want to take a taxi to save yourself the 15-minute walk straight uphill). This place is small and simple, with an equally small menu that lists about seven entrées and a few daily specials. If they're on the menu, try the grilled French breast of duck in an apple sauce, the chateaubriand sauce béarnaise, or the rack of lamb in a chanterelle and red wine sauce.

Open: Mon–Sat. noon–3pm and 7pm–midnight. *MTR:* Central. FRENCH

• **Seasons,** 17 On Lan St., Central (tel. 5268429). *Prices:* Average dinner HK$200 ($26); fixed-price lunch HK$80 ($10.50). AE, DC, MC, V.

This trendy, smart restaurant serves an Italian-influenced nouvelle cuisine, specializing in light pastas. The chef is also an artist, as is evident in his presentations, and he's not afraid to experiment. The menu changes every three months but always offers fresh seafood and veal, as well as a dreamy selection of great desserts. At last check, there was talk of transforming the place into a club called Midnight Shift on weekend nights, and if the restaurant itself is any indication, it's sure to be a hit. Wear your designer clothes, and make a reservation if you want to eat here for lunch.

Open: Mon–Sat. 11am–3pm and 6–11pm. *Reservations:* Advised, but necessary at lunch. *MTR:* Central. ITALIAN/EUROPEAN

BUDGET

Several restaurants in the moderate category above offer lunches that even the budget-conscious can afford. Luk Yu Tea House, for example, serves dim sum, while the Ashoka, La Taverna, and Seasons dish out inexpensive fixed-price lunches. In addition, check out the sections at the end of this chapter for establishments that serve dim sum or buffet spreads.

Asian Food

• **City Hall Restaurant,** 2nd floor of City Hall, Low Block, Central (tel. 5211303). *Prices:* Average meals HK$50–HK$90 ($6.50–$11.75); dim sum HK$6–HK$10 (80¢–$1.30). AE, V.

Decorated in Chinese red, this large restaurant offers a view of the harbor and is so popular for lunch that you'll probably have to wait to get in if you haven't made a reservation (report immediately to the woman at the desk near the door to get on the waiting list). The clientele is almost exclusively Chinese, and the food is Cantonese, with the usual shark's fin, bird's nest, abalone, pigeon, duck, vegetable, beef, and seafood dishes, as well as dim sum.

Open: Daily 10am–11:30pm (from 8am Sun and hols). *MTR:* Central. CANTONESE

• **Yung Kee,** 32-40 Wellington St., Central (tel. 5221624). *Prices:* Average meal HK$70 ($9.10); dim sum about HK$6–HK$10 (80¢–$1.30). Cash only.

A popular restaurant for decades, Yung Kee started out in 1942 as a small shop selling roast goose, which it did so well that it soon expanded into a very successful Cantonese restaurant. Its specialty is still roast goose with plum sauce, cooked to perfection with tender meat on the inside and crispy skin on the outside. Other specialties include bean curd combined with prawns, shredded chicken, or delicacies; filet of garoupa sauté; sautéed filet of pomfret with chili and black-bean sauce; and hundred-year-old eggs (which come automatically with each meal). Dining is up on the first floor in a restaurant of red and gold, but if all you want is a bowl of congee or other rice dishes, join the office workers who pour in for a quick meal on the ground floor.

Open: Daily 11am–11:30pm. *MTR:* Central. CANTONESE

Western Food

• **Beverly Hills Deli,** 2 Lan Kwai Fong, Central (tel. 5265800). *Prices:* Entrées HK$30–HK$60 ($3.90–$7.80). AE, DC, MC.

Located right in the heart of Central's nightlife district, this, like its namesake in Tsimshatsui, is a good place to satisfy late-night cravings. Although it calls itself Beverly Hills Deli, the menu claims it's "Hong Kong's only New York–style deli." An identity crisis, perhaps, but the fact remains that it's the best place in town for sandwiches, hot dogs, hamburgers, and traditional deli fare. Its menu is huge and includes Texas chili, stuffed and triple-decker sandwiches with a wide selection of fillings, bagels with lox and cream cheese, Cajun chicken, fried chicken, pepper steak, spaghetti, and roast beef, to name only a few. It even has some Middle Eastern dishes, and there are also a few choices for the vegetarian. The atmosphere is informal diner, and all foods are available for take-out and delivery anywhere in Hong Kong.

Open: Daily 11am–midnight (till 11pm Sun and hols). *MTR:* Central. SANDWICHES/DELI

• **Spaghetti House,** Malahon Centre, 10 Stanley St., Central (tel. 5231372). *Prices:* Pizza from HK$25 ($3.25); spaghetti from HK$21 ($2.75). AE, MC, V.

Part of a Hong Kong chain specializing in spaghetti and pizza cooked American style, it serves 14 different kinds of spaghetti, and pizzas ranging from individual to large sizes, as well as lasagne, sandwiches, chili con carne, and fried chicken. Items can be prepared for take-out.

Open: Daily 11am–11pm. *MTR:* Central. ITALIAN

6. Restaurants in Wanchai/Causeway Bay

The most famous dining area in Causeway Bay is a pedestrian lane known as Food Street. It's bordered on both sides by restaurant after restaurant serving all kinds of different foods, from Chinese and Japanese to Western and fast foods. Several of these restaurants are listed in this section, but if you're undecided, simply walk around and choose what fits your fancy and your budget. Altogether there are more than 30 restaurants on Food Street and neighboring side streets, so you shouldn't have any problem finding a place to eat.

EXPENSIVE

Asian Food

■ **Sunning Unicorn,** Sunning Plaza, 1 Sunning Rd., Causeway Bay (tel. 5776620). *Prices:* Average meal from HK$200 ($26). AE, MC, V.

Located near the Lee Gardens Hotel, this elegant and modern Cantonese restaurant caters to business people during lunch and to discerning diners at night, and the service is nothing short of excellent. You could spend a fortune for shark's fin or bird's nest here, but the specialties of the house, drunken prawns and crispy chicken, are equally satisfying and not as pricey. Although it's a Cantonese restaurant, you won't find any dim sum here. Rather, this is a good restaurant if you're looking for quiet, intimate dining and well-prepared food.

Open: Daily noon–3pm and 6–11:30pm. *Reservations:* Recommended. *MTR:* Causeway Bay. CANTONESE

Western Food

■ **Excelsior Grill,** Excelsior Hotel, 281 Gloucester Rd., Causeway Bay (tel. 5767365). *Prices:* Average dinner HK$250 ($32.50), fixed-price dinners from HK$190 ($24.75); fixed-price lunch HK$130 ($17). AE, DC, MC, V.

The Excelsior Grill offers refined European dining with a great view of the harbor (be sure to request a window seat when making your reservation). The tables are well spaced, there are fresh flowers and candles on every table, and the service is excellent. Live piano music is piped in from the Noon Gun Bar (where you might want to stop off for a cocktail before or after your meal). The à la carte menu features U.S. prime rib, rack of lamb, duck, and a wide array of seafood dishes, many cooked in unusual ways. One of its best, for example, is medallions of Scottish salmon and turbot with crayfish and caviar in a saffron-flavored chablis wine sauce laced with chives. The rack of lamb is baked with eucalyptus leaves and port wine in a clay pot. Grilled dishes and main entrées include a trip through the salad bar, but if you have a small appetite you can have the salad bar by itself for only HK$55 ($7.15), a real bargain.

Open: Daily noon–3pm and 7–11:30pm. *Reservations:* Recommended. *MTR:* Causeway Bay. EUROPEAN/GRILLED FOODS

■ **Landau's,** 2nd floor of Sun Hung Kai Centre, 30 Harbour Rd., Wanchai (tel. 8912901). *Prices:* Entrées HK$80–HK$100 ($10.50–$13); average dinner HK$200 ($26).

Owned by the same company as Jimmy's Kitchen, Landau's is

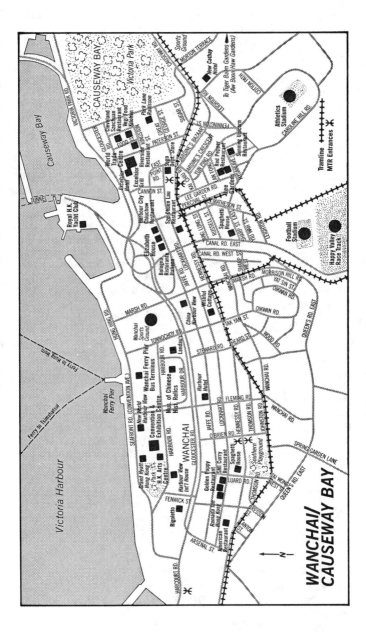

very popular among Hong Kong's expatriates for its hearty European fare. The dining area itself is nothing spectacular, but the atmosphere is convivial and the service is attentive. Entrées include black-pepper steak, duck marinated in port wine, New Zealand lamb chops, wienerschnitzel, beef Stroganoff, Australian rock oysters, paprika veal goulash, corned beef and cabbage, fresh Macau sole, and smoked Norwegian salmon. Don't forget to check out the blackboards announcing the daily specials.

Open: Daily noon–3pm and 7–11:30pm. *Reservations:* Recommended, especially weekend nights. *MTR:* Wanchai. EUROPEAN

• **Rigoletto,** 14-16 Fenwick St., Wanchai (tel. 5277144). *Prices:* Average meal HK$180 ($23.50); pizzas and pastas from HK$45 ($5.85). AE, MC, V.

Ask any Hong Kong resident to recommend an Italian eatery in Wanchai, and most likely Rigoletto will be it. Long an old standby, it seems a bit old-fashioned with its Italian pendants and souvenirs and rather loud orange-and-green tablecloths, but the lighting is pleasantly dark and large front windows offer an interesting perspective on the action of Wanchai. Entrées consist mainly of northern Italian dishes and include calves' liver, veal, steaks, and seafood. For starters you might want to try one of the pizza or pasta dishes.

Open: Mon–Sat noon–3pm and daily 6pm–midnight. *MTR:* Wanchai. ITALIAN

MODERATE

Asian Food

• **Harbour City Chiuchow Restaurant,** 2nd floor of Elizabeth House, 254 Gloucester Rd., Causeway Bay (tel. 8336678 and 8936788). *Prices:* Average meal HK$110 ($14.25). AE, DC, MC, V.

Located about a five-minute walk west of the Excelsior Hotel, this modern, pink-and-black restaurant is one of the many new Chiu Chow establishments recently to hit the Hong Kong scene. There are almost 200 selections on its menu, including lobster, crab, scallops, squid, goose, duck, abalone, whelk, and chicken dishes. Specialties include fresh fish, sliced soya goose, and shark's-fin soup, though the least expensive shark's-fin dish is a soup mixture with chicken for HK$75 ($9.75).

Open: Daily 11am–3pm and 5pm–midnight. *MTR:* Causeway Bay. CHIU CHOW

• **Red Pepper,** 7 Lan Fong Rd., Causeway Bay (tel. 5768046). *Prices:* Average meal HK$130–HK$160 ($17–$20.75). AE, DC, MC, V.

Open since 1970, the Red Pepper has a large following among the colony's expatriates, many of whom seem to come so often they know everyone else in the place. It's a very relaxing, small restaurant, with a rather quaint decor: Chinese lanterns, Chinese straight-backed chairs, and a red ceiling with gold dragon motifs. It specializes in fried prawns with chili sauce on a sizzling platter, sour-pepper soup, smoked duck marinated with oranges, and shredded chicken with hot garlic sauce and dry-fried string beans. Since it's so popular with Western residents living in Hong Kong, I strongly recommend that you make reservations if you want to come for dinner. Lunch is usually less crowded.

Open: Daily noon–midnight. *Reservations:* Recommended, especially for dinner. *MTR:* Causeway Bay. SZECHUAN

- **Sze Chuen Lau Restaurant,** 466 Lockhart Rd., Wanchai (tel. 8919027). *Prices:* Average meal HK$100 ($13). MC, V.

This is a small, rather nondescript restaurant, similar to many family-run neighborhood eateries all over Hong Kong. It serves the normal Szechuan specialties, including chili prawns on a sizzling plate, smoked duck, smoked pigeon, braised eel, sliced beef with kumkwat-orange peel and hot pepper, sliced pork with hot garlic dressing, and cold chicken with chili-sesame sauce. Dishes come in three different sizes, making it a good place for the lone diner.

Open: Daily 11:30am–midnight. *MTR:* Causeway Bay. SZECHUAN

- **Riverside,** 13-15 Cleveland St., Causeway Bay (tel. 5779733). *Prices:* Dinners average HK$130 ($17); lunches average HK$50 ($6.50); fixed-price lunch for two HK$180 ($23.50). AE, V.

Located at the end of Food Street, this Cantonese restaurant is a bit formal with its Chinese screens and black lacquered chairs, and is known for good cuisine. It offers an abundant selection of bird's nest, abalone, scallop, shark's fin, crab, duck, vegetable, and seafood dishes. Especially recommended are the roast chicken, steamed prawns with garlic sauce, deep-fried stuffed crab claws, boneless duck with mashed lotus taro, or garoupa balls sauté.

Open: Mon–Fri 11am–3pm and 5:30pm–midnight; Sat, Sun, and hols 11am–midnight. *MTR:* Causeway Bay. CANTONESE

- **Vegi Food Kitchen,** 8 Cleveland St., Causeway Bay (tel. 8906660 or 8906603). *Prices:* Average meal HK$100 ($13). AE, V.

Located just off Food Street, this small and ornate restaurant serves only vegetarian food, with combinations of mushrooms, fungus, nuts, bean curd, and seasonal vegetables. It's famous for its Buddhist Carnival, a plate of assorted vegetables, as well as its vegetarian "shark's-fin" soup, made with vermicelli and shredded mushrooms. Another popular soup is its white fungus with either sweet corn or asparagus. Since this place is small, you should make a reservation.

Open: Daily 11am–midnight. *MTR:* Causeway Bay. VEGETARIAN

- **Golden Poppy,** 90-92 Jaffe Rd., Wanchai (tel. 5283128). *Prices:* Average meal HK$110–HK$150 ($14.25–$19.50); lunch buffet HK$60 ($7.80). AE, MC, V.

Lovers of Thai food will find paradise here, since its food is authentic, good, and spicy, and prices are very reasonable. It's actually two restaurants in one. The lower floor is a bar and is the place to head if you want to gorge yourself on its great buffet-style Thai lunch, served weekdays from 12:30 to 2:30pm. After 5pm the bar transforms itself, oddly enough, into a Japanese drinking bar, complete with sake and Japanese-style snacks. Upstairs is the formal Thai dining room with an à la carte menu listing more than 100 selections. For drinks, try the Thai Singha beer, or if you're suicidal, experiment with Mekhong whisky.

Open: Daily noon–2:30pm and 6–11pm. *MTR:* Wanchai. **THAI**

Western Food

• **Bologna Ristorante Italiano,** ground floor of Elizabeth House, 250 Gloucester Rd., Causeway Bay (tel. 5746808 or 5747282). *Prices:* Average meals HK$100–HK$150 ($13–$19.50); fixed-price lunch HK$49 ($6.25). AE, DC, MC, V.

This is a cheerful and spacious Italian restaurant, complete with red tablecloths, candles on the tables, and scores of wine bottles hanging from the ceiling. You could splurge and go for grilled king prawns, veal escalope with asparagus, calves' liver, steaks, or lobster, but you'd be no less content with the pasta or pizza. Portions are large, and to wash it all down there's a good selection of Italian wines.

Open: Daily 11am–2:30pm and 6–11:30pm. *MTR:* Causeway Bay. **ITALIAN**

BUDGET

In addition to the recommendations below, be sure to go through the "Specialty Dining" sections on buffets and dim sum for more hints on inexpensive dining. And don't forget Food Street in Causeway Bay, where you'll find a wide assortment of informal eateries.

Asian Food

• **American Restaurant,** 20 Lockhart Rd., Wanchai (tel. 5271000 or 5277277). *Prices:* Small dishes HK$24–HK$40 ($3.10–$5.20), medium HK$35–HK$60 ($4.55–$7.80), large HK$40–HK$80 ($5.20–$10.50); average meal HK$70 ($9.10). Cash only.

Despite its name, the American Restaurant serves hearty Pekinese food and has been doing so since it opened right after World War II. In fact, not much has changed in this restaurant in the past four decades, including its bright green-and-red façade, red-and-gold interior, and Chinese waiters of the old school (a bit gruff, and not even an attempt at English—one friend told me that it's not unusual for the waiters here to actually throw the plates onto the table). Still, the restaurant continues to draw in a faithful clientele of both Chinese and Western residents, who come because the food is good. The English menu, with almost 200 dishes, includes barbecued Peking duck, beggar's chicken (which must be ordered a day in advance), prawns in chili sauce, and various beef, chicken, pork, and seafood dishes. Peking duck remains the favorite and comes in one size only, at HK$140 ($18.25), and can be shared by two or more people.

Open: Daily 11:30am–11pm. *MTR:* Wanchai. PEKINESE

• **Cleveland Szechuan Restaurant,** 6 Cleveland St., Causeway Bay (tel. 5763876). *Prices:* Average meal HK$70–HK$100 ($9.10 –$13). AE, V.

Located near Food Street, this Szechuan restaurant is popular with local Chinese, especially families with children. Its decor is rather plain, but prices are good and most dishes come in two sizes. The small size is good for two people, while the medium is enough for four (remember, if there are two of you, you'll want to order at least two small-size dishes and then share). The specialty of the house is its smoked duck with camphor tea. Other highly recom-mended dishes are fried king shrimp on a sizzling plate, fried diced chicken with black beans and pepper, deep-fried fish with sweet-and-sour sauce, cold sliced pork with garlic sauce, and beef filet with hot garlic sauce.

Open: Mon–Fri 11am–2:30pm and 5:30pm–midnight, and Sat and Sun 11am–midnight. *MTR:* Causeway Bay. SZECHUAN

• **SMI Curry Restaurant,** 81-85 Lockhart Rd., Wanchai (tel. 5273107 or 5299111). *Prices:* Average meal HK$50 ($6.50). DC, MC, V.

This curry house is a true find, the kind of place that will set your taste buds quivering even before you reach the upstairs dining room. It's crowded, informal, and great fun, filled with people who seemingly want nothing more out of life than their favorite curry. And there are curries plenty. SMI supposedly stands for Singapore, Malaysia, and India, but that doesn't cover the chicken, beef, mut-ton, prawn, and vegetable curries from a score of other countries. Chicken selections alone, for example, include dry chicken tandoori, dry masala chicken, East Indies curry chicken, Southeast Asian hot curry chicken, Tamil curry chicken, Pakistani curry chick-en, chicken korma, and Singhalese white-curry chicken. The list is almost endless, and you'll find yourself wistfully wishing you could try every one.

Open: Daily noon–11:30pm. *MTR:* Wanchai. SOUTH ASIAN

• **Sogo Department Store,** 555 Hennessy Rd., Causeway Bay (tel. 8338338). *Prices:* Average meal HK$25 ($3.25). Cash only.

If you're looking for a cheap cafeteria, head for the second base-ment of the Sogo Department Store, located right next to the Causeway Bay MTR subway station. There are various counters here serving salads, Chinese noodles, satays, Oriental noodles, congee, sushi, and other Chinese and Japanese snacks. For dessert you can even top it off with Häagen-Dazs ice cream. Simply decide what you want, pay the cashier, and then return to the appropriate counter to pick up your ordered dish. There are tables in the middle of the room, and though the surroundings are a far cry from fancy, no one can deny that prices are low.

Open: Daily 10am–10pm daily. *MTR:* Causeway Bay. CHINESE/JAPANESE CAFETERIA

• **Wishful Cottage Vegetarian Restaurant,** 336-340 Lockhart Rd., Wanchai (tel. 5735645). *Prices:* Average meal HK$60 ($7.80). Cash only.

You could spend a fortune eating its most expensive delicacy, bamboo fungus in brown sauce, which costs HK$270 ($35). Otherwise, most dishes at this vegetarian restaurant are priced between HK$30 and HK$60 ($3.90 and $7.80). Opened in 1967, this is one of Hong Kong's oldtimers, where diners dine under the watchful gaze of a Buddhist statue. It serves seasonal vegetables, noodles, and bean-curd dishes.

Open: Daily 10am–10pm. *MTR:* Wanchai or Causeway Bay. VEGETARIAN

Western Food

• **Spaghetti House,** 5 Sharp St., Causeway Bay (tel. 7952245), and Hennessy and Luard Rds., Wanchai (tel. 5290901). *Prices:* Pizza from HK$25 ($3.25); spaghetti from HK$21 ($2.75). AE, MC, V.

This chain of spaghetti houses offers cheap pizza and pasta, including take-out.

Open: Daily 11am–11pm. *MTR:* Causeway Bay and Wanchai respectively. ITALIAN.

---

7. More Restaurants on Hong Kong Island

HAPPY VALLEY

• **Amigo Restaurant,** 79A Wong Nei Chong Rd., Happy Valley (tel. 5772202). *Prices:* Average meal HK$350 ($45.50); fixed-price lunch HK$130 ($17). AE, DC, MC, V.

Amigo conjures up images of a sombrero-filled Mexican restaurant, but Amigo Restaurant is actually a very smart French establishment. In fact, some people consider this the best French restaurant in town. It certainly feels like a top contender, with a timbered dining room with the finest of crystal and china, Hong Kong's elite dressed to kill (jacket and tie are a must), and service that leaves nothing lacking. Romantic and, of course, very expensive. Practically everything on the menu is a specialty, though as a starter you don't want to neglect its oyster soup baked in puff pastry. Steaks, lobster, and other seafood make up most of the entrées, complemented by a fine wine list and heavenly desserts. An experience you won't forget.

Open: Daily noon–2:30pm and 6–11:30pm. *Reservations:* A must, especially on horse-racing days. FRENCH

• **Pep N' Chili,** 12-22 Blue Pool Rd., Happy Valley (tel. 5738251). *Prices:* Average meal HK$150 ($19.50). AE, DC, MC, V.

A favorite with many Szechuan-food fanatics, this restaurant is almost European in appearance. Catering largely to expatriates, it also tones down its food, but somehow manages to do so without compromising on taste. Try the eggplant with garlic, crispy pork strips, hot-and-sour seafood soup, or the duck smoked in camphor leaves. This is a fun place to dine.

Open: Daily noon–2:30pm and 6–11pm. *Reservations:* Recommended, especially on racing days. SZECHUAN

THE PEAK

- **Peak Tower Restaurant,** Peak Tower, Victoria Peak (tel. 8497260). *Prices:* Average dinner HK$160–HK$200 ($20.75–$26); fixed-price dinner HK$150 ($19.50); buffet lunch HK$115 ($15). AE, MC, V.

The main thing this restaurant has going for it is the view—it's the highest spot in the colony for a meal. Located in Peak Tower, the top terminus of the peak tram, it offers a bird's-eye view of Central, Wanchai, and Kowloon, undoubtedly the best view in Hong Kong. Otherwise its food is rather ordinary and includes fish, steaks, lamb, and duck. Be sure to request a window seat when you make your reservation. Incidentally, one floor lower than the Peak Tower Restaurant is the Peak Tower Coffee Shop, open daily from 9am to 11:30pm and serving breakfast, pastas, sandwiches, hamburgers, and Chinese dishes. A meal here will cost about HK$60 ($7.80).

Open: Daily 11:30am–2:30pm and 6–11:30pm. *Reservations:* Recommended, especially for a window seat. *Directions:* Peak tram. CONTINENTAL/GRILLED FOODS

- **Peak Café,** Victoria Peak (tel. 8496168 or 8496161). *Prices:* HK$30–HK$50 ($3.90–$6.50). Cash only.

Located across the street from Peak Tower is the small Peak Café, practically hidden among the overgrown bushes and trees that surround it. Formerly a rickshaw station, it's a delightful place for a snack or drink, and there's even an outdoor patio set amid the lush growth where you can actually hear birds singing. The menu is small—sandwiches, rice dishes, hamburgers, ice cream, floats, coffee, and beer. At last check, there was indication that the café may close for extensive remodeling.

Open: Daily 10am–11:30pm. SNACKS/SANDWICHES/RICE DISHES

STANLEY

- **Stanley's Restaurant,** 86-88 Stanley Main St., Stanley (tel. 8138873). *Prices:* Average meal HK$200 ($26). AE, DC, MC, V.

Whatever you save by bargain-shopping at Stanley Market may well go toward a meal at Stanley's Restaurant, and I can't think of a better place to spend it. This is an absolutely charming French restaurant, refined, cozy, romantic—the adjectives could go on and on. There are several floors of dining, all in small rooms that look like they're part of someone's house. There are flowers on the tables, pictures on the walls, and there's even an upstairs outdoor patio.

For starters you might try its Caesar salad, considered a house specialty, or smoked salmon pâté. For soup there's the zucchini and dill soup. Entrées include sautéed Tasmanian scallops and calamari in lemon-garlic butter, blackened filet of pomfret, roast whole spring chicken, chicken-and-yogurt curry, blackened prime rib eye of beef with Cajun hollandaise, rack of lamb provençal, and Macau sole. There are also daily specials. This restaurant is tucked away in a corner of the market, beside Stanley beach.

Open: Daily 10am–noon for breakfast, noon–3pm for lunch, 3–5pm for afternoon tea, and 7–10:30pm for dinner. *Reservations:* A must. FRENCH

---

8. Specialty Dining

FLOATING RESTAURANTS

Aberdeen

No doubt you've heard about Hong Kong's floating restaurants in Aberdeen. Although they are often included in Hong Kong's nighttime organized tours, they are no longer touted by the tourist office as one place every tourist has to see—there are simply too many other restaurants that are less touristy, more authentic, better priced, with better food. However, if it has been your lifetime fantasy to eat in a floating restaurant, try one of the two listed below. Simply take the bus to Aberdeen and board the restaurant's own shuttle boat to the restaurant.

• **Jumbo Floating Restaurant** (tel. 5539111). *Prices:* Average meal HK$150 ($19.50); dim sum from HK$8 ($1.05). AE, MC, V.

Probably the largest and most garish of the floating restaurants, this Cantonese restaurant also serves dim sum from 7:30am to 4pm, which is certainly the least expensive way to enjoy the experience.

Open: Daily 7:30am–midnight. CANTONESE/DIM SUM

• **Tai Pak Seafood Restaurant** (tel. 5525953). *Prices:* Average meal HK$150 ($19.50). AE, MC, V.

Similar to Jumbo Floating Restaurant with its huge, high-ceilinged dining room with traditional Chinese decor. Portions are large and the Cantonese menu is diverse, offering the usual shark's-fin soup, braised garoupa (a local fish), sautéed scallops, sliced beef in oyster sauce, and steamed chicken with vegetables.

Open: Daily 11am–11pm. CANTONESE

Causeway Bay

If it's during the warm summer months from May to October, a good alternative to the floating restaurants of Aberdeen is a meal on a rustic **sampan** in Causeway Bay. Simply head for the Typhoon Shelter (located across from the Excelsior Hotel) and board one of the flat-bottomed skiffs, where your captain will propel you through the waters of the Typhoon Shelter, filled with yachts and other sampans. The sampans are outfitted with table and chairs (and a very rudimentary makeshift bathroom) but do not serve food. Rather, meals are provided by other sampans laden with Cantonese food, including fish, prawns, and other seafood, and vegetables. Other boats sell beer. But the most memorable boat is the one that holds the musicians, who ask for donations in return for tunes. All in all, it's very festive, making for a fun evening. Boats rent for HK$165 ($21.50) an hour, so try to get a group together. Hours of operation are 7pm to midnight, in summer only.

PLACES FOR DIM SUM

Everyone should try a dim sum meal at least once, as much for the atmosphere as the food. Prices are low, you order only as much or as little as you wish to eat, and restaurants offer a true experience in Chinese dining. (Refer to the beginning of this chapter for suggestions of various dim sum.) Simply look over the steaming baskets being pushed around by trolley and choose what looks best. Prices per basket range from about HK$6 to HK$15 (80¢ to $1.95), with HK$8 to HK$10 ($1.05 to $1.30) the average price.

Kowloon

• **Capital Restaurant,** 2nd floor of Chungking Mansion, 40-44 Nathan Rd., Tsimshatsui (tel. 3681844).

One of the oldtimers, this cavernous Cantonese restaurant is just like a dim sum place should be—noisy, crowded, informal, and chaotic. It's also one of the cheapest places around for dim sum.

Open: Daily 7am–5pm for dim sum. *MTR:* Tsimshatsui.

• **The Chinese,** Hyatt Regency Hotel, 67 Nathan Rd., Tsimshatsui (tel. 3662321). AE, DC, MC, V.

A refined, modern, and fancy setting for dim sum. There are no trolleys here, but there's a great dim sum lunch for HK$60 ($7.80) which gives you several different varieties.

Open: Daily noon–3pm for dim sum. *MTR:* Tsimshatsui.

• **City Chiuchow Restaurant,** East Ocean Centre, 98 Granville Rd., East Tsimshatsui (tel. 7236226). AE, DC, MC, V.

Although it's a Chiu Chow restaurant, it serves its own dim sum.

Open: Daily 11am–3pm (till 5pm Sunday) for dim sum. *MTR:* Tsimshatsui.

• **East Ocean Seafood Restaurant,** 16th floor of the Ambassador Hotel, 4 Middle Rd., Tsimshatsui (tel. 3666321).

Conveniently located right off Nathan Road, this comfortable and pleasant Cantonese restaurant offers a good view of the city and the harbor. It's small but lively.

Open: Daily 11am–2:30pm for dim sum. *MTR:* Tsimshatsui.

• **Fook Lam Moon,** 31-35A Mody Rd., Tsimshatsui (tel. 3660286). Cash only.

Another Hong Kong oldtimer, but much more formal than

the Capital Restaurant. The atmosphere is of another era.
Open: Daily 11:30am–2:30pm for dim sum. *MTR:* Tsimshatsui.

- **Full Moon,** 102 Barnton Court, Harbour City, Tsimshatsui (tel. 7309131); and Empire Center, 68 Mody Rd., East Tsimshatsui (tel. 7392868). Cash only.
    This modern, trendy Cantonese restaurant has two locations.
    Open: Daily 11:30am–3pm for dim sum. *MTR:* Tsimshatsui.

- **Jade Garden Chinese Restaurant,** 4th floor of Star House, 3 Salisbury Rd., Tsimshatsui (tel. 7226888). AE, DC, MC.
    An easy place for the uninitiated, this Cantonese chain is used to tourists and is conveniently located across from the Star Ferry terminus.
    Open: Daily 11:30am–6pm for dim sum. *MTR:* Tsimshatsui.

- **Lotus Pond,** 15 Harbour City, Canton Rd., Tsimshatsui (tel. 7308688). AE, V.
    Although a Szechuan restaurant, it serves its own style of dim sum.
    Open: Daily 11am–3pm for dim sum. *MTR:* Tsimshatsui.

- **Shang Palace,** Shangri-La Hotel, 64 Mody Rd., East Tsimshatsui (tel. 7212111). AE, CB, DC, MC, V.
    One of Kowloon's most elaborate Chinese restaurants, complete with red-lacquered walls and Chinese lanterns hanging from the ceiling. Because it has a menu in English, this is a great place to try dim sum for the first time, not to mention the fact that it has some of the best dim sum in town—a bit more expensive, but worth it. Choose your dim sum from the menu, which changes every two weeks and always includes more than a dozen varieties of dim sum.
    Open: Daily noon–3pm (from 11am Sun and hols) for dim sum. *MTR:* Tsimshatsui.

- **Tsui Hang Village Restaurant,** 15th floor of Keewan Tower, Park Lane Square, 132-134 Nathan Rd., Tsimshatsui (tel. 3686363). AE, MC, V.
    Another Cantonese restaurant with a view, recently remodeled.
    Open: Mon–Sat 11am–2:30pm, Sun 10am–5pm, for dim sum. *MTR:* Tsimshatsui.

Central

- **Blue Heaven,** 48 Queen's Rd., Central (tel. 5243001).
    This second-floor Cantonese restaurant is well known for its dim sum.
    Open: Daily 7am–5pm for dim sum. *MTR:* Central.

- **City Hall Restaurant,** 2nd floor of City Hall, Low Block, Connaught Rd., Central (tel. 5211303). AE, V.
    A popular place and often crowded, filled with shoppers and office workers.

Open: Daily 10am–3pm (from 8am Sun and hols) for dim sum. *MTR:* Central.

- **Luk Yu Tea House,** 24-26 Stanley St., Central (tel. 5235464). Cash only.

The most authentic dim sum tea house in Hong Kong, but often so packed with regulars that mere tourists can't get a seat. In addition, trolleys with dim sum are pushed through the place only until 11am, after which there's only a Cantonese restaurant. Try to bring along a Chinese friend.

Open: Daily 7am–5pm for dim sum. *MTR:* Central.

- **United,** 6th floor of the United Centre, 95 Queensway, Central (tel. 5295010). Cash only.

A huge place, popular with local Chinese.

Open: Daily 7:30 am–4pm for dim sum. *MTR:* Admiralty.

- **Yung Kee,** 32-40 Wellington St., Central (tel. 5221624).

Famous for its roast goose, but also has dim sum in the afternoon.

Open: Daily 2–5pm for dim sum. *MTR:* Central.

Causeway Bay

- **Dim Sum Kitchen,** Food Street, Causeway Bay (tel. 5777286).

Located on Food Street, a pedestrian lane lined with restaurants, this small cafeteria is one of the cheapest places for dim sum. Simply pay for what you want beforehand at the ticket window and then present your food ticket to someone at the counter.

Open: Daily 7:30am–midnight for dim sum. *MTR:* Causeway Bay.

BUFFET SPREADS

Buffets have really caught on in Hong Kong, a bonus for diners with large appetites or lone diners who want to sample various dishes. They are often much cheaper than full-course meals. Note that most buffets are offered only for lunch.

Kowloon

- **Golden Elephant Thai Restaurant,** 3 Barnton Court, Harbour City, Tsimshatsui (tel. 7350733). *Prices:* Lunch buffet HK$75 ($9.75) Mon–Sat, HK$85 ($11) Sun. AE, DC, MC, V.

Open: Daily noon–3pm. *MTR:* Tsimshatsui. THAI

- **Nathan's,** Hyatt Regency Hong Kong, 67 Nathan Rd., Tsimshatsui (tel. 3662321). *Prices:* Lunch buffet HK$88 ($11.50). AE, DC, MC, V.

Open: Daily noon–2:30pm. *MTR:* Tsimshatsui. INDIAN/CONTINENTAL

- **The Pizzeria,** Kowloon Hotel, 19-21 Nathan Rd., Tsimshatsui (tel. 3698698). *Prices:* Lunch buffet HK$63 ($8.20); salad bar HK$39 ($5.05) extra. AE, CB, DC, MC, V.

Open: Daily 11:45am–2:30pm. *MTR:* Tsimshatsui. PASTA/SALAD

• **The Salisbury,** YMCA, Salisbury Rd., Tsimshatsui (tel. 3692211). *Prices:* Breakfast buffet HK$42 ($5.45); lunch buffet HK$38 ($4.95) weekdays, HK$55 ($7.15) Sat and Sun. AE, MC, V.

Open: Daily 7–10:30am and noon–2:30pm. *MTR:* Tsimshatsui. WESTERN/CHINESE

• **The Spice Market,** 3rd floor of Harbour City, Canton Rd., (near the Omni Hongkong Hotel), Tsimshatsui (tel. 7306238). *Prices:* Lunch buffet HK$75 ($9.75) weekdays, HK$90 ($11.75) Sat and Sun; dinner buffet HK$90 ($11.75) weekdays, HK$100 ($13) Sat and Sun.

A great view of the harbor!

Open: Daily 11am–3pm and 6–10pm. *MTR:* Tsimshatsui. CURRIES AND DISHES OF ASIA

Central

• **Dragon Boat,** Hong Kong Hilton Hotel, 2 Queen's Rd., Central (tel. 5233111). *Prices:* Lunch buffet HK$108 ($14). AE,CB, DC, MC, V.

Open: Mon–Fri only, noon–2:30pm. *MTR:* Central. WESTERN/CHINESE

• **Jade Lotus,** Hong Kong Hilton Hotel, 2 Queen's Rd., Central (tel. 5233111). *Prices:* Lunch buffet HK$140 ($18.25). AE, CB, DC, MC, V.

Open: Mon–Fri only, noon–2:30pm. *MTR:* Central. WESTERN/CHINESE/INDIAN/VEGETARIAN

• **La Ronda,** 30th floor on the Furama Inter-Continental Hotel, 1 Connaught Rd., Central (tel. 5255111). *Prices:* Lunch buffet HK$150 ($19.50); dinner buffet HK$215 ($27.75). AE, CB, DC, MC, V.

A revolving restaurant, with stunning views!

Open: Daily noon–3pm and 7–11pm. *Reservations:* Recommended. *MTR:* Tsimshatsui. WESTERN/CHINESE/INDIAN/INTERNATIONAL

Wanchai/Causeway Bay

• **Dicken's Bar,** Excelsior Hotel, 281 Gloucester Rd., Causeway Bay (tel. 5767365). *Prices:* Lunch buffet HK$65 ($8.45). AE, DC, MC, V.

Open: Mon–Fri only, noon–2pm. *MTR:* Causeway Bay. INDIAN

• **Golden Poppy,** 90-92 Jaffe Rd., Wanchai (tel. 5283128). *Prices:* Lunch buffet HK$60 ($7.80) AE, MC, V.

Open: Mon–Fri only, 12:30–2:30pm. *MTR:* Wanchai. THAI

EXPLORING HONG KONG

To help you get the most out of your stay in Hong Kong, this chapter is organized to suggest sightseeing strategies for stays of one to five days, introduce you to the top sights, and lead you on walking tours through both Hong Kong Island and Kowloon. There are also sections on places of interest to children, organized tours, and sports.

1. Sightseeing Strategies

If you want to do Hong Kong justice, you should plan on staying here at least a week. Barring that, if you're active from dawn until past dusk, you can see quite a bit of the city and its outlying attractions in three to five days, simply because the colony is so compact and transportation is so efficient. To help you get the most out of your stay, the suggested itineraries below will guide you to the most important attractions.

IF YOU HAVE ONE DAY

If you have only one day to spend in Hong Kong—what can I say, I feel sorry for you. I think I'd have a coronary racing around in a panic trying to see everything, growing more anxious by the minute as I realized that there were so many more things I wouldn't be able to see. Thus the best thing to do if you have only one day is to devote the morning to a half-day sightseeing tour. The typical Hong Kong Island tour, for example, includes a trip up to Victoria Peak, followed by a drive to the southern end of the island to Stanley Market where visitors can do a little bargain hunting, and to Aberdeen.

The afternoon should be structured to your own tastes, but should include a ride on the famous Star Ferry across Victoria Harbour. To get a feel of Hong Kong, you might want to board the double-decker tram on Hong Kong Island, or follow part of the walking tour for either the Central and Western District or Kowloon (see Section 3, "Walking Tours of Hong Kong," farther on in this chapter). For one-stop shopping, try one of the large stores specializing in Chinese products such as Chinese Arts & Crafts Ltd., China Products Co., or Yue Hwa (check the shopping chapter, Chapter VIII).

Since you have only one evening, you might consider joining one of the organized evening tours. If you haven't yet visited Aberdeen, you might consider a sunset cruise which includes a meal at one of the floating restaurants in Aberdeen. Tours can be booked through most tourist hotels in Hong Kong (for more information on evening tours, check the nightlife chapter, Chapter IX).

IF YOU HAVE TWO DAYS

Because two days still isn't much time, spend your very first morning on a half-day tour of Hong Kong Island, as outlined above. Spend the rest of the afternoon on Hong Kong Island according to your interests—Stanley for bargain shopping; a tram ride to Causeway Bay; a do-it-yourself tour of the Central District and Western District for insight into traditional Chinese life; or Ocean Park and the Middle Kingdom. In the evening, join one of the many organized evening tours. There's a six-hour tour, for example, that gives participants a ride from Causeway Bay through Central in an antique tram, followed either by a dinner cruise in the harbor or dancing and dinner at La Ronda revolving restaurant. There are also sunset harbor cruises.

Start the next morning at a Chinese restaurant with dim sum. If you haven't yet ridden the Star Ferry, do so, or take a one-hour cruise of the harbor. Spend the rest of the day exploring Kowloon, with visits to the Space Museum, Museum of History, the many shops along Nathan Road, and the Jade Market. Begin the evening with a cocktail at one of Hong Kong's many lounges with a view of the harbor, followed by dinner at a Chinese or Western restaurant. Retire afterward to a pub or disco, or attend a performance at one of Hong Kong's several theaters.

IF YOU HAVE THREE DAYS

Start the day with a dim-sum breakfast in a Chinese restaurant. Then, for your first breathtaking view of Hong Kong, ride the famous Star Ferry across Victoria Harbour. For even better views, take the peak tram to the top of Victoria Peak, where you'll be rewarded with a spectacular view of the city—that is, if the weather is clear. Take an hour's walk along the circular path around Victoria Peak, where you'll have changing vistas of Central, Kowloon, Aberdeen, and even Cheung Chau and other islands.

Have lunch at one of Central's many restaurants or one of its English-style pubs, followed by a do-it-yourself walking tour of Central and the Western District, where you can observe traditional Chinese life firsthand. For your first evening, try one of Hong Kong's excellent evening tours, such as a sunset cruise or the combination tram-and-cruise tour.

Devote your second day to Kowloon. Start with a do-it-yourself tour of Tsimshatsui and Yaumatei, where you'll visit the Space Museum, Museum of History, and the Jade Market. Reserve time later in the day for shopping, including the many shops along Nathan Road and the huge shopping complexes such as Harbour City. Visit the factory outlets in Tsimshatsui or Hung Hom in Kowloon. When evening comes, head for a cocktail lounge with a view, followed by dinner and entertainment in a pub or disco.

For your last morning in Hong Kong, head for one of the outlying islands. Cheung Chau is good for short excursions; Lamma is good if you want to do some hiking. (See Chapter X for descriptions of the outlying islands.) Spend the afternoon following your own persuasions: Stanley for shopping; Aberdeen for a sampan ride; a tram ride to Causeway Bay; Ocean Park and the Middle Kingdom; or Aw Boon Haw Gardens. After dinner at a traditional Chinese restaurant, take a stroll through one of the night markets, either Poor Man's Nightclub near the Macau Ferry Terminal in Hong Kong or Temple Street Night Market in Kowloon.

IF YOU HAVE FIVE DAYS OR MORE

Consider yourself lucky! Spend the first three days as outlined above. Note, however, that if you're having something tailor-made, visit a tailor on your first day to discuss needs and fittings. On the fourth day, take a trip to the New Territories (see Chapter X for more information). The easiest way to see this vast area is by joining the seven-hour organized tour called "The Land Between" Tour, but you may wish to explore the New Territories on your own via the Kowloon–Canton Railway. If you're interested in historical settings, an alternative is to visit Sam Tung Uk Museum in Tsuen Wan, a restored Hakka walled village, followed by a bus trip to Kam Tin, a walled village still inhabited by the Hakka. If you have children or like organized tours, you might be more interested in joining a tour of Sung Dynasty Village, a re-creation of how a Chinese village may have looked 1,000 years ago. If you're not too tired come evening, take the Peak Tram to Victoria Peak for a romantic nighttime view of Hong Kong, ablaze with glittering lights, or stroll the promenade along the Tsimshatsui waterfront.

On the fifth day, spend the morning visiting another island you haven't yet seen. Devote the afternoon to all those things you haven't yet been able to do, whether more shopping, sightseeing, or unstructured exploration. If you haven't yet been to Stanley, Ocean Park, or Causeway Bay, for example, this is your last chance. If it's horse-racing season, try to get in on the action. If you've had something custom-made, don't forget to pick it up.

For a memorable last evening in Hong Kong, splurge at one of Hong Kong's fine Chinese or Western restaurants, or experience the festivities of a sampan dinner at the Typhoon Shelter in Causeway Bay.

If you have more days to spare, cross the Pearl River Estuary by jetfoil to the ancient Portuguese city of Macau, the first European settlement in the Far East (see Chapter XI on Macau). There are a number of great restaurants there, as well as expensive and moderately priced accommodations. Or, if you wish, cross the border in the New Territories for a one-day or longer trip to China.

2. Top Attractions

Although Hong Kong is compact and easy to navigate around, it makes sense to divide the city into sections when planning your sightseeing itineraries. To make your life easier, the information below on various sightseeing attractions is presented according to area. Likewise, the chapters on restaurants and nightlife are also divided into areas, making it easy to coordinate the day's activities with lunch, dinner, and evening entertainment. Don't forget to read over the recommended walking tours later on in this chapter, since they include stops at several of Hong Kong's top attractions.

For sightseeing on the outlying islands and the New Territories, refer to Chapter X, "Exploring the Environs."

THE FOUR MUSTS

There are four things every visitor to Hong Kong should do, and they all involve the colony's public transportation system. They are: ride the Star Ferry across the harbor; go up to Victoria Peak in the Peak Tram; take a rickety old tram on Hong Kong Island; and ride one of the ferries to the outlying islands (see Chapter X, "Exploring the Environs," for information on the various islands, the ferries, and the fares). Nothing can beat the thrill of these four experiences, nor give better insight into the essence of Hong Kong and its people. What's more, riding the ferries and trams are trips in themselves and are all inexpensive.

The Star Ferries

The stars of the show, of course, are the Star Ferries, a group of green-and-white vessels that have been carrying passengers back and forth between Kowloon and Hong Kong Island since 1898. At only HK$.60 (8¢) for the ordinary fare, it's one of the cheapest—and yet most dramatic—seven-minute rides in the world. For tips on using the Star Ferry, refer to Chapter IV under "Getting Around."

Since a seven-minute ride isn't nearly enough time to soak up the ambience of Victoria Harbour, you may wish to board a special Star Ferry for a one-hour harbor cruise. These cruises depart six times daily from both the Kowloon and Hong Kong sides. For more information on this and other cruises, read on to Section 3 on "Organized Tours" later in this chapter.

Victoria Peak

At 1,308 feet, Victoria Peak is Hong Kong Island's tallest hill and offers the best and most spectacular views of Hong Kong. It's always been one of the colony's most exclusive places to live, since in the days before air conditioning the Peak was usually a few degrees cooler than the sweltering city below. A hundred years ago, the rich reached the Peak after a three-hour trip in sedan chairs, powered to the top by coolies. Then, in 1888, the **peak tram** opened, cutting the journey from a grueling three hours to eight minutes.

In 1989 the original, cast-iron green funicular cars with mahogany seats were replaced by new, modern cars imported from Switzerland, increasing passenger load from 72 to 120 people. I was sorry to see the old cars go, but I guess it will make life easier for the residents. After all, the peak tram is used by residents and tourists alike. Making several stops along the way, the peak tram takes children to school and commuters to work and delivers them back home again.

The easiest way to reach the peak tram, located on Garden Road behind the Hilton Hotel, is to take one of the free shuttle buses that operate between the tram terminal and the Star Ferry in Central. Shuttle buses run every 20 minutes from 9am to 7pm. Otherwise, it's about a 10-minute walk from Chater Garden.

The peak tram costs HK$6 (80¢) one way, HK$10 ($1.30) round trip. It departs every 10 minutes and is in operation daily from 7am to midnight. The tram climbs almost vertically to the top of the Peak—don't worry, there's never been an accident in its entire 100-some years of operation. At the top there's the **Peak Tower,** where you will find souvenir shops, an observation deck, the Peak Tower Restaurant, and the Peak Tower Coffee Shop.

The best thing to do atop Victoria Peak is to take a walk. If you're feeling particularly energetic, you might want to hike up Mount Austin Road to where the governor's summer lodge used to stand—usually shrouded in mist. Only the formal gardens remain, carefully tended and offering a pleasant respite from the crowdedness of Hong Kong down below.

My favorite walk on Victoria Peak is the hour-long circular hike on Lugard Road and Harlech Road (as you exit from Peak Tower, take an immediate right). Mainly a foot path, it snakes along the side of the cliff, offering great views of the Central District down below, the harbor, Kowloon, and eventually Aberdeen and outlying islands on the other side. This is one of the best walks in the colony.

A Tram Ride

Just as the Star Ferry is the most colorful and cheapest way to see the harbor, the tram is the most colorful and cheapest way to see the northern end of Hong Kong Island. In fact, the tram is so much a part of Hong Kong life that it was chosen for Hong Kong's exhibit at the Vancouver '86 Expo. Dating from 1904, the tram line follows what used to be the waterfront before the days of land reclamation. Old, narrow, double-decker affairs, the trams cut through the heart of the city, from Kennedy Town in the west to Shau Kei Wan in the east. There's only one detour—off to Happy Valley—so it's impossible to get lost.

In any case, if you're in Central, you can board the tram on Des Voeux Road Central. Climb to the upper deck and try to get a seat in the front row. For more information on the fare and how to ride the tram, refer to Chapter IV, Section 2, "Getting Around." In addition, the HKTA distributes a free leaflet called "Tram Travel," which describes the various neighborhoods passed along the way. If you're a tram nut, you may even want to take an organized tram tour, offered with dim sum, lunch, afternoon tea, or in the evening (see the "Organized Tours" section later in this chapter for more information).

Ferries to the Outlying Islands

While most of Hong Kong's 235 outlying islands are uninhabited, trips by ferry to the most interesting ones are described in Chapter X, "Exploring the Environs."

CULTURAL SHOWS

If you're interested in traditional Chinese performing arts, one of the first things you'll want to do upon arrival in Hong Kong is inquire at the **Hong Kong Tourist Association** about its schedule of free cultural entertainment. The HKTA organizes one-hour Chinese cultural shows twice a week, with one performance at Taikoo Shing's Cityplaza, Hong Kong (MTR: Taikoo Shing), and the other at Tsimshatsui's New World Centre, Kowloon (MTR: Tsimshatsui). The programs vary, but may include performances of Chinese instrumental music, shadow puppetry, Fukienese glove puppetry, Chinese magic and acrobatics, folk songs and dances, or Chinese martial arts. At last check, shows were at noon at Cityplaza and at 6pm at the New World Centre, but contact the HKTA (tel. 7225555) for exact times, dates, and information on the day's program.

Free cultural shows are also staged daily at the **Full Moon Village Folk-Craft Centre** in the Empire Centre, 68 Mody Rd., East Tsimshatsui (tel. 7240587). Shows include performances of Chinese traditional dance, folk songs, and acrobatics. Call for information on performance times.

HONG KONG ISLAND SIGHTS

With its 30 square miles, Hong Kong Island holds the most attractions for the visitor. This is where the colony's history began, and there's everything here from museums to gardens to beaches and amusement parks.

Central District and Vicinity

Hong Kong Museum of Art, 10th and 11th floors, High Block, City Hall, Connaught Rd. and Edinburgh Pl., Central (tel. 5224127).

Located just a two-minute walk east of the Star Ferry terminus in Central, the Museum of Art features changing exhibitions of art and antiquities. Its collection is vast, and includes Chinese ceramics, bronzes, jade, cloisonné, lacquerware, bamboo carvings, snuff bottles, and embroidery, as well as paintings and calligraphy dating from the 17th century to the early 20th century. The collection also houses more than 980 paintings, prints, drawings, lithographs, and engravings, providing a vivid pictorial account of Sino-British contacts in the 18th and 19th centuries.

However, don't come to the museum expecting to see all of the above. This museum has no permanent exhibition, only special exhibitions, usually of a month's duration. Sometimes the display is from overseas and has nothing to do with Chinese art or antiquities, so you might want to call beforehand if you're interested only in things Chinese. The museum also serves as a venue for contemporary Hong Kong artists and sells their work. (Note: The Museum of Art is scheduled to move in 1991 to a new home near the Hong Kong Cultural Centre in Tsimshatsui. Contact the HKTA for the exact date.)

Open: Fri–Wed 10am–6pm. *Closed:* Thurs, New Year's Day, the first three days of the Chinese New Year, and Dec 25 and 26. *Admission:* Free. *MTR:* Central.

Flagstaff House Museum of Tea Ware, Victoria Barracks (enter from Cotton Tree Drive), Central (tel. 8690690).

Flagstaff House is the oldest colonial building in Hong Kong and thus is the best place to go if you want to see architecture typical of Hong Kong more than 100 years ago. It was built in 1844 as the home of the commander of the British forces. Its collection includes about 500 pieces of teaware, primarily of Chinese origin, dating from the 7th century to the present day.

Open: Thurs–Tues 10am–5pm. *Closed:* Wed, New Year's Day, the first three days of the Chinese New Year, and Dec 25 and 26. *Admission:* Free. *Directions:* Bus 3, 12, 23, 23B, 40, or 103, getting off at the first stop on Cotton Tree Drive; or 20-minute walk from Chater Garden in Central.

Zoological and Botanical Gardens, Garden Rd., Central (tel. 8625579).

Established in 1864, these gardens on the slope of Victoria Peak are a popular park and respite for the residents of Hong Kong. Come here early, around 8am, and you'll see Chinese going through the slow motions of tai chi, or shadow boxing, a kind of disciplined physical exercise designed to bring a sense of peace and balance to its practitioners. Flowers are almost always in bloom, from azaleas in spring to wisteria and bauhinea in summer and fall; plants in the botanical gardens include Burmese rosewood trees, Indian rubber trees, camphor trees, and the Hong Kong orchid. The small zoo houses mountain lions, jaguars, orangutans, and monkeys, and there's an aviary with about 800 birds representing 300 species, including Palawan peacocks, birds of paradise from Papua New Guinea, cranes, and Mandarin ducks. If you're tired of Central and its traffic, this is a pleasant place to regain your sanity.

Open: Daily 6am–7pm for the zoological garden, 6am–10pm for the botanical garden. *Admission:* Free. *MTR:* Central, then a 15-minute walk past the Hilton on Garden Road.

Sai Ying Pun

Fung Ping Shan Museum, 94 Bonham Rd., University of Hong Kong (tel. 8592114).

This university museum, located to the west of Central, has collections of Chinese art, primarily ceramics and bronzes. The bronze collection includes Shang and Zhou ritual vessels, decorative mirrors, and Nestorian crosses of the Yuan Dynasty.

The ceramics collection includes painted pottery of the third millennium B.C., tomb pottery of the Han, three-color glazes of the Tang, wares of the Song kilns, blue and white wares, monochromes and polychromes of the Ming and Qing Dynasties, and recent works by Jingdezhen and Shiwan potters.

Open: Mon–Sat 9:30am–6pm. *Closed:* Sun, public hols, Chinese New Year's Eve, March 16, Christmas Eve, and New Year's Eve. *Admission:* Free. *Directions:* Bus 3 from the Connaught Road Central bus stop in front of Jardine House; get off at the Bonham Road bus stop opposite St. Paul's College.

Wanchai and Causeway Bay

Pao Sui Loong Galleries, 4th and 5th floors, Hong Kong Arts Centre, Harbour Rd., Wanchai (tel. 8230200).

Changing exhibitions of contemporary international and local art, including paintings, graphic art, sculpture, photography, crafts, and calligraphy.

Open: Daily 10am–8pm (closed the first three days of the Chinese New Year). *Admission:* Free. *MTR:* Wanchai.

Museum of Chinese Historical Relics, Causeway Centre, 28 Harcourt Rd., Wanchai (tel. 5742692).

Changing exhibitions relating to China, its products, and its art. A recent exhibition, for example, showcased products produced in Shanghai, from machinery to clothing. Be sure to call in advance for information of current exhibitions, admission price, and opening times.

MTR: Wanchai.

Noon Day Gun, Gloucester Rd., Causeway Bay.

It may not be worth going out of your way to see, but if you're in the neighborhood of the Excelsior Hotel, look for a small garden opposite the hotel near the harbor. There you'll find a gun, a well-known historical landmark associated with Jardine, Matheson & Co., Hong Kong's oldest trading house. Pointing out over the Royal Hong Kong Yacht Club, the gun is fired every day at noon, an act immortalized in Noel Coward's "Mad Dogs and Englishmen": "In Hong Kong they strike a gong and fire off the noon day gun." The tradition, so they say, started in the last century when the Jardine trading company fired off a double-gun salute to welcome returning bosses. The salute, usually reserved for the military, so incensed a senior British naval officer that he ordered the Jardines to fire the gun every day at noon as punishment.

MTR: Causeway Bay.

Victoria Park, Causeway Rd. and Gloucester Rd., Causeway Bay.

This 19-acre park is one of Hong Kong's largest, serving as the green lungs of the city. Constructed on land reclaimed from a typhoon shelter, it has tennis and squash courts, a 50-meter swimming pool, basketball courts, a skating rink, and a jogging track. The Mid-Autumn Festival is held here, as well as a flower market a few days before Chinese New Year.

MTR: Causeway Bay.

Aw Boon Haw Gardens, Tai Hang Rd., Causeway Bay.

Formerly known as the Tiger Balm Gardens, these are probably the most bizarre gardens you'll ever see. They were built in 1935 by Chinese millionaire and philanthropist Aw Boon Haw, who made his fortune with a cure-all ointment called Tiger Balm. The 7½ acres of these gardens feature colorfully painted statues from Chinese mythology, some of them rather grotesque, especially those depicting unfortunate souls being tortured in hell. The message here is quite clear: behave yourself, or else! Because the gardens are so colorful, you can get some great photographs to show the folks back home. For more information, contact the HKTA.

Open: Daily 10am–4pm. *Admission:* Free. *Directions:* Bus 11 from the Central Bus Terminus or Causeway Bay MTR Station; get off after passing the Lai Tak Tsuen public housing project and when you can see a white pagoda ahead of you on the left.

Aberdeen

Located on the south side of Hong Kong Island, Aberdeen is a town nestled around a naturally protected harbor. Famous for its colorful floating seafood restaurants and boat people who live on junks in Aberdeen harbor, Aberdeen has undergone massive changes in recent years. Originally a typhoon shelter and landbase for seafarers, it used to be a charming fishing village and boatbuilding port, supported primarily by several thousand junks and boat people. Many of the boat people, however, have been moved to massive housing projects, and the waterfront surrounding Aberdeen is now crowded with high-rises.

Still, Aberdeen continues to be popular with the tourist crowd because of its remaining boat population and floating restaurants. Women operating sampans will vie for your dollars to tour you around the harbor, which is definitely worth the cost since it's about the only thing to do here and is the best way to see the junks. A 30-minute tour will cost HK$80 ($10.50) per person and is offered daily between 8am to 6pm. Watertours also offers a 20-minute tour of Aberdeen for HK$40 ($5.20).

You'll pass huge boats housing extended families with men repairing fishing nets, women hanging out their laundry, dogs barking and children playing, families eating, and people fishing in the murky waters. There was a time when a boat person could be born, live, marry, and die on board without ever setting a foot on shore. Nowadays, however, young people are moving to shore to take advantage of job opportunities.

Other attractions of Aberdeen include its floating restaurants Jumbo and Tai Pak (see Section 8 in Chapter VI) and a Tin Hau temple. Built in 1851, it's dedicated to Tin Hau, protectress of fishing folk, and is located at the junction of Aberdeen Main Road and Aberdeen Reservoir Road.

To get to Aberdeen, take bus 70 from the Central Bus Terminal.

Deep Water Bay

Ocean Park (tel. 5520291).

If you're a kid or a kid at heart, you'll love Ocean Park. Situated along a dramatic rocky coastline on the island's southern shore, the park is divided into two areas, a "lowland" and a "headland."

The lowland boasts greenhouses with cacti, foliage, orchids, and other flowering plants; a butterfly house (shaped, interestingly enough, like a caterpillar) with 1,000 free-flying butterflies; and the Golden Pagoda, with more varieties of goldfish than you ever imagined possible, most of them from China. The Pompomed Bull goldfish, for example, has large pompomlike growths on its head, while the Dragon Eyes has huge buglike eyes. And then there's the Lamp Dragon Eyes, too bizarre for words. For children, there's Adventure World, with jungle gyms to climb on and animals to observe.

From the lowland, visitors board cable cars for a spectacular 10-minute ride over a hill to the headland, while being treated to great views along the way. The headland area, situated on a peninsula that juts into the sea, has an artificial wave cove that is home to seals, sea lions, and penguins, as well as various thrill rides that includes a roller coaster that turns upside down. Ocean Theatre features shows by talented dolphins, sea lions, and a killer whale. Other exhibits include the Shark Aquarium, with 40 species of sharks, and the Aviary, with 2,000 birds. But my favorite is the Atoll Reef, one of the world's largest aquariums, with 5,000 fish of 500 different species. The observation passageway circles three stories outside the aquarium, giving you views from different angles of everything from giant turtles to schools of tropical fish.

Open: Mon–Sat 10am–6pm, Sun 9am–6pm. *Admission:* HK$100 ($13) for adults, HK$50 ($6.50) for children under 15. *Directions:* Ocean Park Citybus from the Admiralty MTR station (buy tickets at major MTR stations); or bus 70 or 90 from Exchange Square in Central.

Middle Kingdom, Tai Shue Wan (tel. 5555222).

Opened in 1989, the Middle Kingdom is a small, re-created village of China's past with full-size temples, shrines, pavilions, pagodas, street scenes, and public squares. Its streets lead visitors past 13 dynasties of Chinese history, each represented by a building, statue, or object. Representing the Ming Dynasty (A.D. 1369–1644), for example, is a replica of a boat used by Admiral Cheng

Ho, who traveled as far west as the Red Sea. Throughout the Middle Kingdom are various craftspeople at work making paper, silk weavings, iron castings, pottery, and glass. Shops sell a variety of Chinese products, from writing instruments to tea, engravings, and incense.

The Middle Kingdom is located next to the headland entrance of Ocean Park. You can visit the Middle Kingdom on your own, or, if you wish, join an English tour that will give information and insight into China's various dynasties.

Open: Daily 10am–6pm. *Admission:* HK$140 ($18.25) for adults, HK$70 ($9.10) for children. *Tours:* HK$220–HK$280 ($28.50–$36.25) for adults, HK$150–HK$210 ($19.50–$27.25) for children.

Water World (tel. 5556055).

Located next to Ocean Park's main (lowland) entrance, Water World is a good place to cool off on a hot summer's day. It contains several pools with various slides and diving platforms, and even has a pool with a sandy beach and waves. Be sure to bring your bathing suit.

Open: summer daily 10am–10pm; spring and autumn 10am–5pm. *Closed:* Nov–March. *Admission:* HK$45 ($5.85). *Directions:* Bus 70 or 90 from Exchange Square in Central.

Stanley

Back when Hong Kong Island was ceded to the British in the 1840s, Stanley was one of the largest fishing villages on the island, with a population of 2,000. Today it's a residential area of about 6,000 and has become a rather fashionable address.

The best-known attraction in Stanley is its market, a mecca for those in search of inexpensive jeans, silk, and sportswear. Other attractions include a Tin Hau temple, built in 1767; a Kwun Yum temple, with a 20-foot statue of Kwun Yum, the goddess of mercy; and Stanley Main Beach, popular in the summer for swimming.

To get there, take bus 6 or 260 from Exchange Square in Central.

KOWLOON SIGHTS

In addition to its myriad hotels, restaurants, and shops, southern Kowloon has a number of specific sights worth visiting. More information on Kowloon, especially in its northern end near the border with the New Territories, is given in Chapter X in Section 1, "The New Territories."

Space Museum, 10 Salisbury Rd., Tsimshatsui (tel. 7212361 or 5739595).

Located in front of the Peninsula Hotel on the Tsimshatsui waterfront, the Space Museum is easy to spot with its white-domed planetarium. The museum is divided into three parts: the Exhibition Hall, the Hall of Solar Sciences, and the Space Theatre. The Exhibition Hall on the ground floor provides an introduction to man's progress in astronomy and space, including information on the various constellations and an explanation of Stonehenge. If you've ever wondered what you'd weigh on the moon or Mars, this is your chance to find out. The Hall of Solar Sciences, located on the first floor, is devoted to our nearest star, the sun.

The Space Theatre, a planetarium with a 75-foot domed roof, has a Zeiss star projector that can project up to about 9,000 stars and an Omnimax projection system that produces an almost 360° panorama. Hour-long shows, which range from celestial phenomena to such wonders of the world as the Great Barrier Reef, are held throughout the afternoon and early evening and cost HK$15 ($1.95) per person. Some shows are narrated in English, but those that aren't provide free headsets with simultaneous English translations. Buy your ticket at least a day in advance.

Open: Mon and Wed–Fri 2–9:30pm, Sat 1–9:30pm, Sun 10:30am–9:30pm. *Closed:* Tues. *Admission:* Free to Exhibition Hall and Hall of Solar Sciences; Space Theatre HK$15 ($1.95). *MTR:* Tsimshatsui.

Hong Kong Museum of History, Kowloon Park, Haiphong Rd. or Nathan Rd., Tsimshatsui (tel. 3671124).

Housed in two buildings dating from the late 19th century, this museum outlines the history of Hong Kong, including the political, cultural, social, and economic development of the colony. Its collection includes archeological finds, ethnographic collections, natural history displays, and historical photographs.

Open: Mon–Thurs and Sat 10am–6pm, Sun and hols 1–6pm. *Closed:* Fri, New Year's Day, the first three days of the Chinese New Year, and Dec 25 and 26. *Admission:* Free. *MTR:* Tsimshatsui (Haiphong Road exit).

Jade Market, Kansu St., Yaumatei.

More than 400 vendors sell jade and freshwater pearls, laying out their wares on everything from cloths spread out on the sidewalk to satin-lined display cases. Before you buy anything here, however, read the "Chinese Crafts and Products," "Jade Market," and "Jewelry" sections in Chapter VIII, "Hong Kong Shopping."

Open: Daily 10am–2pm. *Admission:* Free. *MTR:* Halfway between the Yaumatei and Jordan stations.

Bird Market, Hong Lok St., Mongkok.

Two blocks west of Nathan Road off Argyle Street, there's a fascinating lane filled with the Bird Market. Thousands of birds, hundreds of cages, millions of crickets, and scores of people buying and selling birds and their accoutrements. Very Chinese, and lots of fun.

Open: Daily 9am-5pm. *Closed:* Chinese New Year. *Admission:* free. *MTR:* Monkok.

Sung Dynasty Village, Mei Lai Rd., Kowloon (tel. 7415111).

This small replica of how a Chinese village may have looked 1,000 years ago during the Sung Dynasty took five years to construct and cost the equivalent of $2 million U.S. Re-created with close attention to architectural detail, the village consists of open-fronted wooden shops, stalls, and buildings grouped around a willow-lined stream. Staffed by villagers dressed in Sung Dynasty costumes, each shop is based on a different theme and offers a different product, from almond cookies and Chinese tea to hand-painted fans and incense. There's a rice wine shop, a herbal medicine shop, a Chinese restaurant, and a replica of a rich man's house. There's also entertainment, from a monkey show to Chinese acrobatics and opera.

Included in the village is Hong Kong's largest wax museum, with famous personalities from Chinese history. The explanations that accompany each figure are quite entertaining. We learn, for example, that Kou Chien, who lived around 421 B.C., suffered defeat by his enemies and as self-punishment "he slept on faggots and constantly tasted gall." It must have worked because we're told that after 20 years he finally succeeded in defeating his enemy.

If you want to visit Sung Dynasty Village on a weekday, you can do so only on an organized tour (see Section 4, later in this chapter). Sung Dynasty Village is located rather far from Tsimshatsui, though the MTR delivers you there within 30 minutes.

Open: Sat and Sun 12:30–5pm (weekdays organized tours only). *Admission:* HK$50 ($6.50) for adults, HK$30 ($3.90) for children. *Directions:* Bus 6A from Star Ferry, then a four minute walk; or MTR to Mei Foo Station, then a 15-minute walk north along Lai Wan Road and Mei Lai Road.

---

3. Walking Tours of Hong Kong

Surprisingly compact, Hong Kong is an easy city to explore on foot. If it weren't for the harbor, you'd never need anything but your own two feet to cover Tsimshatsui, the Central District, Wanchai, and Causeway Bay. Walking affords a more intimate relationship with your surroundings, allows chance encounters with the unexpected, and lets you discover that vegetable market, temple, or shop you otherwise never would have seen.

If, for example, you're in the Central District and want to eat dinner on Food Street in Causeway Bay, you can walk there in less than an hour, passing through colorful Wanchai on the way. Causeway Bay is good for unstructured exploring, since it's full of little sidewalk markets, street vendors, restaurants, and shops patronized by the locals. Another great place for a hike is the Western District, fascinating because it encompasses a wide spectrum of Chinese traditional shops, from chop makers to egg shops to ginseng wholesalers. If you like views, nothing can beat the hour-long circular walk on Victoria Peak (see Section 2, above, in this chapter).

On the other side of the harbor, a walk up Nathan Road from the harbor to the Yaumatei subway station takes less than 30 minutes, although it would be hard to resist all the shops and department stores you pass on the way. And Yaumatei itself is another good place for wandering, since it, too, offers insight into the Chinese way of life with its markets and traditional shops.

What follows are two recommended strolls, one through the Central District and Western District on Hong Kong Island, the other from Tsimshatsui to Yaumatei in Kowloon. If you want detailed maps of these two areas, you may want to purchase two nifty booklets put out by the Hong Kong Tourist Association and available at HKTA offices. One is called "Central and Western District Walking Tour," which describes a three-hour walk through Central and the Western District, while the other is called "Yau Ma Tei Walking Tour," with visits to the Jade Market, traditional shops, and the Temple Street Night Market. Each costs HK$15 ($1.95) and comes complete with a map and detailed information of the various sights and shops you'll see along the way.

EXPLORING THE CENTRAL AND WESTERN DISTRICTS

The birthplace of modern Hong Kong, the Central District used to be called Victoria and boasted elegant colonial-style buildings with sweeping verandas and narrow streets filled with pigtailed men pulling rickshaws. That's hard to imagine nowadays. With its gleaming skyscrapers of glass and concrete, there's almost nothing left of its colonial beginnings. Still, it's the logical beginning for a tour of Hong Kong.

During the summer, you could begin your tour of the Central District by stopping off for a relaxing drink or snack on the upper deck of the public **Blake Pier,** located just to the west of the Star Ferry terminus. This is one of the cheapest and best places to enjoy a great view of the harbor and of the familiar green-and-white Star Ferries as they come and go. Popular at lunchtime with office workers, the snackbar here sells sandwiches, spaghetti, salads, ice cream, beer, coffee, and soft drinks. As you sit here soaking up some of the waterfront ambience, consider the fact that the waterfront used to be much farther back, at Queen's Road. In the 1800s land reclamation added first Des Voeux Road and then Connaught Road. Land reclamation has also been carried on extensively across the harbor on Kowloon—all of East Tsimshatsui is reclaimed land. One Hong Kong local I met joked that so much land was being reclaimed it wouldn't be long before you could walk across the harbor.

If you haven't yet been to the tourist office, you'll want to stop by the **Jardine House** (formerly Connaught Centre), located in front of the Star Ferry terminus. In the basement in Shop 8 is the main headquarters of the Hong Kong Tourist Association. Also near Star Ferry, just to the east, is **City Hall,** where on the 10th and 11th floors you'll find the **Hong Kong Museum of Art.** Admission here is free, so it's worth stopping by to see what the current exhibition is. Past exhibitions have displayed Chinese art and antiquities, including jade, cloisonné, lacquerware, and ceramics, as well as works by contemporary Hong Kong artists. (Note: The Museum of Art is scheduled to move in 1991 to a new location near the Hong Kong Cultural Centre in Tsimshatsui; contact the HKTA to find out the exact date.)

From here it's just a short walk inland to **Des Voeux Road Central,** with its fashionable boutiques, banks, and office buildings, as well as the classy **Landmark complex** with its shops and restaurants. Heading west, you'll soon reach Li Yuen Street East and Li Yuen Street West, two parallel pedestrian lanes which rise up steeply

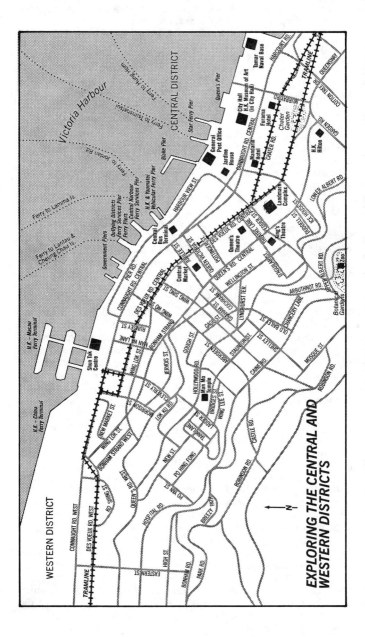

EXPLORING THE CENTRAL AND WESTERN DISTRICTS

to your left and are packed with stalls selling clothing and accessories, including handbags, belts, and even bras.

Farther down Des Voeux is **Central Market,** a four-story building that serves as Hong Kong's largest public market for everything from seafood and live poultry to fruits and vegetables. Although it's open from 6am to 2pm and again from 4:30 to 8pm, try to get here in the morning, when it's at its busiest with housewives buying the day's meal and chefs purchasing the daily specials. With the Chinese penchant for freshness, chickens are killed on the spot, boiled, and then thrown into machines that pluck them. Almost every part of every animal is for sale, including the liver, heart, and intestines. Wicker baskets may contain the discarded horns and skulls of bulls, with even the brains carved out—not for the fainthearted. If all you want to see are fruit and vegetables, head for the third floor.

The next interesting place to watch out for is **Wing On Street,** which is actually a covered, hidden bazaarlike alley that's easy to miss if you don't keep your eyes peeled. It has earned the nickname **Cloth Alley** because of its long string of stalls selling fabrics from around the world, including cotton, silk, denim, wool, linen, knits, and even upholstery weights. You might want to buy cloth here for those tailor-made suits.

Farther along is **Wing Sing Street,** also called **Egg Street,** where tons of eggs are distributed every morning to restaurants and retail outlets. Imported mainly from China, all kinds of eggs are sold here, from 100-year-old eggs and quail eggs to pigeon and goose eggs. The 100-year-old eggs are actually much younger, having first been soaked with tea leaves, salt, and chemicals for one month before being covered with mud and rice husks. They can be preserved in this mud-covered state for as long as six months without refrigeration. At any rate, both Egg Street and Cloth Alley demonstrate the Chinese way of doing business: retailers and wholesalers sharing the same kind of business set up shop together in a specific area, so customers know where to find their product.

Not far from Wing Sing Street is **Man Wa Lane,** home of one of China's oldest trades—"chop" or carved-seal making. Made from stone, ivory, jade, clay, marble, bronze, porcelain, bamboo, wood, soapstone, and even plastic, these chops can be carved with a name and are used by the Chinese to stamp their identification, much like a written signature. If you want, you can have your own chop made, with your name translated into Chinese characters. It takes about an hour for a chop to be made, so you may want to stop by again later after you've finished your walk.

Man Wa Lane empties onto **Bonham Strand East,** home of Central's **snake shops,** which do a roaring business during the winter months from October to February. Eaten as protection against the winter cold, snakes are favored also for their gall bladders, which are mixed with Chinese wine as cures for rheumatism. One of the most famous snake shops is at 91 Bonham Strand East, with more shops on both Jervois Street and Hillier Street. Snake shops are easily identifiable either by cages of pythons, cobras, and banded kraits piled on the sidewalk or by the wooden drawers lining the walls of the shop. Who knows, you might see a customer's order being filled, in which the shopkeeper deftly grabs a snake out of one of the drawers, extracts the gall bladder, and mixes it in yellow wine. The snake survives the operation, but who knows what other fate awaits it. A vial of three gall bladders mixed with wine begins at about HK$110 ($14.25). The more poisonous the snake, so they say, the better the cure. The mixture is also believed to be an aphrodisiac.

Back on Bonham Strand, you'll pass several rattan shops before reaching the most interesting shops of all—those **shops selling medicinal herbs and ginseng.**

Based on the Oriental concept of maintaining a healthy balance between the *yin* and *yang* forces in the body, medicinal herbs include a startling range of ingredients, including roots, barks, twigs, dried leaves, seeds, pods, flowers, grasses, insects (such as discarded cicada shells), deer antlers, dried sea horses, dried fish bladders, and rhinoceros horns. The herbalist, after discussing a customer's symptoms and checking the pulses in both wrists, prescribes the appropriate remedy, using perhaps a bit of bark here and a seed there, based on thousands of years of passed-down wisdom.

The king of trade on **Bonham Strand** is clearly the Chinese ginseng root. More than 30 varieties are handled in this wholesale trading area: The most prized are the red ginseng from North Korea, white ginseng from North America, and a very rare ginseng that grows wild in the mountains of northeastern China. It's the red ginseng that's considered to aid in male virility, while the white variety is good for treating hangovers.

At the end of Bonham Strand, turn left on **Des Voeux Road West,** where you'll see shop after shop selling **preserved foods.** Dried and salted fish, flattened squid, oysters, scallops, abalone, sea slugs, fish bladders, starfish, shrimp, and many other kinds of seafood have been dried and preserved. You can buy bird's nest here, as well as shark's fin, and in winter there's also pressed duck and Chinese sausages made from pork meat and liver. At the top of **Sutherland Street** where it meets Queen's Road West, you might be lucky enough to see a sidewalk barber at work, once plentiful but now going the way of the rickshaw. The old woman who works here uses a string to pull out the facial hairs of her customers, an ancient method only a few barbers can still do.

Next comes **Hollywood Road,** with its strange mixture of shops selling coffins and funeral items, as well as furniture and antique shops offering real antiques as well as excellent imitations. Here you'll find everything from woodblock prints and rosewood furniture to snuff bottles, porcelain, and round-bellied smiling Buddhas.

Next to **Ladder Street,** an extremely steep flight of stairs, is **Man Mo Temple,** Hong Kong Island's oldest and most important temple. It was around this area that the movie *The World of Suzie Wong* was filmed. The temple, which dates back to the 1840s and is open daily from 7am to 5pm, is dedicated to two deities, the god of literature (Man) and the god of war (Mo). Oddly enough, Mo finds patronage among the members of the police force (shrines in his honor can be found in all Hong Kong police stations)—as well as among members of the underworld. Two ornately carved sedan chairs are kept in the temple to carry the gods around the neighborhood during festivals.

If you follow the steps leading downhill on Ladder Street, you'll see **Upper Lascar Row** leading off to the left, better known as **Cat Street.** For almost a century Cat Street was famous for its antiques, which could be had for a pittance, but with the new antiques shops on Hollywood Road and the nearby Cat Street Galleries, Cat Street today offers a fantastic study in junk, where most dealers lay their wares out on the sidewalk. Pleasantly dotted with potted palms, this pedestrian lane is worth a browse for jade, snuff bottles, watches, pictures, copper and brass kettles, old eyeglasses, bird cages, and odds and ends.

Back on Queen's Road and heading toward Central, you'll pass traditional art-supply shops, more street markets, and a spattering of *dai pai dong,* or street food stalls. These food stalls do a brisk business in noodles, deep-fried dough sticks, soups, and other fast foods for a populace always on the go.

EXPLORING TSIMSHATSUI AND YAUMATEI

A logical tour of Tsimshatsui begins with the **Star Ferry,** since for more than a century it served as the only link with Hong Kong Island. That colonial-looking clock tower you see near the ferry terminus, now dwarfed by the new Cultural Centre, was once the final stop for those traveling overland from London on the *Orient Express.* If you haven't yet stopped by the tourist office, you can do so at the HKTA office in the Star Ferry concourse.

As you leave the Star Ferry concourse and walk through the plaza with its many buses and taxis, you'll see a busy road going north to your left. This is **Canton Road,** home of several hotels as well as Hong Kong's biggest shopping complex, **Harbour City,** which houses the Ocean Terminal, Ocean Galleries, and Ocean City. Altogether there are 600 shops here, all connected by air-conditioned walkways. Enter it, and you may never escape during this lifetime.

Better to save shopping for another day, and head east instead down **Salisbury Road.** That huge, modern building on your right is the new **Hong Kong Cultural Centre,** the colony's largest arena for the performing arts. Opened in 1989, it boasts a concert hall, theaters, exhibition areas, restaurants, and bars. In 1991 the Hong Kong Museum of Art will also find a new home near the Cultural Centre.

Next to the Cultural Centre is the **Space Museum,** easy to spot with its white-domed planetarium. The museum is divided into three parts—the Space Theatre's planetarium, where films are projected onto the 75-foot domed roof, the Hall of Solar Sciences on solar phenomena, and an exhibition hall that explores man's progress in astronomy and space. Shows at Space Theatre are held throughout the afternoon and early evening and cost HK$15 ($1.95) per person. Since these are popular and each day's showings are often sold out in advance, you might want to stop off now and

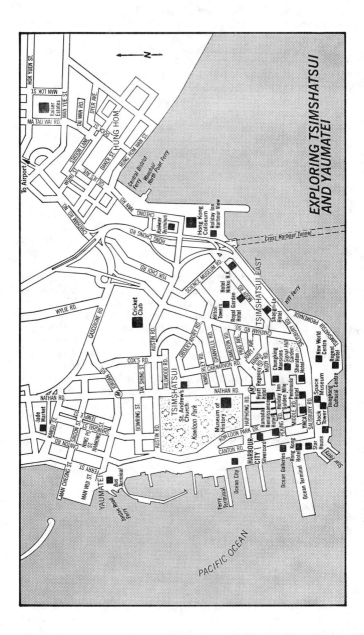

EXPLORING TSIMSHATSUI
AND YAUMATEI

buy your ticket for a later performance. The museum itself is free and is open every day except Tuesday until 9:30pm, opening at 2pm on weekdays, at 1pm on Saturday, and at 10:30am on Sunday.

The Space Museum has stolen the view from Tsimshatsui's most famous landmark, the venerable **Peninsula Hotel** right across the street. Built in 1928 and guarded by a fleet of black Rolls-Royces, the Peninsula is Hong Kong's grandest old hotel. Its lobby, reminiscent of a Parisian palace with its high gilded ceilings, pillars, and ferns, has long been a favored spot for a cup of coffee and people-watching.

Turn left on **Nathan Road,** Kowloon's most famous street. It is also one of the colony's widest, and runs almost 2½ miles straight up the spine of Kowloon all the way to Boundary Road, the official border of the New Territories. Nathan Road is named after Sir Matthew Nathan, who served as governor at the time of the road's construction. After it was completed, it was nicknamed "Nathan's Folly." After all, why build such a wide road, here in the middle of seemingly nowhere? Kowloon didn't have many people back then and had even less traffic. Now, of course, Nathan Road is known as the **"Golden Mile"** of shopping, because of the boutiques and shops that line it.

You'll pass jewelry stores, electronics shops, optical shops, clothing boutiques, and other enterprises as you head north on Nathan Road. After about 15 minutes (assuming you don't shop on the way), you'll soon see a mosque on your left, followed by a lineup of shops called **Park Lane Shopper's Boulevard.** Behind this boulevard is **Kowloon Park,** a good place to bring children for a romp through its playgrounds and open spaces. In addition to its water garden, sculpture garden, and a woodland trail, Kowloon Park is also home to the **Hong Kong Museum of History.** Housed in two buildings dating from the 19th century, this museum gives a brief introduction to Hong Kong's history and is open every day except Friday from 10am to 6pm (on Sunday and holidays from 1 to 6pm). Opposite the park, on the other side of Nathan, are **Kimberley Street** and **Granville Road,** popular among young Chinese for their inexpensive clothing boutiques.

Continuing up Nathan Road, you should keep on the lookout for two traditional Chinese products stores on this busy thoroughfare: **Chinese Arts and Crafts Ltd.,** 233-239 Nathan Road, and **Yue Hwa,** 301-309 Nathan Road. These large stores are emporiums for goods from China, including silk, antiques, china, jade, embroidered tablecloths, and Chinese medicinal herbs.

Once you've passed Yue Hwa, you'll find yourself in **Yaumatei.** Its name roughly translates as "the place for growing sesame plants," but you won't see any such cultivation today. Rather, like the Western District, Yaumatei offers a look at traditional Chinese life, with shops selling tea, chopping blocks, joss, bamboo steamers, baked goods, embroidery, herbs, and dried seafood. Shanghai Street, Canton Road, and Woosung Street are where you'll find most of the traditional shops, but the best-known site of Yaumatei is the Jade Market.

Located along Kansu Street underneath the overpass, the **Jade**

Market consists of some 400 stalls selling jade as well as pearls, and is open from about 10am to 2pm daily. The jade on sale here comes in a bewildering range of quality. The highest quality should be cold to the touch and translucent, but unless you know your jade you're better off just coming here for a look. It's possible to infuse jade with color so that inferior stones acquire the brightness and translucence associated with more expensive jade. If you want a souvenir, pick up a pendant or bangle, but don't spend more than a few dollars on it. (Serious jade buyers should refer to the "Chinese Crafts and Products," "Jade Market," and "Jewelry" sections in Chapter VIII, "Hong Kong Shopping.") The freshwater pearls are also good bargains. Watch how the Chinese bargain—they often do it secretly using hand signals concealed underneath a newspaper, so that none of the onlookers will know the final price.

Across from the Jade Market is **Yaumatei Market,** as well as **Reclamation Street,** where all kinds of fresh vegetables are sold from open-air stalls. This is an interesting area for unstructured strolls.

At any rate, you may want to wander around for several more hours or go back to your hotel room to recuperate and rest up, because Yaumatei's most famous night attraction doesn't get underway until after 6pm, with most of the action taking place after 8pm.

Called **Temple Street Night Market** after the street it runs along, this market is a wonderful place to spend an evening. There are countless stalls here, selling clothing, watches, lighters, sunglasses, sweaters, cassettes, and more; and the name of the game is to bargain. There are also many seafood stalls here, where you can have cheap meals of clams, shrimp, mussels, and crab. Be sure to follow Temple Street to its northern end past the overpass, where you'll find palm readers, musicians, and street singers. Cantonese operas and pop songs are among the favorites in their repertoire.

4. Organized Tours

Hong Kong is well developed in the organized-tour department, so if you're pressed for time this may be the best way to go. For general sightseeing, the Hong Kong Island Tour is a four-hour trip offered both morning and afternoon and may include stops at Victoria Peak, Aberdeen, Stanley, and Aw Boon Haw Gardens. On the Kowloon side, there are four-hour tours of residential and industrial areas, new satellite towns, farm villages, scenic New Territories countryside, and Lok Ma Chau near the Chinese border. Prices for tours of either Hong Kong Island or Kowloon are HK$90 ($11.75) for adults and HK$74 ($9.60) for children.

There are also organized tours to Stanley, Ocean Park, Cheung Chau, and Lantau, but I personally think you're much better off exploring these areas on your own. Tours to the People's Republic of China are discussed in Chapter X, Section 3. Special-interest tours worth joining, however, are listed below.

All tours can be booked through your hotel, a travel agent, or the HKTA.

BOAT TOURS

Hong Kong, with so many of its attractions on the water, has a wide variety of boat tours available to its visitors. The most popular and plentiful are the harbor cruise, but there are countless others that last from 1 to 7½ hours ranging from the harbor itself to Aberdeen and the outlying islands and including lunch, sunset, and evening cruises as well as combination water-and-land tours. For complete information on them all, consult the sightseeing desk in your hotel, a travel agent, or the HKTA; hotels and travel agents can help you with bookings.

One of the most popular cruises is the one-hour cruise aboard a **Star Ferry.** Departing from the Star Ferry piers in both Central and Tsimshatsui, the cruise takes passengers past the Macau Ferry Terminal, the Central District, Causeway Bay Typhoon Shelter, North Point, the airport runway, and East Tsimshatsui. There are six departures daily: 11:15am and 12:30, 2:15, 3:30, 7, and 9:15pm (it would be wise to check the times again). The two evening cruises include complimentary white wine, while the day cruises include coffee and refreshments. The cost of all the cruises are HK$110 ($14.25) for adults and HK$80 ($10.50) for children.

Watertours (tel. 5254808 or 5263538), Hong Kong's largest tour operator of boat and junk cruises, also offers a one-hour cruise for HK$55 ($7.15) for adults and HK$45 ($5.85) for children. They also have about 20 other longer boat trips that include a wide range sightseeing possibilities.

Another popular boat cruise is that aboard the ***Duk Ling,*** a 35-year-old authentic Chinese sailing junk, typical of fishing vessels built in Hong Kong 150 years ago. Originally owned by a local fisherman, the *Duk Ling* has been restored and now offers 1½-hour cruises of the harbor. Visitors board at Queen's Pier in the Central District and the cost is HK$150 ($19.50) per person, which includes unlimited drinks on board. This junk has already been featured in several films, including *Taipan* and *Noble House.* To book a tour, contact Detours Ltd. (tel. 3311611).

Finally, the Hong Kong Hilton offers cruises aboard its own 110-foot brigantine, named the ***Wan Fu.*** Built in Taiwan in 1959, it offers breakfast, lunch, and dinner cruises, with trips usually taking in the sights of Aberdeen and Victoria Harbour. Prices start at HK$230 ($29.75) for adults and HK$190 ($24.75) for children. Contact the Hilton (tel. 5233111) for more information.

NIGHT TOURS

For more information about organized evening tours, see the last section of Chapter IX, "Hong Kong After Dark."

TRAM TOURS

Two of Hong Kong's original trams from the early part of this century have been refurbished for the **Antique Tram Tour,** a two-hour tour. For HK$120 ($15.50) for adults and HK$80 ($10.50) for children, participants can partake of dim sum or afternoon cakes and tea while they rumble through colorful neighborhoods on Hong Kong Island. There's also a lunchtime tour at HK$170 ($22) for adults and HK$120 ($15.50) for children.

A different tram tour is available in the evenings, which includes visits to Poor Man's Nightclub, an open-air night market, and then either a dinner cruise or dinner at the La Ronda revolving restaurant.

SUNG DYNASTY VILLAGE TOUR

Sung Dynasty, a replica of a 1,000-year-old Chinese village, is open to individual visitors only on weekends, so if you're in Hong Kong on a weekday, an organized tour is the only way to see the village. Tours are offered daily. Prices are HK$170 ($22) for adults and HK$125 ($16.25) for children, increasing to HK$220 ($28.50) and HK$150 ($19.50) respectively for those tours that include lunch or dinner.

"THE LAND BETWEEN" TOUR

Organized by the HKTA, this seven-hour trip takes guests via air-conditioned motorcoach on a trip through the New Territories. Passing satellite towns with high-rise apartment buildings, farms, and villages, the bus makes stops at a Cantonese restaurant for lunch, a Buddhist temple, and a produce market. Price of this tour is HK$220 ($28.50) for adults and HK$170 ($22) for children.

"COME HORSE RACING" TOUR

Another HKTA-organized tour, this one allows visitors to experience the excitement of the races, at either Happy Valley or Shatin, an excitement that grows proportionately according to how much you bet. Tours are only during the horse-racing season, which is from September through May on Wednesday evenings and on Saturday and/or Sunday afternoons. Included in the tour price is a pre-race Chinese lunch or dinner, personal entry badge to the Members' Enclosure, transportation, guide services, and even hints to help you place your bets. Tours are limited to individuals over 18 years of age who have been in Hong Kong fewer than 21 days. More information on the horse races is given in Section 6, "Sports," below. Price of tour: HK$250 ($32.50).

SPORTS AND RECREATION TOUR

Sports enthusiasts may want to take advantage of the Sports and Recreation Tour, which involves a day spent at the Clearwater Bay Golf and Country Club. Tours are offered only on Tuesday and Friday and last approximately eight hours, including travel time. Included is transportation to and from the club, lunch, and the admission fee to the club. Facilities at the club include a golf course, indoor and outdoor tennis courts, an outdoor swimming pool, saunas, and a Jacuzzi. Use of the pool, table tennis, saunas, and Jacuzzi is free. The tour costs HK$240 ($31.25), plus greens fees of HK$320 ($41.50) or HK$33 ($4.30) per hour for tennis courts (both clubs and racquets are available for rent).

5. Kids' Hong Kong

There are several attractions listed above that children would enjoy. On the Kowloon side, the **Space Museum** is very much geared toward children, with buttons to push, telescopes to look through, and computer quizzes to test what they've learned, not to mention the films featured in the Space Theatre. **Sung Dynasty,** a replica of a Chinese village, is a fantasy-filled experience for children, who love the monkey and acrobatic shows. Next door to Sung Dynasty is **Lai Chi Kok,** a small, rather old-fashioned amusement park popular with Chinese families and open from noon to 10pm weekdays, 11am to 11pm on Saturday, and 10am to 11pm on Sunday and holidays. Admission is HK$5 (65¢) for adults and HK$3 (40¢) for children. And don't forget **Kowloon Park** right on Nathan Road, which has a playground for children and lots of space to run.

On Hong Kong Island, the biggest draw for kids of all ages is **Ocean Park,** which recently completed a children's Adventure Land at a cost of HK$12 million ($1.56 million), with lots of things to climb on and animals to observe, not to mention the many other attractions of Hong Kong's largest theme park. Next door is **Water World,** with its swimming pools and slides. For free entertainment, visit the **Zoological and Botanical Gardens** with its monkeys, birds, and other animals, and **Aw Boon Haw Gardens.**

6. Sports

Despite the fact that Hong Kong is rather small with a sizable population, there's enough open space to pursue everything from golf to hiking to windsurfing. For the hard-working Chinese and expatriates, recreation and leisure are important for winding down after a hard week's work and for rejuvenation for the week ahead. With that in mind, try to schedule your golfing, swimming, or hiking trips on weekdays unless you enjoy jostling elbows with the crowds.

If you want to golf, swim, or play tennis and don't want to hassle about making arrangements yourself and getting there, you might want to join the Sports and Recreation Tour, outlined above.

THE HORSE RACES

If you'd rather watch sports than participate, and if you're in Hong Kong anytime from September through May, join the rest of Hong Kong at the horse races. Horse racing got its start in the colony in Happy Valley more than 100 years ago, making the Happy Valley track the oldest racecourse in Asia outside China. There is also a newer, modern track in Shatin in the New Territories.

Without a doubt, horse racing is by far the most popular sporting event in Hong Kong. It's not, perhaps, the sport itself that draws so much enthusiasm, but rather the fact that, outside of the local lottery, racing is the only legal form of gambling in Hong Kong. The Chinese love to gamble, and there are even 129 off-course betting centers throughout the colony for those unable to make it to the races.

Races are held at Happy Valley on Wednesday evenings and at either Shatin or Happy Valley on most Saturday and some Sunday afternoons. Both tracks feature giant color screens that show closeups of the race. It's fun and easy to get in on the betting action, and you don't have to bet much—HK$10 ($1.30) per race is enough.

The cheapest admission fee is HK$10 ($1.30), which is for the general public and is standing room only. If you want to watch from the Hong Kong Royal Jockey Club members' stand, are older than 18 years old, and have been in Hong Kong fewer than 21 days, you can purchase a temporary member's badge for HK$50 ($6.50). It's available upon display of your passport at either the Badge Enquiry Office at both tracks' main entrances to the members' private enclosures or at the off-course betting center near the Star Ferry concourse in Central. Tickets are sold on a first-come, first-served basis.

If you don't want to go to the races but would still like to bet on the outcomes, you can place bets at one of the many off-course betting centers. Two convenient ones are near the Star Ferry concourse in the Central District and at 2-4 Prat Avenue in Tsimshatsui.

On the other hand, the most effortless way to see the races is to join an HKTA tour to the tracks, described in the "Organized Tours" section, above.

GOLF

If you enjoy watching golf, the highlight of the year is the **Hong Kong Open Golf Championships,** held in February at the Royal Hong Kong Golf Club in Fanling in the New Territories.

If you want to play, it's not as cheap as it used to be. Greens fees have doubled in the past two years, driven up no doubt by the flocks of golfing enthusiasts from Japan, where the cost of a game is through the roof. But compared to golfing in Japan, Hong Kong is a giveaway.

The **Royal Hong Kong Golf Club** maintains courses in both Fanling (tel. 0901211) and Deep Water Bay (tel. 8127070) and welcomes visitors on weekdays only. No advance reservations are taken, so visitors should arrive early. There are three 18-hole courses in Fanling, with greens fees at HK$800 ($109). Deep Water Bay, on Hong Kong Island, is a nine-hole course, with greens fees at HK$200 ($26). Club rentals are extra, about HK$100 ($13) per set per day.

The **Discovery Bay Golf Club,** on Lantau Island (tel. 9877271), has a beautiful 18-hole course developed by Robert Trent Jones, Jr., with great views of Hong Kong and the harbor. Visitors are allowed to play here Monday through Friday with the exception of public holidays, and greens fees are HK$350 ($45.50), though clubs and carts cost extra.

Another scenic course, operated by the **Clearwater Bay Golf**

and Country Club (tel. 7192454), is located near Sai Kung. Visitor's greens fees are HK$400 ($52). On weekends, guests must be signed in by a member, but greens fees remain the same. If you're interested in playing golf here but want to let someone else worry about arranging transportation, contact the HKTA for its Sports and Recreation Tour, described in the "Organized Tours" section, above.

TENNIS

Public courts in Hong Kong are in much demand, simply because there are not enough. Prices average about HK$25 ($3.25) an hour during the day and HK$40 ($5.20) in the evenings. For information, inquire at **Victoria Park,** in Causeway Bay (tel. 5706186); **King's Park,** in Yaumatei, Kowloon (tel. 3858985); the **Tennis Centre,** on Wong Nei Chong Gap Road in Happy Valley, Hong Kong (tel. 5749122); and **Jubilee Sports Centre,** Shatin, New Territories (tel. 6051212).

ROLLER AND ICE SKATING

Two easily accessible **roller-skating rinks** are the **Sportsworld Association,** located inside the Telford Gardens adjacent to the Kowloon Bay MTR station in Kowloon (tel. 7572211); and **Rollerworld,** located in Cityplaza at the Taikoo Shing MTR station on Hong Kong Island (tel. 5670391).

For **ice skating, Cityplaza Phase II,** at Taikoo Shing (tel. 5675388), has an ice-skating rink, as does **Lai Chi Kok,** an amusement park in Kowloon (tel. 7414281).

JOGGING

The best places to jog on Hong Kong Island without dodging traffic are **Victoria Park** in Causeway Bay and **Bowen Road,** which stretches from Stubbs Road to Magazine Gap Road and offers great views over the harbor. On the other side of the harbor, there's **Kowloon Park,** as well as the **waterfront promenade** along Tsimshatsui and East Tsimshatsui. Remember that it can be quite hot and humid during the summer months, so try to jog early in the morning or in the evening.

HIKING

There are many trails of varying levels of difficulty throughout Hong Kong. Serious hikers, for example, may want to consider the **MacLehose Trail** in Sai Kung, which stretches about 60 miles through eight country parks in the New Territories, or **Lantau Trail,** a 43-mile circular trail on Lantau Island. The Lantau Trail begins and ends at Mui Wo (also called Silvermine Bay), passing several popular scenic spots along the way. Both the MacLehose and Lantau trails are divided into smaller sections of varying difficulty, which means that you can tailor your hike to suit your own abilities and time constrictions. The Hong Kong Government Publications Office, located on the ground floor of the main post office in Central right next to the Star Ferry concourse, has leaflets on county parks and maps. For more information about hiking in Hong Kong, contact the HKTA.

BEACHES

There are about 40 beaches in Hong Kong open free for public use, most of which have lifeguards on duty in the summer, changing rooms, and snack stands or restaurants. Even on Hong Kong Island itself you can find a number of beaches, including **Big Wave Bay** and **Shek O** on the east coast, and **Stanley, Deep Water Bay,** and **Repulse Bay** on the southern coast. Repulse Bay is by far the most popular beach in Hong Kong and gets unbelievably crowded on a summer weekend. Prettier beaches are found on the outlying islands, including **Hung Shing Ye** on Lamma, **Tung Wan** on Cheung Chau, and **Cheung Sha** on Lantau. It is, however, advisable to check on the condition of the water for pollution before plunging in, especially on the islands.

Windsurfing boards can be rented at several of the beaches, including Stanley and Tung Wan. Although prices may vary slightly, cost of a board for one hour is HK$45 ($5.85) to HK$60 ($7.80) at Stanley.

HONG KONG SHOPPING

No doubt about it—one of the main reasons people come to Hong Kong is to shop. According to the Hong Kong Tourist Association (HKTA), visitors to the colony spend more than 50% of their money on shopping, an amount that totals more than HK$15 billion ($1.95 billion) annually. In fact, Hong Kong is such a popular shopping destination that many luxury cruise liners dock longer here than they do anywhere else on their tour. I doubt that there's ever been a visitor to Hong Kong who left empty-handed.

1. What to Buy

Hong Kong is a duty-free port, which means that all imported goods are free of duty in Hong Kong with the exception of some luxury goods, including tobacco, alcohol, perfume, cosmetics, cars, and some petroleum products. Thus you can get many items cheaper in Hong Kong than you can in the country where they were made. What's more, there is no sales tax in Hong Kong. It's cheaper, for example, to buy Japanese products such as designer clothing, cameras, electronic goods, and pearls in Hong Kong than in Japan itself. In fact, all my friends living in Japan make it a point to visit Hong Kong at least once or twice a year to buy their business clothes, cosmetics, and other accessories.

You can also buy products from the People's Republic of China sometimes cheaper in Hong Kong than you can in China itself. Great buys include porcelain, jade, cloisonné, silk clothing, jewelry, and artwork. You'll also find crafts and goods from other parts of Asia, including Thailand, India, the Philippines, and Indonesia.

But one of the best buys in Hong Kong remains its clothes. If you've looked at the labels of clothes sold in your own hometown stores and shopping malls, you've probably noticed the labels "Made in Hong Kong." Both custom-made and designer clothes are a real bargain in Hong Kong, including three-piece business suits, leather outfits, furs, sportswear, and jeans. Hong Kong is one of the world's foremost producer of knits, and there are also factory outlets and small stores where you can pick up inexpensive fashions for a song. For your guidance, there is a chart of clothing size conversions in the Appendix at the end of this book.

Other good buys include shoes, jewelry, furniture, carpets, leather goods, luggage, handbags, briefcases, Chinese herbs, and eyeglasses. Hong Kong is also one of the world's largest exporters of watches and toys. And of course, if you're interested in fake name-brand watches, handbags, or clothing to impress the folks back home, you've come to the right place. Although illegal, fake name-brand items were still being sold at Hong Kong's night markets during my last visit by vendors ready to take flight at the first sight of officials.

As for electronic goods and cameras, they are not the bargain they once were. Make sure, therefore, to comparison-shop at home before traveling to Hong Kong so that you know how to spot a bargain. The best deals are in models recently discontinued, such as last year's Sony Walkman.

As for sales, the biggest and best seasonal sale takes place in the period after Christmas and before the Chinese lunar New Year. All the major department stores, as well as shops in many of the huge shopping complexes, hold sales during this period. There are also end-of-season sales in early spring and early autumn.

2. Hunting Grounds

Tsimshatsui has the greatest concentration of shops in Hong Kong. Nathan Road, which stretches up the backbone of Kowloon for 2½ miles from the harbor to the border of the New Territories, is lined with stores selling clothing, jewelry, eyeglasses, cameras, electronic goods, crafts from China, shoes, handbags, luggage, watches, and more. There are also tailors, tattoo artists, and even shops that will carve your name into a wooden chop, a stamp used in place of a signature in official documents. Be sure to explore the side streets radiating off Nathan Road, especially Granville Road and Kimberley Street which abound in small, family-owned clothing stores. There are also department stores and shopping arcades, as well as three huge shopping malls.

Another happy hunting ground is Causeway Bay on Hong Kong Island. In contrast to Tsimshatsui, it caters more to a local market rather than to tourists, and prices are generally quite low. In addition to small shops selling everything from shoes to clothing to

Chinese herbs, there are Japanese department stores, a Lane Crawford department store, and the China Products store with imports from mainland China. Check the backstreets of Causeway Bay, such as Lockhart Road and Jaffe Road, as well as the area around Jardine's Bazaar and Jardine's Crescent, an open-air market with cheap clothing, food, and produce. For shoes, get on the tram and head for Happy Valley, where on Leighton Road and Wong Nai Chung Road near the race course there are rows of shoe and handbag shops.

---

3. Shopping Tips

Because shopping is such big business in Hong Kong, most shops are open seven days a week, closing only for two or three days during the Chinese New Year. Exceptions are a few large department stores that close on Sunday, and some Japanese department stores that are closed one day of the week. Most shops open at 10am, and remain open until 6pm in Central, 9pm in Tsimshatsui, and 9:30pm in Causeway Bay. Street markets are open every day.

However, Hong Kong is a buyer-beware market. Name brands are sometimes fakes, that cheap jade you bought may be glass, and equipment may not work. To make things worse, the general practice is that goods are usually not returnable and deposits paid are not refundable.

HKTA MEMBER STORES

To be on the safe side, try to make your major purchases at HKTA member stores, which display their logo (a round circle with a red Chinese junk in the middle) on their storefronts. Altogether there are more than 750 member shops, all listed in a directory provided free by HKTA offices called "The Official Guide to Shopping, Eating Out and Services in Hong Kong." This booklet gives the names, addresses, and phone numbers of shops for everything from audio-video equipment to musical instruments, hairpieces, antiques, and wines. Even more important, it lists the sole agents for specific products, such as the sole agent for Sony, Chanel, or Nikon, along with their telephone numbers. HKTA member stores are required to give accurate representation of the products they sell and prompt rectification of justified complaints. If you have any complaints against a member store, contact the Membership Department of the HKTA, 35th floor, Jardine House, Connaught Rd., Central District (tel. 5244191, ext. 278).

GUARANTEES

In any case, if you're buying a camera, electronic goods, electrical items, watches, or any other expensive product, be sure to ask the shopkeeper for a guarantee, which should include a description of the model and serial number, date of purchase, name and address of the shop where you bought it, and the shop's official chop or stamp. Different products and models of the same brand may carry different guarantees, some valid worldwide, others valid only in Hong Kong. Worldwide guarantees must carry the name and/or symbol of the sole agents in Hong Kong for the product concerned. If you're in doubt, check with the relevant Hong Kong sole agent. And be sure to ask for a receipt from the shopkeeper detailing a description of your purchase.

COMPARISON-SHOPPING AND BARGAINING

But the cardinal rule of shopping in Hong Kong is to shop around. Unless you're considering antiques or art, you'll probably see the same items in shop after shop, on both sides of the harbor. And with the exception of department stores and designer boutiques, you'll be able to bargain for that purchase. You most certainly must bargain at all street markets, as well as at many of the smaller, family-owned shops. Thus the bargains you walk away with will depend on your bargaining skills. Begin your comparison-shopping as soon as you arrive in Hong Kong, so that you can get an idea of the differences in prices. And generally speaking, you can get a better price if you pay with cash than by credit card.

SHIPPING

Many shops, especially the larger ones, will pack and ship your purchases home for you. In addition, all upper-bracket and most medium-range hotels offer a parcel-wrapping and mailing service. Packages sent to the United States generally take six to eight weeks by surface mail and one week by airmail. For major purchases, you should buy an all-risks insurance policy to cover the possibility of damage or loss in transit. As these policies can be expensive, check into whether using your credit card to make your purchase will provide automatic free insurance.

---

4. Markets

Markets offer the best deals in Hong Kong, though a lot depends on how well you can bargain. Be sure to check over the items carefully, since you won't be able to return them. Check clothing for faults, tears, cuts, marks, and uneven seams and hemlines.

HONG KONG ISLAND

Stanley

Stanley Market is probably the most popular and best-known market in Hong Kong and it's a trendy place for foreign residents to live. Located on the southern coast of Hong Kong Island on a small peninsula, it's a great place to pick up inexpensive clothing. The best buys here are jeans, sportswear, swimming suits, sweaters, casual clothing, and silk blouses, dresses, and suits. There are also shops selling such accessories as belts and handbags, as well as household goods and souvenirs from China. During my last visit, shopkeepers were not keen on bargaining, no doubt because tourists come here by the busload. In fact, Stanley is not as cheap as it once was, and many shops are remodeling and becoming more chic and expensive. Still, you're bound to find at least something you're wild about, and most visitors leave with bundles and bags of purchases. I buy more of my clothes here than anywhere else in Hong Kong, especially when it comes to cheap, fun fashions, and raw-silk suits.

To reach Stanley, take bus 6 or 260 from Central's bus terminal by the Star Ferry. The bus ride to Stanley takes approximately 30 minutes. Shops are open daily from 10am to 7pm.

Li Yuen Street East and West

These two streets are parallel pedestrian lanes in the heart of the Central District, very narrow and often congested with human traffic. Its stalls are packed full with handbags, clothes, scarves, sweaters, toys, babyclothes, watches, makeup, umbrellas, knick-knacks, and even brassieres. They're popular with the locals and tourists alike. Don't neglect the open-fronted shops behind the stalls. Some of these are boutiques selling fashionable but cheap clothing as well as shoes, purses, and accessories. These two streets are located just a couple of minutes' walk from the Tsimshatsui MTR station or the Star Ferry.

Jardine's Bazaar and Jardine's Crescent

The open-air market that spreads along these two streets in Causeway Bay and spills into the surrounding area is a traditional Chinese market for produce and cheap clothing. Though you may not find something worth taking home, it's fun just to walk around. The nearest MTR station is Causeway Bay, but you can also reach this area easily by tram.

KOWLOON

Jade Market

Jade, considered by the Chinese to hold mystical powers, is available in all sizes, colors, and prices at the Jade Market, located on Kansu Street in the Yaumatei District. The jade comes from Burma, China, Australia, and Taiwan. Unless you know your jade, you won't want to make any expensive purchases here, but it's great for bangles, pendants, earrings, and inexpensive gifts. This market is also great for pearls, especially inexpensive freshwater pearls from China. In 1989 I bought two 20-inch three-strand necklaces, one for HK$70 ($9.10) and another with much larger pearls for HK$150 ($19.50). They may not last forever, but they're certainly good buys.

The Jade Market is open daily from 10am to about 2pm, though some vendors stay until 3 or 4pm. It's located near the Jordan MTR station or less than a 30-minute walk from the Star Ferry.

NIGHT MARKETS

Both **Temple Street** in the Yaumatei District of Kowloon and **Poor Man's Nightclub** in front of the Macau Ferry Terminal on Hong Kong Island are night markets that open up when the sun goes down. Of the two, Temple Street is the larger. Both sell the usual stuff street vendors sell, including T-shirts, jeans, watches, lighters, socks, jewelry and jewelry boxes, cassette tapes, sweaters, and imitation Lacoste shirts. Be sure to bargain fiercely, and check products to make sure they're not faulty or poorly made.

The night markets are at their busiest from about 8 to 11pm. Temple Street market is located near the Jordan MTR station, while the Poor Man's Nightclub is near the Sheung Wan MTR station.

5. Shopping A to Z

The shops listed below are just a few of the thousands upon thousands of shops in Hong Kong. For a more detailed listing of shops throughout the colony, refer to "The Official Guide to Shopping, Eating Out and Services in Hong Kong," which lists some 700 shops that are members of the HKTA.

ANTIQUES AND CURIOS

Several of the Chinese products stores, listed below under "Chinese Crafts and Products," stock antiques. The most famous area for antiques, however, is in the **Hollywood Road** area above the Central District. It gained fame in the 1950s, following the 1949 revolution in China which flooded the market with family possessions. Hollywood Road twists along for a little more than half a mile, with shops selling porcelain, silver, and rosewood and blackwood furniture, as well as fakes and curios. Near its western end is Upper Lascar Row, popularly known as Cat Street, where vendors sell snuff bottles, curios, and odds and ends. Here is also where you'll find **Cat Street Galleries,** 38 Lok Ku Road (tel. 5431609), which houses several individually owned booths of arts and crafts and expensive antiques. At the eastern end of Hollywood Road near Pottinger Street is a cluster of chic antiques shops displaying furniture and blue-and-white porcelain.

On the Kowloon side, there's **Charlotte Horstmann and Gerald Godfrey,** Shop 2104, Ocean Terminal, Harbour City (tel. 3677167). This large store, located in the Ocean Terminal shopping mall on Canton Road, is an emporium of expensive, top-quality Oriental antiques.

CARPETS

Hong Kong is a good place to shop for Chinese, Indian, Persian, and other types of carpets and rugs. The **Hollywood Road** and **Wyndham Hill Street** areas in Central are the best places to search for shops dealing in imported carpets. **Harbour City,** the huge mega-mall at 5 Canton Road in Tsimshatsui, is another good place to look, and shops here include the Banyan Tree, the Carpet House, Carpet World, and Chinese Carpet Centre.

CERAMICS

Chinaware, a fine, translucent earthenware, was first brought from China to Europe by the Portuguese in the 16th century. Its name was subsequently shortened to "china," and Hong Kong remains one of the best places in the world to shop for both antique (mainly from the Ching Dynasty, 1644–1911) and contemporary Chinese porcelain. Traditional motifs include bamboo, flowers, dragons, carp, and cranes, which adorn everything from dinner plates to vases, lamps, and jars. Probably the best place to begin looking for china is at one of the Chinese products stores, listed below under "Chinese Crafts and Products." If you're looking for contemporary china or replicas, you might wish to visit one of the porcelain factories below.

Ah Chow, Block B, Hong Kong Industrial Centre, 489-491 Castle Peak Rd., Lai Chi Kok, Kowloon (tel. 7451511).

A small outlet for modern chinaware.

Open: Mon–Sat 10am–7pm. *MTR:* Lai Chi Kok station, then follow the signs for the Leighton Textile Building/Thung Chau West Street.

Overjoy Porcelain Factory, Block A-B, Kwai Hing Industrial Building, 10-18 Chun Pin St., Kwai Chung, New Territories (tel. 4870615, 0204838, or 0265429).

With more than 400 stock designs, dinner services are the specialty. You may also mix and match, or even create your very own design. Sets are usually commissioned for either 6, 8, or 12 diners and take four to six weeks to complete.

Open: Mon–Sat 9am–6pm *MTR:* Kwai Hing station, then taxi.

Sheung Yu Ceramic Arts, Room Cl, Vita Tower, 29 Wong Chuk Hang Rd., Aberdeen, Hong Kong Island (tel. 5551881).

It specializes in replicas from the great Chinese dynasties and also produces contemporary designs.

Open: Mon–Fri 10am–noon and 1:30–5pm, Sat 9am–1pm. *Directions:* Bus 70 from Central.

Wah Tung China Company, 12-17 Floors, Grand Marine Industrial Building, 3 Yue Fung St., Tin Wan Hill Rd., Aberdeen, Hong Kong Island (tel. 8732232).

Reputedly the largest company specializing in antique porcelain reproductions, especially huge pieces like vases and garden stools.

Open: Daily 9am–6pm. *Directions:* Bus 70 from Central.

CHINESE CRAFTS AND PRODUCTS

Three store names to watch out for if you're looking for imports from China are Chinese Arts and Crafts Ltd., Yue Hwa Chinese Products, and Chinese Products Co. They have the best and widest selection I have found.

Chinese Arts and Crafts Ltd., with branches in the Silvercord building, 30 Canton Rd., Tsimshatsui (tel. 7226655); Star House, 3 Salisbury Rd., Tsimshatsui (tel. 7354061); the New World Centre, Shop G34-35, Salisbury Rd., Tsimshatsui (tel. 3697760); 233-239 Nathan Rd., Yaumatei (tel. 7300061); Shell House, Queen's Rd., Central (tel. 5223621); and the China Resources Building, 26 Harbour Rd., Wanchai (tel. 8344567).

In business for more than 30 years, this is the top upper-end shop for Chinese arts and crafts. This is one of the best and safest places to purchase jade, and you can also buy silk dresses and blouses, arts and crafts, antiques, jewelry, carpets, cloisonné, furs, Chinese medicine, rosewood furniture, ceramics, Chinese teas, and embroidered tablecloths or pillowcases. It's a great place for gifts in all price ranges. The largest stores are in the Silvercord building and in Wanchai.

Open: Mon–Sat 10am–6pm and Sun noon–6pm (Yaumatei branch, Mon–Sat 10am–9pm and Sun noon–6pm). *MTR:* Tsimshatsui for the Silvercord, Star House, and New World Centre branches; Jordan for the Yaumatei branch; Central for the Shell House branch; and Wanchai for the Wanchai branch.

China Products Co., with branches at 19-13 Yee Wo St. (tel. 8908321) and at 488-500 Hennessey Rd. (tel. 5770222), both in Causeway Bay.

This store sells more ordinary household items, including small appliances, porcelain, everyday clothing, shoes, traditional padded Chinese coats, furniture, silk, and embroidered kimono.

Open: Daily, 10:30 am to 9:30 pm (both branches). *MTR:* Causeway Bay for both branches.

Yue Hwa Chinese Products, with its main store at 301-309 Nathan Rd. in Yaumatei (tel. 3840084), and branches in the Park Lane Shopper's Boulevard at 143-161 Nathan Rd. (tel. 7393888) and at 54-64 Nathan Rd. (tel. 3689165), both in Tsimshatsui.

Yue Hwa is a cross between the other two. Its main shop in Yaumatei stocks everything from household goods to clothing, jewelry, arts and crafts, china, and medicines and herbs. It was here that I bought some friends a gag wedding gift—Chinese whisky with preserved lizards in it, all for only HK$25 ($3.25), definitely a bargain. The Tsimshatsui stores deal primarily with Chinese handcrafts and jewels.

Open: Daily, 10am–9:30pm at the main store, 10am–8:30pm at the Park Lane branch, and 9:30am–8pm at the 54-64 Nathan Rd. branch. *MTR:* Jordan for the main store, Tsimshatsui for the other two branches.

CLOTH

Many tailors stock their own bolts of fabric, but for one-stop fabric shopping with larger selections, the place to go is **Wing On Street** in the Central District, popularly called Cloth Alley. This narrow, covered pedestrian lane is lined with shop after shop selling every imaginable type of cloth, including cottons, linens, silks, velvets, and satins. The salesmen can advise almost to the inch how much fabric you'll need for any outfit, even if all you have to show them is a drawing.

COSMETICS AND PERFUME

Because you must pay duty on such luxury items as cosmetics and perfume, I'm not sure there's much of a savings on these goods. I priced several Lancôme products, for example, and found prices slightly cheaper back in my hometown than in Hong Kong. However, there are several products that might be more readily available in Hong Kong than elsewhere, such as Retin-A, which is available in Hong Kong without a prescription. Be sure to comparison-shop. I found that Tack Long, for example, had cheaper prices than Watson's but not the diversity.

Watson's has more than 30 locations in Hong Kong. Check Section 3, "Fast Facts About Hong Kong," in Chapter IV for specific addresses of this drugstore.

Tack Long is located at 33 Hankow Road, Tsimshatsui (tel. 3671768 or 3672564).

DEPARTMENT STORES

It probably comes as no surprise to learn that Hong Kong has a great many department stores. Wing On and Lane Crawford are two upmarket chain department stores with a good selection of clothing, accessories, local and imported designer fashions, gift items, and cosmetics. Japanese department stores have also made great headway in Hong Kong and are very popular with locals. Causeway Bay has the largest concentration of Japanese department stores, including Daimaru, Matsuzakaya, Sogo, and Mitsukoshi. On the Kowloon side, there's Isetan and Tokyu. Hours for department stores are the same for other stores in the area (refer to this chapter's Section 3, "Shopping Tips," for business hours).

Local Department Stores

Lane Crawford Ltd. has branches at Lane Crawford House, 70 Queen's Road, Central (tel. 5266121); Windsor House, Gloucester Road, Causeway Bay (tel. 8909533); 74 Nathan Road, Tsimshatsui (tel. 7219668); and Ocean Terminal, Shop 2100, Harbour City, 5 Canton Road, Tsimshatsui (tel. 7393393). *MTR:* Central for the Lane Crawford House shop, Causeway Bay for the Windsor House branch, and Tsimshatsui for the Nathan Road and Harbour City branches.

Wing On has branches at 211 Des Voeux Road Central, Western District (tel. 8521888); 26 Des Voeux Road Central, Central (tel. 5247171); Hopewell Centre, 183 Queen's Road East, Wanchai (tel. 5291060); and 361 Nathan Road, Yaumatei (tel. 7804341). *MTR:* Sheung Wan, Central, Wanchai, and Jordan, respectively.

Japanese Department Stores

Daimaru, Great George St., Causeway Bay (tel. 5767321). *MTR:* Causeway Bay.

Isetan, Sheraton Hotel Shopping Mall, Salisbury Rd.,

Tsimshatsui (tel. 3690111). *MTR:* Tsimshatsui.

Matsuzakaya, 2-20 Paterson St., Causeway Bay (tel. 8906622). *MTR:* Causeway Bay.

Sogo, East Point Centre, 555 Hennessy Rd., Causeway Bay (tel. 8338338). *MTR:* Causeway Bay.

DESIGNER BOUTIQUES

If you're looking for international name brands and don't care about price, check out the boutiques in the Landmark, Swire House, and Prince's Building, all located in the heart of Central.

The **Landmark,** located on Des Voeux Road Central, is an ultra-chic shopping complex, with shops for Gucci, Kansai, Burberry's, Claude Montana, Krizia, Sonia Rykiel, Hermès, Louis Vuitton, Givenchy, Lanvin, Christian Dior, Bally, and Wedgwood, as well as restaurants.

Not to be outdone is the nearby **Swire House** on Connaught Road, with a large range of Japanese designers, including Matsuda, Kenzo, Issey Miyake, and Yohji Yamamoto. The **Prince's Building,** on Chater Road, Statue Square, located across from the Mandarin Oriental Hotel, showcases five floors of boutiques by Dunhill, Cartier, Cerruti, Chanel, Christian Dior, Aquascutum, Daks Simpson, and Diane Freis.

Meanwhile, across the harbor, the **Peninsula Hotel,** on Salisbury Road in Tsimshatsui, boasts a shopping arcade with designer boutiques for Charles Jourdan, Louis Vuitton, Loewe, Bally, Chanel, and Dunhill, to name only a few. Expect to spend a lot of money and you won't be disappointed. Other boutiques are located in Tsimshatsui's huge shopping malls such as **Harbour City** (see "Mega-Malls," below).

For **Hong Kong designers,** check out the fashions of Eddie Lau, sold at Chinese Arts and Crafts stores (see "Chinese Crafts and Products," above). Another popular Hong Kong designer, Diane Freis, has outlets in the Prince's Building, Ocean Terminal and Ocean Galleries (both in Tsimshatsui's Harbour City shopping complex), and the Hyatt Regent Hotel's shopping arcade in Tsimshatsui.

FACTORY OUTLETS

Shoppers in the know head for Hong Kong's factory outlets to buy many of their clothes. Although scattered in various parts of the territory, the most convenient ones are either in the Central District on Hong Kong Island or Hung Hom and Tsimshatsui in Kowloon. The best-known buildings that contain factory-outlet showrooms are the **Pedder Building,** 12 Pedder Street, Central; a large group of warehouse buildings called **Kaiser Estates** in Hung Hom; and **Shui Hing House** at 23-25 Nathan Road, **Star House,** on Salisbury Road, and the **Sands Building** at 17 Hankow Road, all in Tsimshatsui.

Factory outlets sell excess stock, overruns, and quality-control rejects, and because they are made for the export market, sizes are Western. Be sure to examine garments inside out. Bargains include clothes made of silk, cashmere, leather, cotton, and wool, and some outlets have men's clothing as well. These can be great places to buy well-tailored and expensive-looking business outfits.

However, you never know what's for sale until you get there, and sometimes the selection is disappointing. What's more, some outlets are indistinguishable from upmarket boutiques, with prices to match. It seems that some shops simply call themselves factory outlets because that's what tourists are looking for. Thus unless you have lots of time to search through outlet after outlet before finding that gem, it's debatable whether it's worth your while to go chasing up to the ones in Hung Hom in search of a good deal. Check some of the more conveniently located stores first, and then make up your mind whether or not you want to pursue them further.

For a list of factory outlets along with their addresses, telephone numbers, types of wares, and hours, pick up a pamphlet called "Factory Outlets" available free at HKTA offices. Most outlets are open from 9 or 10am to 6pm Monday through Friday, and some are open on Saturday and Sunday as well.

JEWELRY

According to the HKTA, Hong Kong has more jewelry stores per square mile than any other city in the world. Gems are imported duty free from all over the world, and Hong Kong is reputedly the world's third-largest trading center for diamonds. **Gold jewelry,** both imported and locally made pieces, is required by law to carry a stamp with the accurate gold content.

Jade, of course, remains the most popular with both visitors and Chinese. It's considered to protect wearers against illness. There are two categories of jade. Jadeite jade (also called Burmese jade) is generally white to apple green in color, although it is also found in hues of brown, red, orange, yellow, and even lavender. It may be mottled in color, but the most expensive jade is a translucent emerald green. Less expensive is the second category of jade, nephrite jade, which is usually a dark green or off-white. In any case, true jade is so hard that supposedly even a knife leaves no scratch. Unless you know your jade, you're safest shopping in one of the Chinese products stores, listed above under "Chinese Crafts and Products," above. For less expensive pieces, visit the Jade Market, described earlier under "Markets."

Pearls, almost all of which are cultured, are another favorite item among shoppers in Hong Kong. There are both sea- and freshwater pearls, available in all shapes, sizes, colors, and lustre. For inexpensive strands, check the vendors at the Jade Market. There are also many shops along Nathan Road in Tsimshatsui that sell them.

For more information on jewelry, pick up a free pamphlet at HKTA offices called "Shopping Guide to Jewelry," which contains useful information about gold, diamonds, emeralds, rubies, sapphires, jade, pearls, birthstones, and other precious stones. Also included are shopping hints and advice on the care and protection of jewelry.

There are also factory outlets specializing in jewelry. These are listed in "Factory Outlets," a free pamphlet also available at HKTA offices.

MEGA-MALLS

Hong Kong boasts large shopping complexes that are so huge I call them mega-malls. They are open daily, with most businesses operating from 10am to 7 or 8pm.

The largest one in the territory, and probably Asia, is a particularly large complex called **Harbour City** on Canton Road in Tsimshatsui, conveniently located right next to the dock that disgorges passengers from cruise liners and just to the east of the Star Ferry. It encompasses Ocean Terminal, Ocean Galleries, and Ocean City, all interconnected by air-conditioned walkways. Altogether there are 600 outlets here, with shops selling clothing, accessories, jewelry, cosmetics, antiques, electronic goods, furniture, housewares, Asian arts and crafts, and much more. There's enough to keep you occupied here for the rest of your life, but it's especially good on a rainy or humid day when you'd rather be inside than out.

Other mega-malls in Hong Kong include the **New World Centre,** located next to the Regent Hotel in Tsimshatsui, the **New Town Plaza** in Shatin in the New Territories, and the **Taikoo Shing City Plaza,** located at the Taikoo MTR station on Hong Kong Island.

POSTCARDS AND PRINTS

You can buy postcards of Hong Kong at virtually every souvenir stand in the colony, but for unique, historical postcards and prints, drop by the **Government Publications Centre,** on the ground floor of General Post Office, Connaught Place, Central (tel. 5231071), right in front of the Star Ferry concourse. It has postcards of Hong Kong's colorful festivals, photographs of the colony in its early years, and prints of original paintings done in the 1800s of life in the South China seas. Prints start at HK$3 (40¢), and a set of 10 postcards runs about HK$6.50 (85¢).

Open: Mon–Fri 9am–6pm, Sat 9am–1pm. *MTR:* Central.

SOUVENIRS

In addition to the two shops here, the Chinese products stores listed above under "Chinese Crafts and Products," above, offer a wide array of souvenirs and gifts. Other places to look for souvenirs include hotel shopping arcades, Nathan Road in Tsimshatsui, the Peak Tower on Victoria Peak, and the mega-malls.

Amazing Grace Elephant Co., with branches at 3236-3242 Ocean Terminal, Harbour City, 5 Canton Rd., Tsimshatsui (tel. 7227275); 348-349 Ocean Centre, Harbour City, 5 Canton Rd., Tsimshatsui (tel. 7215455); the Excelsior Hotel lobby and arcade, Gloucester Rd., Causeway Bay (tel. 5764420); and B6 Gloucester Tower, the Landmark, Des Voeux Rd., Central (tel. 5229527).

Begun in the 1970s by an American who started by selling ceramic elephants from Vietnam, it has since expanded into arts and crafts from China, Thailand, Indonesia, the Philippines, and other Asian countries. Among the beautiful, but expensive, decorations for the home that are offered here are brassware, rattan products, jewelry, clothing, ceramics, and silks. There's also a factory outlet at

4 Kin Fung Street, Tuen Mun, New Territories (tel. 0838156); to get there, take the MTR to the Tsuen Wan station, then bus 68M to Tuen Mun. *MTR:* Tsimshatsui for the two Harbour City branches, Causeway Bay for the Excelsior Hotel branch, and Central for the Landmark branch.

Welfare Handicrafts Shop, on Salisbury Rd. (between the YMCA and the Star Ferry concourse) in Tsimshatsui (tel. 3666979) and on the lower ground floor of Jardine House, Connaught Rd., Central (tel. 5243356).

The proceeds of these two small shops go to charity. Items for sale include T-shirts, porcelain, silk coin purses, pin cushions, small cast-iron statues, and other souvenirs.

Open: Mon–Sat 9am–5:45pm at the Salisbury Rd. shop; Mon–Fri 9am–5:30pm and Sat 9am–noon at the Jardine House shop. *MTR:* Tsimshatsui for the Salisbury Rd. shop; Central for the Jardine House shop.

TAILORS

The 24-hour suit is a thing of the past, but you can still have clothes custom-made in a few days. In fact, rare is the visitor to Hong Kong who doesn't have at least one thing custom-made. Tailoring in Hong Kong got its first running start in the 1950s, when tailor families from Shanghai fled China in 1949 and set up shop in Hong Kong. Today, prices are no longer as cheap as they once were. Still, they often run about what you'd pay for a similar ready-made garment back home, but the difference, of course, is that this one should fit you perfectly. The standards of the better, established shops rival even those of London's Savile Row—at about half the price. A top-class men's suit will run about HK$4,000 ($519), including fabric, while a silk shirt can cost HK$450 ($58.50).

Tailors in Hong Kong will make anything you want, from business suits and evening gowns to wedding dresses, leather jackets, and monogrammed shirts. Some stores will allow you to bring in your fabric, while others require that you buy theirs. Many tailors have a wide range of cloth from which to choose, from cotton and linen to very fine wools, cashmere, and silk. Kong tailors are excellent at copying fashions, even if all you have is a picture or drawing of what you want.

On average, you should allow three to five days to have something custom-made, with at least two or three fittings. Be specific about what you want, such as lining, tightness of fit, buttons, and length. If you aren't satisfied during the fittings, speak up. Alterations should be included in the original price (ask about this beforehand during your first negotiations). If in the end you still don't like the finished product, you don't have to accept it. However, you do forfeit the deposit you were required to pay before the tailor began working, usually about 50% of the total cost.

With more than 2,500 tailoring establishments in Hong Kong, it shouldn't be any problem finding one. Some of the most famous ones are located in hotel shopping arcades and shopping complexes, but the more upmarket the location, the higher the prices.

Tsimshatsui abounds with tailor shops. In any case, your best bet is to deal only with shops that are members of the HKTA or ones you've used before. Member shops are listed in "The Official Guide to Shopping, Eating Out and Services in Hong Kong."

Once you've had something custom-made and your tailor has your measurements, you will more than likely be able to order more later after you've returned home.

TOYS

Even though Hong Kong is one of the world's leading exporters of toys, toys seem in short supply in Hong Kong itself.

Toys "Я" Us, Ocean Terminal, Harbour City, 5 Canton Rd., Tsimshatsui (tel. 7309462), is one of the largest, if not *the* largest, toy stores in Hong Kong. A huge department store of toys, it claims to have 20,000 items for sale, including games, sporting goods, hobby goods, baby furniture, books, clothing, and of course, toys.

Open: Mon–Sat 10am–8pm. *MTR:* Tsimshatsui.

VIDEO PRODUCTS

If you're interested in buying video cassette recorders, camcorders/players, laser disc and compact disc videos, laser disc players, or other video-related products, pick up a pamphlet called "Shopping Guide to Video Products," available free at HKTA offices. It gives hints for shopping for these products, lists sole agents in Hong Kong for various brand names, and tells which HKTA member shops sell video products.

HONG KONG AFTER DARK

1. HINTS FOR INEXPENSIVE PURSUITS
2. THE PERFORMING ARTS
3. COCKTAIL LOUNGES
4. PUBS AND BARS
5. DISCOS
6. TOPLESS BARS AND HOSTESS CLUBS
7. NIGHT TOURS

Nightlife in Hong Kong seems pretty tame when compared with Tokyo, Bangkok, and several other Asian cities. With the world of Suzie Wong in Wanchai now a shadow of its former self, Hong Kong nowadays seems somewhat reserved, rather British, and, perhaps to some minds, yawningly dull. For the people who live here, exclusive clubs are where many expatriates entertain their guests, while the Chinese are likely to spend their entire evening at one of those huge lively restaurants.

Yet it would be wrong to assume that Hong Kong has nothing to offer by way of nightlife—it's just that you probably won't get into any trouble enjoying yourself. To liven things up, Hong Kong stages several annual events, including the Hong Kong Arts Festival held in January or February, the Hong Kong International Film Festival which usually occurs in April, and the biennial Festival of Asian Arts, generally staged sometime in autumn. In addition, there are plenty of that finest of British institutions—the British pub—not to mention sophisticated cocktail lounges, discos, hostess clubs, and topless bars. There's even a nightlife district, so to speak, in the area of Lan Kwai Fong Street and D'Aguilar Street in the Central District, where a modest number of bars and restaurants have added a spark to Hong Kong's financial district. Remember that a 10% service charge will be added to your bill.

1. Hints for Inexpensive Pursuits

If you're watching your Hong Kong dollars, keep in mind that one of the best traditions in the colony is its "happy hour," when many bars offer two drinks for the price of one or drinks at lower prices. Actually, "happy hours" would be more appropriate, since they're generally from 5 to 7pm and sometimes even longer than that. In addition, many pubs, bars, and lounges offer live entertainment, from jazz to Filipino combos, which you can enjoy simply for the price of a beer.

NIGHT STROLLS
One of the most beautiful and romantic sights in the world must be that afforded from **Victoria Peak** at night. The peak tram, which costs only HK$10 ($1.30) round trip and runs daily until midnight, deposits passengers at the Peak Tower terminal. Take a right out of the terminal, and then another right onto a pedestrian footpath. This path, which follows Lugard Road and Harlech Road, circles around the Peak, giving great views of glittering Hong Kong. Popular with both lovers and joggers, the path is lit at night and leads past expensive villas and primeval-looking jungles. Definitely the best stroll in Hong Kong, it takes about an hour.

On the other side of the harbor, there's a promenade along the Tsimshatsui waterfront, popular with young Chinese couples.

NIGHT MARKETS
If you're looking for colorful atmosphere, head for one of Hong Kong's two night markets. **Temple Street Night Market,** near the Jordan MTR station on Kowloon, extends for several blocks and has stalls selling clothing, accessories, toys, cassettes, household items, and much more. Be sure to bargain fiercely if you decide to buy anything, and be sure to check the merchandise to make sure it isn't going to fall apart in two weeks. This is also a good place for an inexpensive meal at one of the dai pai dong, roadside food stalls, which here specialize in seafood, including clams, shrimp, mussels, and crab.

But the most wonderful part of the market is its northern end, to the right around the white parking area. There, near the Tin Hau temple, is where you'll find palm readers and fortune tellers, as well as street musicians and singers. You'll have to hunt for the tiny alleyway of musicians, where group after group has set up its own stage and is surrounded by its own appreciative audience. Cantonese pop songs and operas are among the favorites in their repertoire, and when they do an especially good job they are rewarded with tips.

Another nighttime market is the **Poor Man's Nightclub** on

Hong Kong Island, which was unfortunately drastically reduced in size with the completion of the Macau Ferry Terminal next to it. Still, you can pick up some good buys here, and there are also plenty of dai pai dong to snack from.

The night markets are under full swing from about 8 to 11pm daily.

MORE SUGGESTIONS

If you're in Hong Kong anytime from September through May on a Wednesday evening, you can go to the **horse races in Happy Valley** for as little as HK$10 ($1.30). It's standing room only, but you'll be surrounded by betting fanatics and a giant screen displays the races. For more information, see Section 6, "Sports," in Chapter VII.

Lai Chi Kok, an amusement park near the Mei Foo MTR station and the Sung Dynasty Village in the New Territories, has the usual thrills, and is open every evening until 10pm weekdays and 11pm on Saturday and Sunday. Admission is a mere HK$5 (65¢).

Finally, the Hong Kong Tourist Association sponsors **free cultural shows** every Friday from 6 to 7 pm at the New World Centre in Kowloon. Changing weekly, they include such traditional Chinese performances as acrobatics, Fukienese rod puppets, martial arts, or Chinese instrumental music. Contact the HKTA for an updated schedule and to confirm the time.

---

2. The Performing Arts

The busiest time of the year for the performing arts is the month-long **Hong Kong Arts Festival,** held every year in January or February. This international affair features artists from various parts of the globe with performances of orchestras, dance troupes, opera companies, and chamber ensembles. Performing at the 1990 festival, for example, were the Hong Kong Philharmonic Orchestra, the Philharmonic from London, the Empire Brass from Boston, the Hong Kong Chinese Orchestra, the Stuttgart Ballet, the Paul Taylor Dance Company, and the Georgian State Dance Company from the USSR. City Hall, located in Central just east of the Star Ferry concourse, sells tickets to performances, which are priced from HK$50 ($6.50) to HK$300 ($39). For information about the program of the Hong Kong Arts Festival and future dates, call 5229928; for ticket inquiries, call 5739595.

Throughout the year there are other cultural activities and entertainment, including theater productions, pop concerts, and Chinese opera and dance performances. To find out what's going on, check Hong Kong's two newspapers, the *South China Morning Post* and the *Hong Kong Standard*. In addition, the two tourist newspapers, *Orient* and *Hong Kong,* also carry information on what's being shown where, as well as the "Upfront" section of the

Official Hong Kong Guide. For more information on artistic and cultural events, drop by City Hall on Connaught Road in Central or the Arts Centre on Harbour Road in Wanchai to pick up a free brochure called "City News."

THE MAJOR CONCERT/PERFORMANCE HALLS

Hong Kong Academy for Performing Arts, Gloucester Rd., Wanchai (tel. 8231500).

Located across the street from the Arts Centre, the Academy is Hong Kong's institution for vocational training in the performing arts. It also features regular performances in theater and dance, either by local or international playwrights and choreographers. Its Theatre Block is composed of six venues, including the Lyric Theatre, Drama Theatre, Orchestral Hall, and Recital Hall.

MTR: Wanchai.

Arts Centre, Harbour Rd., Wanchai (tel. 8230230).

Built on Wanchai's new waterfront of reclaimed land, the Arts Centre hosts the Hong Kong Arts Festival and other international presentations, as well as performances by Hong Kong's own amateur and professional companies. It has regular programs of plays or dances, exhibition galleries, and showings of foreign films. There are three auditoriums: Shouson Theatre, Studio Theatre, and the Recital Hall.

MTR: Wanchai.

City Hall, Connaught Rd., Central District (tel. 5739595).

Located right beside the Star Ferry concourse, its Low Block has a 1,500-seat balconied concert hall, as well as a 470-seat theater used for plays and chamber music.

MTR: Central.

Hong Kong Cultural Centre, Salisbury Rd., Tsimshatsui (tel. 5227704).

Sandwiched in between the Space Museum and the Star Ferry concourse, the Hong Kong Cultural Centre is the territory's newest and largest arena for the arts. Opened in 1989, this complex boasts both a Western and a Chinese restaurant, exhibition areas, and practice and rehearsal rooms, but its pride is its 2,100-seat Concert Hall, home of the Hong Kong Philharmonic Orchestra. It features a 93-stop 8,000-pipe Austrian Rieger organ, one of the world's largest organs. The stage, set near the center of the oval hall, is surrounded by seating at two levels.

There are also two theaters. The Grand Theatre seats 1,750 and is used for musicals, large-scale drama, dance, film shows, and Chinese opera. It is fitted with a revolving stage wagon, an orchestra pit for 110 musicians, a five-language simultaneous interpretation system (for conventions and conferences), and cinematic projection equipment. Smaller is the Studio Theatre, designed for experimental theater and dance. Its stage configuration can be changed to end, thrust, center, and transverse, and can seat from 326 to 542.

MTR: Tsimshatsui.

Coliseum, East Tsimshatsui (tel. 7659233).

Located on the waterfront near the Hung Hom railway terminus, this 12,500-seat arena is designed in an inverted pyramid and features rock and pop concerts, ice shows, and sporting events.

Directions: Bus 5A from Star Ferry.

Ko Shan Theatre, Ko Shan Rd., near Kowloon City (tel. 3342331).

A former quarry site, this open-air theater in a large park is favored for Chinese opera, variety shows, and major film screenings. It seats 3,000 people.

Directions: Bus 5 or 5A from Star Ferry.

Queen Elizabeth Stadium, Happy Valley (tel. 5756793).

Located near the race track, this 3,500-seat air-conditioned arena sponsors rock concerts and other musical performances.

Directions: Bus 5, 5A, 10, or 103; or tram.

CHINESE OPERA

Chinese opera predates the first Western opera by about 600 years, although it wasn't until the 13th and 14th centuries that performances began to develop into a structured operatic form, with rules of composition and fixed role characterization. Opera then began developing into different styles all over China, and even today there are marked differences between the operas performed in, say, Peking, Canton, Shanghai, Fukien, Chiu Chow, and Szechuan.

The most popular, however, is the Peking-style opera, with its spectacular costumes and elaborate makeup, familiar stories, and feats of acrobatics and swordmanship. The plots are usually of legends and historical events, extolling loyalty, filial piety, and righteousness. Accompanied by seven or eight musicians, the performers, especially the females, sing in shrill, high-pitched falsetto, a sound Westerners sometimes do not appreciate initially.

In any case, Chinese opera is immensely popular in Hong Kong, so much so that tickets sell out well in advance, making it almost impossible for visiting tourists to get their hands on any. If you're still determined to see a performance, contact the HKTA to see whether anything's going on, or check with one of the tourist publications. Or ask your travel agent or hotel to try to get you tickets when you first make your travel plans. Ko Shan Theatre and Lai Chi Kok's Paladium Opera House both stage performances of Chinese opera.

THEATER

Local repertory companies include Actors' Rep, the Garrison Players, the Hong Kong Stage Club, the American Community Theatre, and the Hong Kong Singers, which specializes in musical comedies.

In addition to plays performed at the Hong Kong Cultural Centre in Tsimshatsui and the Arts Centre and Academy for the Performing Arts in Wanchai, fine acting is also regularly featured at the **Hilton Playhouse,** a dinner theater located in the Hilton Hotel, 2

Queen's Road, Central District (tel. 5233111). It stages well-known and popular plays, usually from London's West End and Broadway.

Another place to check for theatrical events is the **Fringe Club,** located on Lower Albert Road in Central (tel. 5217251). Actually a private club which offers a temporary, one-night membership for HK$10 ($1.30), it specializes in experimental drama, music, comedy, and other happenings.

DANCE AND MUSIC

The Hong Kong Cultural Centre is home of the **Hong Kong Philharmonic Orchestra,** founded in 1975 and performing regularly in the colony from September to June and at other scheduled events throughout the year. Its music director is American composer-conductor Kenneth Schermerhorn. For more information, call 8327121.

Not to be outdone is the equally acclaimed **Hong Kong Chinese Orchestra,** which features 85 musicians playing a wide range of traditional and modern Chinese instruments, combining them with Western orchestrations. For more information, call 3348465.

If you're interested in jazz, there are several pubs that feature concerts regularly. **Ned Kelly's Last Stand,** 11A Ashley Road, Tsimshatsui (tel. 3660562), has its own in-house band with Dixieland jazz or swing every night from 9 pm. The **Godown,** located in the Admiralty Centre in the Central District (tel. 8661166), features jazz every Wednesday from 9:30pm. And finally, for some jazz on Sunday afternoon, head for the **Dickens Bar,** located in the basement of the Excelsior Hotel, 281 Gloucester Road, in Causeway Bay (tel. 5767365), where there's the big-band sound from 3 to 6pm.

There's also live music at several of Hong Kong's cocktail lounges, including the **Sky Lounge** in the Sheraton Hotel and the **Chin Chin** in the Hyatt, both on Nathan Road, and the **Tiara** in the Shangri-La on Mody Road. For more information, see "Cocktail Lounges," later in this chapter.

As for dance, both the **Hong Kong Ballet Company** and the **Hong Kong Dance Company** have extensive repertoires. The Hong Kong Dance Company specializes in the development of Chinese dance in modern forms. Finally, another troupe is the **City Contemporary Dance Company,** which expresses contemporary Hong Kong culture through dance.

MOVIES

The biggest event in the film year is the **Hong Kong International Film Festival,** held in April and May. This festival features a wide variety of films from all over the world.

Otherwise, film is never far from the minds of Hong Kong residents, as the city is famous in Asia as a center for film production. There are some 30 cinemas all over the territory, with tickets costing

HK$25 to HK$35 ($3.25 to $4.55) for assigned seats. Chinese films are naturally the most popular, especially in the genre of "Bruce Lee" kung fu movies. There are also showings of the latest Western films. For information on what's playing, check the local newspapers.

3. Cocktail Lounges

KOWLOON

Chin Chin, Hyatt Regency, 67 Nathan Rd., Tsimhsatsui (tel. 3111234).

Located just off the lobby of the Hyatt Regency hotel, the Chin Chin is one of Hong Kong's longtime favorites. Very Chinese in decor, it features Filipino musicians from 5pm.

Open: Daily 11am–2am. *Prices:* Beer from HK$23 ($3); cocktails HK$33 ($4.30). Happy hour 11am–8pm with drinks for half price. *MTR:* Tsimshatsui.

Sky Lounge, Sheraton Hotel, 20 Nathan Rd., Tsimshatsui (tel. 3691111).

This plush and comfortable lounge is located on the top floor of the Sheraton, affording one of the best and most romantic views of the harbor and glittering Hong Kong Island. There's soft live music beginning at 5:30pm Monday through Saturday and at 8:30pm on Sunday. Unless you're a hotel guest, from 8pm onward there's a minimum drink charge of HK$77 ($10) per person.

Open: Daily 11am–1am (to 2am Fri and Sat). *Prices:* Beer HK$25 ($3.25); cocktails HK$33 ($4.30). *MTR:* Tsimshatsui.

Tiara, 21st floor of the Shangri-La Hotel, 64 Mody Rd., East Tsimshatsui (tel. 7212111).

Its high location assures customers a spectacular view of Victoria Harbour, but get here early if you want to be sure of getting a window seat at dusk. Piano music sets the mood for this intimate and cozy lounge. After 8pm there's a minimum drink charge of HK$95 ($12.25) per person.

Open: Daily 5pm–2am. *Prices:* Beer and cocktails average HK$35 ($4.55). *MTR:* Tsimshatsui.

CENTRAL DISTRICT

La Ronda Lounge, 30th floor of the Furama Hotel, 1 Connaught Rd., Central (tel. 5255111).

On the Hong Kong side, this lounge offers spectacular closeup views of Central, the harbor, and Kowloon beyond. Although it's located next to a revolving restaurant, the bar itself is stationary (a blessing, perhaps, if one is drinking).

Open: Daily 5:30–11pm. *Prices:* Cocktails average HK$40 ($5.20). *MTR:* Central.

4. Pubs and Bars

KOWLOON

Beefy's Cabin, 70 Canton Rd., Tsimshatsui (tel. 7214689).

This place looks like a bar anywhere, with no money wasted on decor. On the walls hang posters of Rod Stewart, Elvis, Buddy Holly, and James Dean. If you're hungry, its menu lists beef stew, bacon and eggs, burritos, beef satay, corned beef sandwiches, chili, nachos, Mexican pizza, spaghetti, spring rolls, tacos, and more. There's a live Filipino band from 5pm until the wee hour of 5am—so as you might guess, the real action here starts late. Wonder of wonders, there's no cover or music charge.

Open: 24 hours daily! *Prices:* Beer from HK$24 ($3.10) for a pint. Happy hour is 5–9pm, with two drinks for the price of one. *MTR:* Tsimshatsui.

The Blacksmith's Arms, 16 Minden Ave., Tsimshatsui (tel. 3696696).

This English-style pub complete with a dart board is inexpensive compared with other Hong Kong bars and serves mainly beer and whisky.

Open: Daily noon–1:30am. *Prices:* Most beers HK$15–HK$17 ($1.95–$2.20). Happy hour is Mon–Sat 5–8pm with discounts on drinks; beer from HK$11 ($1.45). *MTR:* Tsimshatsui.

Kangaroo Pub, 15 Chatham Rd., Tsimshatsui (tel. 7238293).

This pub also serves the same menu as the adjacent Windjammer Restaurant, but you save 10% by eating at the pub because there's no service charge. Its menu lists steaks, seafood, spaghetti, sandwiches, and other dishes, and it also serves breakfast. If you want a beer first thing in the morning, this is the place.

Open: Daily 8am–2am. *Prices:* Beer from HK$20 ($2.60); cocktails HK$27–HK$38 ($3.50–$4.95). *MTR:* Tsimshatsui.

Mariner's Club, 3rd floor, Middle Rd., Tsimshatsui (tel. 3688261).

This has got to be one of the cheapest places for a drink in all of Hong Kong. The Mariner's Club serves as accommodation for seamen, but it seems that anyone can use the bar, judging from the crowd of college-age coeds, backpackers, oldtimers, and salty dogs who were there during my last visit. The place is simple and bare, reminding me of a students' cafeteria.

Open: Daily 11am–midnight. *Prices:* Beers from HK$11 ($1.45); cocktails HK$26 ($3.40). *MTR:* Tsimshatsui.

Ned Kelly's Last Stand, 11A Ashley Rd., Tsimshatsui (tel. 3660562).

This is a lively Australian saloon, with live Dixieland jazz or swing nightly from 9pm to 2am. It serves Australian chow, including juicy pork sausages served with mashed potatoes and onion gravy; stew; liver, bacon, and fried onions; chicken; Australian sirloin steak; hamburgers; and meat pie with mashed potatoes and onion gravy.

Open: Daily 11:30am–2am. *Prices:* Beer from HK$16 ($2.10). Happy hour is 11:30am–7pm, with beer from HK$11 ($1.45). *MTR:* Tsimshatsui.

Red Lips Bar, Lock Rd. and Peking Rd., Tsimshatsui (tel. 7217098).

This bar is an institution, the last holdout of what used to be quite common back in the Vietnam era's heyday: a cheap and tacky hostess bar. In operation more than 22 years, this small hole-in-the-wall is decorated with red lights and red furniture, and from the looks of some of the women plying their trade, they were old before they even started working here. Nonetheless, the ladies are sweet and full of information about the old days, and all they ask is that you buy them a drink, from which they receive a commission. Their drinks cost HK$33 ($4.30) for a cup of tea, HK$55 ($7.15) for something stronger. In any case, the place seems fairly innocent and couples are welcome, but the women really pour on the charm for their male customers. This one-room bar is located down a narrow passageway on the corner of Lock Road and Peking Road. At the entrance of the passageway are usually a couple hostesses, trying to entice passersby to come inside.

Open: Daily 10am–3am. *Prices:* Beer from HK$13 ($1.70); spirits from HK$20 ($2.60). *MTR:* Tsimshatsui.

Rick's Café, 4 Hart Ave., Tsimshatsui (tel. 3672939).

Taking its name from the bar in the movie *Casablanca,* this basement oasis features potted palm trees, ceiling fans, and posters of Bogie and Bergman. Although it's more of a bar than a restaurant, it also serves great tacos, enchiladas, chili con carne, sandwiches, African ribs, and other exotic fare. Prices are rather high for what you get, but after 9pm there's a disc jockey and a small dance floor.

Open: Mon–Sat 3pm–3am and Sun 6pm–2am. *Prices:* Beer from HK$17 ($2.20) for a half pint; cocktails from HK$39 ($5.05). Happy hour is 3–9pm (from 6pm Sun), with two drinks for the price of one. *MTR:* Tsimshatsui.

Someplace Else, basement of the Sheraton Hotel, 20 Nathan Rd., Tsimshatsui (tel. 3691111).

This is one of Tsimshatsui's most popular watering holes, especially during happy hour when it's standing room only. This two-level bar/restaurant is decorated with stained-glass lampshades and ceiling fans, and its menu is extensive, offering everything from satay, samosas, and tacos to fish and chips, spareribs, and hamburgers.

Open: Daily 11am–1am (to 2am Fri and Sat). *Prices:* Beer from HK$17 ($2.20); cocktails average HK$33 ($4.30). Happy hour is 4–7pm, with two drinks for the price of one. *MTR:* Tsimshatsui.

White Stag, 72 Canton Rd., Tsimshatsui (tel. 3661951).

This English-style pub caters to a mixed clientele of both Westerners and Chinese. A nice, quiet place where you can actually hear yourself talk, this place sports wooden tables and a few deer heads and antlers. A blackboard announces the entrées of the day, which might include such things as corned beef hash and eggs, spring rolls, Shanghainese fried noodles, or tuna-fish salad. There are also hamburgers, and fish and chips.

Open: Daily 10am–2am. *Prices:* Beer from HK$12 ($1.60) for a half pint. *MTR:* Tsimshatsui.

CENTRAL DISTRICT

California, 24-26 Lan Kwai Fong St., Central (tel. 5211345).

Located in Central's nightlife district of Lan Kwai Fong Street and D'Aguilar Street, this very chic bar is the place to see and be seen, the place of the young nouveaux riches in search of a definition. The atmosphere is modern and sophisticated, with silent TV screens showing movies almost everywhere you look. It's a bar most of the week, except on Wednesday, Friday, and Saturday nights when it's transformed into a happening disco. Its menu lists everything from hamburgers (the house specialty) to pastas, seafood, and chicken.

Open: Daily noon–1am (on Wed, Fri, and Sat 11:30pm–4am is the disco). *Prices:* Beer from HK$33 ($4.30); cocktails from HK$49 ($6.35). Happy hour is 5–7pm, with two drinks for the price of one. Disco cover charge is HK$108 ($14), which includes two drinks; ladies free on Wed. *MTR:* Central.

Bull and Bear, Hutchinson House, 10 Harcourt Rd., Central (tel. 5257436).

This huge, sprawling place was at the forefront of Hong Kong's English-pub craze, opening back in 1974. Notorious from the beginning, it gets pretty rowdy on weekend nights, and draws everyone from businessmen in suits to servicemen on leave. It seems to draw more men than women, and one British expatriate described it as a meat market. Maybe that's what you're looking for. I can confirm that it's not a particularly comfortable place for a woman alone, having had to fight off the attentions of a rather inebriated sailor with tattoos up and down his arms. An alternative is to come for lunch or breakfast. The menu includes items like chili con carne, steak-and-kidney pie, salads, sandwiches, and daily specials.

Open: Mon–Sat 7:30am–midnight. *Closed:* Sun and hols. *Prices:* Beer from HK$11 ($1.45) for a half pint. *MTR:* Central.

Captain's Bar, Mandarin Hotel, 5 Connaught Rd., Central (tel. 5220111).

This refined bar is popular with Hong Kong's professional echelon, which comes as no surprise considering that it's in the Mandarin Hotel. It's a small, intimate place, with seating at the bar or on couches. Live music begins nightly at 9pm.

Open: Daily 11am–2am. *Prices:* Beer from HK$22 ($2.85); cocktails from HK$40 ($5.20). *MTR:* Central.

Godown, Admiralty Tower 2, off Rodney St., Central (tel. 8661166).

Located next to the Admiralty MTR station and a bus depot, the Godown is another longtime favorite. Decorated like an old godown (warehouse) with exposed beams and wooden barrels, this popular place offers live jazz on Wednesday from 9:30pm to 12:30am. On other evenings you can dance to disco music. It's a jovial place to come for lunch as well, for a menu listing steak-and-kidney pie, Irish stew, lasagne, liver, seafood, fish and chips, steaks, and salads. There are even fixed-price lunches with a trip through the salad bar for HK$80 ($10.50).

Open: Daily 9am–2am. *Prices:* Beer from HK$12 ($1.55) for a half pint. Happy hour is 5–7pm, with two drinks for the price of one. *MTR:* Admiralty.

The Jockey, 1st floor, Swire House, Connaught Rd., Central (tel. 5261478).

This is a quiet and refined English pub, popular with bankers, lawyers, and other white-collar workers. Its theme is obviously racing and jockeys, with a very masculine decor.

Open: Mon–Sat 11am–11pm. *Closed:* Sun. *Prices:* Beer HK$15–HK$28 ($1.95–3.65); cocktails HK$30 ($3.90). *MTR:* Central.

MadDogs, 33 Wyndham St., Central (tel. 5252383).

Catering to a mellow crowd of professional people, this is one of Hong Kong's most pleasant English pubs and my favorite of them all. It's located in an old building and consists of a ground floor, basement, and small patio courtyard in the back. With traditional decor reminiscent of Britain in its imperial heyday, including a picture of a stern Queen Victoria, cane chairs, and ceiling fans, it offers a wide variety of draft beers and scotch malts. Pub fare includes sandwiches, meat pies, and salads. If you want to get away from Queen Victoria's gaze, the downstairs area tends to be a little less staid, the music tends to be louder, and the atmosphere a bit livelier. Incidentally, the easiest way to enter MadDogs, especially if you're coming from the nightlife area around Lan Kwai Fong, is via the back entry just off D'Aguilar Street and Lan Kwai Fong Street.

Open: Sun–Thurs 11:30am–1am, Fri and Sat 11:30am–2am. *Prices:* Small beer from HK$10 ($1.30). Happy hour is Mon–Sat 4–7pm, with discounted drinks. *MTR:* Central.

Schnurrbart, 29 D'Aguilar St., Central (tel. 5234700).

This is the place to come for German beer on tap, as well as a wide selection of bottled German beers. Popular with German expatriates, it serves sausages, sauerkraut, and other hearty German fare, with a menu that changes weekly.

Open: Mon–Sat noon–2am. *Closed:* Sun. *Prices:* German beer from HK$20 ($2.60). *MTR:* Central.

WANCHAI/CAUSEWAY BAY

Dicken's Bar, basement of the Excelsior Hotel, Gloucester Rd., Causeway Bay (tel. 5767365).

A classy place with dark-wood paneling, softly lit lamps, and live music from 9pm to 1am, this English pub is particularly well known for its jazz band that plays every Sunday afternoon from 3 to

6pm. It serves snacks of soups and sandwiches, but especially popular is its curry buffet lunch served weekdays from noon to 2pm.

Open: Daily 11am–2am. *Prices:* Beer from HK$13 ($1.70) for a half pint; cocktails from HK$29 ($3.75). *MTR:* Causeway Bay.

Joe Bananas, 23 Luard Rd., Wanchai (tel. 5291811).

Brought to you by the same people who manage MadDogs, this is one of the most popular and hippest hangouts in Wanchai. Called "JB's" by the locals, it's a tribute to the rock, pop, and movie greats of yesterday and is decorated like an American diner, complete with a jukebox, posters, and music memorabilia. This place is a combination bar/restaurant/disco, with dancing every evening after 9pm.

Open: Mon–Thurs noon–2am, Fri and Sat noon–5am, Sun 6pm–2am. *Prices:* Cocktails HK$28–HK$48 ($3.65–$6.25). Happy hour is daily 3–8pm (3pm–2am Mon and Wed), with two cocktails for the price of one. Cover charge Fri and Sat after 9pm is HK$65 ($8.45), which includes two drinks. *MTR:* Wanchai.

Old China Hand, 104 Lockhart Rd., Wanchai (tel. 5279174).

This is one of the oldtimers in Wanchai, and is an informal English pub with dart boards, a picture of Queen Elizabeth, and a lot of kitsch on the walls. A sign warns customers: "Sorry, we don't serve women—you have to bring your own." In the tradition of the pub lunch, meals are also served, including steak-and-kidney pie, fish and chips, sandwiches, salads, chili con carne, and moussaka.

Open: Daily 11am–2am. *Prices:* Beer from HK$10.50 ($1.35) for a half pint; spirits from HK$17 ($2.20). *MTR:* Wanchai.

---

5. Discos

Discos in Hong Kong generally charge more on weekend nights, but the admission price usually includes one or two free drinks. After that, beer and mixed drinks are often priced the same.

KOWLOON

Boobs, 35-39 Hankow Rd., Tsimshatsui (tel. 3683829).

This nightspot is at its wildest around 2am and is the place to go after the other discos have had the good sense to close down for the night. It's popular with people in their 20s, including Chinese, and Filipino and Western expatriates. There's nothing exciting or unusual about its interior, but at this late hour few people care.

Open: Daily 10pm–5am. *Prices:* Beer and mixed drinks HK$28 ($3.65). *Admission:* HK$88 ($11.50) for men, HK$45 ($5.85) for women, one drink included. *MTR:* Tsimshatsui.

Canton, Canton Rd., 161-163 World Finance Centre, Harbour City, Tsimshatsui (tel. 7350209).

One of Hong Kong's hottest discos and particularly popular with Chinese and Japanese, this innovative disco changes its look often so that the locals keep coming back. There are three big screens with music videos, Chinese poster advertisements from the 1920s, and a big dance floor with lots of technical gadgets and lights.

Open: Sun–Thurs 9pm–3am, Fri and Sat 9pm–4am. *Prices:* Drinks HK$48 ($6.25). *Admission:* Sun–Thurs HK$95 ($12.25); Fri and Sat HK$108 ($14), including two drinks; Tues–Thurs, women admitted free. *MTR:* Tsimshatsui.

Faces, New World Hotel, 22 Salisbury Rd., Tsimshatsui (tel. 3694111).

Located right off the lobby, this disco is decorated in black with mirrors, which helps to offset the fact that it's rather small with several separate little rooms. The dance floor is also small, but the overall atmosphere is cozy and intimate.

Open: Sun–Mon 9pm–2am, Fri and Sat 9pm–3am. *Prices:* Drinks HK$40 ($5.20). *Admission:* Sun–Thurs HK$99 ($12.75); Fri and Sat HK$110 ($14.25). *MTR:* Tsimshatsui.

Falcon Disco, Royal Garden Hotel, 69 Mody Rd., East Tsimshatsui (tel. 7215215).

A sophisticated disco for dancers who like dressing up, this is the place to go if you want to eat, drink, and dance all at the same place. On the top floor is the Falcon Pub, a refined, English-style pub which offers a roast-beef buffet dinner daily—if you eat here, you don't have to pay an admission fee to the disco.

Open: Dinner buffet daily 6:30–9:30pm; disco Sun–Thurs 9:30pm–2am, Fri and Sat 9:30pm–3am. *Prices:* Beer HK$38 ($4.95), cocktails HK$44 ($5.70). Happy hour is Mon–Fri 6:30–8:30pm, with drinks 20% less. Dinner buffet is HK$120 ($15.50). *Disco admission:* Sun–Thurs HK$100 ($13), Fri and Sat HK$130 ($17), including two drinks. *MTR:* Tsimshatsui.

Hollywood East, Regal Meridien Hotel, 71 Mody Rd., East Tsimshatsui (tel. 8936460).

Catering to a young and trendy crowd, Hollywood East is decorated on a Hollywood theme with stage-lighting fixtures, posters of movie stars, and 12 screens that depict the history of Hollywood.

Open: Sun–Thurs 9:30pm–2am, Fri and Sat 9:30pm–3am. *Prices:* Most drinks HK$40 ($5.20). *Admission:* HK$95 ($12.25), including two drinks. *MTR:* Tsimshatsui.

Hot Gossip, World Finance Centre, Canton Rd., Harbour City, Tsimshatsui (tel. 7306884).

Just down the street from Canton, Hot Gossip is another popular disco. Its ground floor is a high-tech restaurant and bar which opens at noon (from 5pm on Sunday) and serves soups, salads, sandwiches, burgers, spaghetti, and more. In the basement is the disco, a huge, cavernous place with laser shows.

Open: Sun–Thurs 9pm–2:30am, Fri and Sat 9pm–3:30am. *Prices:* Most drinks HK$35–HK$40 ($4.55–$5.20). *Admission:* Sun–Thurs HK$96 ($12.50), Fri and Sat HK$108 ($14), including two drinks; Sun and Mon, women admitted free. *MTR:* Tsimshatsui.

In Place, 42-44 Hankow Rd., Tsimshatsui (tel. 7396331).

There's not a lot to say about this place except that it attracts a large following of young Westerners—probably because it's cheaper than most discos. In fact, on Monday and Wednesday nights from 9pm until midnight, the HK$55 ($7.15) admission includes all the beer you can consume.

Open: Sun–Thurs 8pm–4am, Fri and Sat 8pm–5am. *Prices:* Beer HK$22 ($2.85); cocktails HK$30 ($3.90). *Admission:* Sun–Thurs HK$55 ($7.15), Fri HK$60 ($7.80), Sat and hols HK$77 ($10); Tues, women admitted free. *MTR:* Tsimshatsui.

The Music Room, Shangri-La Hotel, 64 Mody Rd., East Tsimshatsui (tel. 7212111).

This is the place to go if you think you're too old for the discos described above but aren't quite ready for the rest home. Aiming for an older, sophisticated crowd, it's designed more for socializing and conversing than for wild partying. With its plush carpets and sofas, it looks like a living room, and the music is concentrated on the dance floor.

Open: Daily 5pm–2am. *Prices:* Drinks HK$30–HK$40 ($3.90–$5.20). *Admission:* Fri and Sat after 9pm HK$107 ($14); otherwise free. *MTR:* Tsimshatsui.

CENTRAL DISTRICT

In addition to the two discos below, **California,** listed above under "Pubs and Bars," transforms into a disco on Wednesday, Friday, and Saturday nights from 11:30pm to 4am. The admission of HK$108 ($14) includes two free drinks, and on Wednesday ladies are admitted free.

Disco Disco, 38 D'Aguilar St., Central (tel. 5248809).

One of the first discos to open in the 1970s when disco fever hit Hong Kong, this disco used to be the hottest place in town. Although it has had its ups and downs during the past decade and has changed management several times, it still attracts a wide mixture of clientele, including gays, straights, expatriates, and Chinese. There are separate rooms for dancing and drinking, and the dance floor is surrounded with mirrors so you can watch yourself, if so inclined. This disco also has one room devoted to *karaoke,* the Japanese singalong concept which allows customers to sing into a microphone and have their voices blended with the taped instrumental music.

Open: Daily 10pm–3am. *Prices:* Drinks HK$35 ($4.55). *Admission:* Sun–Thurs HK$70 ($9.10), Fri and Sat HK$95 ($12.25), including two drinks; Tues and Thurs, men admitted free, and Wed and Fri, women admitted free. *MTR:* Central.

Club 97, 9 Lan Kwai Fong, Central (tel. 8109333).

This small, rather eclectically decorated disco is fun and usually crowded to capacity. In fact, it's so small that it sometimes feels like a private party. It's easy to strike up conversations with your neighbors here.

Open: Sun–Thurs 10pm–4am, Fri and Sat 10pm–6pm. *Prices:*

Drinks average HK$45 ($5.85). *Admission:* Thurs–Sat HK$55 ($7.15), Sun–Wed free. *MTR:* Central.

WANCHAI/CAUSEWAY BAY

Joe Bananas in Wanchai, already described under "Pubs and Bars," is transformed into a disco every evening after 9pm. There's an admission charge only on weekends; and on Monday and Wednesday nights cocktails are two for the price of one.

Talk of the Town, Excelsior Hotel, Gloucester Rd., Causeway Bay (tel. 5767365).

Smartly decorated in art deco style, this upmarket disco has a fantastic view of the harbor and Kowloon, and features a Filipino band. If you're a hotel guest here, there's no admission charge.

Open: Happy hour 5–8:30pm, with discounted drinks. Disco is Sun–Thurs 9pm–2am, Fri and Sat 9pm–3am. *Prices:* Drinks HK$39 ($5.05). *Admission:* Sun–Thurs HK$99 ($12.75), Fri and Sat HK$120 ($15.50), including two drinks. *MTR:* Causeway Bay.

---

6. Topless Bars and Hostess Clubs

Hong Kong's world of hostess clubs and topless bars has changed in the past 20 years. Back in the 1950s and '60s, Wanchai was where the action was, buzzing with sailors fresh off the ship, followed by soldiers on leave from Vietnam. It was a world of two-bit hotels, raunchy bars, narrow streets, and dark alleyways, where men came to drink and brawl and spend money on women.

Today, much of Wanchai has grown respectable, mushrooming into an area of new buildings and high-rises. As for the old nightlife, most of it has moved across the harbor, where it has groomed itself into a higher class of distinction, accompanied, of course, by higher prices. Topless bars and hostess establishments still exist there, but in place of sailors and soldiers are the Japanese. Used to high-class hostess bars in their own country, they do not wince at the prices. At any rate, you've been warned.

Bottoms Up, 14 Hankow Rd., Tsimshatsui (tel. 7214509).

If you can make it past the explicit pictures in the entranceway, this is probably the best place to go if you want to witness a topless joint. Welcoming tourists, couples, and unaccompanied men, it was used as a location shot in the James Bond movie *Man with the Golden Gun.* It features four round counters with a topless waitress in the middle of each, with soft, red lighting. I suggest that you come during happy hour.

Open: Mon–Sat 4pm–3am, Sun 5pm–3am. *Prices:* Beer HK$36 ($4.65); cocktails HK$44 ($5.70). Happy hour is 4–9pm, with drinks half price. *MTR:* Tsimshatsui.

Club Volvo, Mandarin Plaza, East Tsimshatsui (tel. 3692883).

This 70,000-square-foot hostess club claims to be the largest Japanese-style nightclub in the world. In fact, the place is so big that a full-size, electric replica of an antique Rolls-Royce delivers drinks along the "highway." There are nightly stage shows, complete with a rotating stage so that everyone gets a chance to ogle the scantily clad performers. There's also a dance floor large enough for 200 couples. You will be charged according to how long you sit at a table, how many drinks you consume, and how long you entertain a hostess at your table. If you don't watch it, you could spend a fortune here. Prices are lower during the day. There are minimum charges for both day and night.

Open: Daily 2pm–4am. *Day prices:* Minimum charge HK$110 ($14.25), including two drinks. Every six minutes at a table costs HK$14 ($1.80); a hostess costs HK$380 ($49.25) for three hours. *Evening prices:* Minimum charge HK$165 ($21.50), including two drinks. Every hour at a table costs HK$165 ($21.50); a hostess costs HK$45 ($5.85) for every 15 minutes. *MTR:* Tsimshatsui, then taxi.

---

7. Night Tours

If you have only one or two nights in Hong Kong, I suggest taking an organized night tour. **Watertours** offers more than half a dozen different evening tours that combine harbor cruises with various land activities. You can make reservations for tours through your hotel or by calling Watertours directly (tel. 5254808).

The Aberdeen & Lamma Island Seafood Dinner Tour, for example, enables participants to enjoy a cruise through Victoria Harbour and Aberdeen at dusk, followed by a seafood dinner at Sok Kwu Wan on Lamma Island. The price of this tour is HK$330 ($42.75). The Tram and Dinner Tour starts out with a tram ride from Causeway Bay through Wanchai to the Central District, followed by a stroll through Poor Man's Nightclub and then either a Chinese Dinner and cruise through the harbor or a Western buffet meal in La Ronda revolving Restaurant. This tour costs HK$380 ($49.25). Other tours might include a trip up Victoria Peak, dinner in an Aberdeen floating restaurant, a cruise in a traditional Chinese junk, or a ride in an open-top bus.

If you like having some guidance in making your plans but prefer to carry them out on your own, you might want to take advantage of a **do-it-yourself night tour** called "Yum Sing—Night on the Town Tour," organized by the HKTA. After purchasing a small packet of coupons, you decide which establishment to visit from a list of participating discos, pubs, bars, and clubs that are members of the HKTA. When you go, and for how long, is up to you, though there are some restrictions.

Two options are available. With the Grand Tour, you receive a coupon that allows free admission into a participating disco, plus a drink there. The package also comes with two more coupons, each worth one or two standard drinks at participating pubs, bars, or nightclubs. Cost of the Grand Tour is HK$165 ($21.50).

The De Luxe Tour, which costs HK$290 ($37.75), gives you one coupon good for one or two standard drinks at a participating pub, bar, or nightclub, as well as one hostess-club coupon good for two standard drinks, a fruit plate, and one hour with a hostess.

To participate, you must be at least 18 years old and a bonafide overseas visitor. For more information, contact the HKTA.

EXPLORING THE ENVIRONS

1. THE NEW TERRITORIES
2. THE OUTLYING ISLANDS
3. TRIPS TO CHINA

Mention Hong Kong and most people think of Hong Kong Island, the shops and neon of Tsimshatsui, and the high-rises of the Central District. What they don't realize is that Hong Kong Island and Kowloon are rather minute in the scheme of things—only 10% of the entire territory. The New Territories and the outlying islands make up the other whopping 90%.

If you have a day or two to spare, or even just an afternoon, I suggest that you spend it on a trip outside the city in one of Hong Kong's rural areas. Escape the bustle and chaos of the city to one of the colony's small villages in the countryside, especially on the islands, and you'll have the chance to glimpse an older and slower way of life, where traditions still reign supreme and where lifestyles have a rhythm all their own.

1. The New Territories

Before the 1980s the New Territories was a peaceful countryside, with duck farms, fields, and old villages. No longer. A vast 389-square-mile region that stretches from Kowloon to the border of China, the New Territories is Hong Kong's answer to its growing population and refugee crunch. Huge government housing projects have mushroomed throughout the New Territories, especially in towns along the railway and subway lines. Once-sleepy villages have erupted into satellite concrete jungles.

Approximately one-third of Hong Kong's population already lives in the New Territories, with a goal set of half the population eventually residing in its suburbs. The New Territories, therefore, is vitally important to Hong Kong itself, its well-being, and its future. For visitors to ignore it completely would be short-sighted. Many visitors find those huge housing complexes nothing short of astounding.

If, on the other hand, it's peace and quietude you're searching for, don't despair. The New Territories is so huge that not all of it has been turned into housing, and it still makes an interesting day trip for first-timers to the colony.

For information on transportation in the New Territories, drop by the HKTA office to pick up "Round New Territories by Bus," which tells which bus to take and where to get off for some of the major destinations. Be aware, however, that it takes time and patience to travel the New Territories by public bus. Distances are great and service is slow. If you are in it for the adventure and don't care about inconvenience, great. Otherwise, consider taking the organized tour below or stick to places easily reached by train or subway.

"THE LAND BETWEEN" TOUR

The easiest and best way to get a roundup view of the New Territories is to leave the driving to the Hong Kong Tourist Association and join its "The Land Between" Tour. A seven-hour trip via air-conditioned coach, this guided tour emphasizes the rural side of Hong Kong, providing the opportunity to learn about the lifestyle, customs, and beliefs of the local people. The bus takes you past satellite towns into a countryside dotted with ponds, duck farms, and small vegetable gardens planted with Chinese kale, chives, onions, and tomatoes. Every inch of the land in the valleys is used; only the barren hills are empty. Stops on the tour include Cheuk Lam Sim Yuen (Bamboo Forest Monastery), home of three of the largest "Precious Buddha" statues in Hong Kong; the indoor market of Luen Wo in Fanling; and Sam Mun Tsai fishing village. Lunch is at the Yucca de Lac Restaurant, a pleasant Cantonese establishment built on a hill overlooking Tolo Harbour. Cost of the tour, which is operated on weekdays only, is HK$240 ($31.25) for adults and HK$185 ($24) for children. For more information, contact your hotel's sightseeing desk or the HKTA.

KOWLOON–CANTON RAILWAY

For years the thing every visitor did in the New Territories was to take the train to the border for a look into forbidden and mysterious China. Now, of course, it's easy to get permission to enter China (more on that at the end of this chapter). Thus the border lookout has lost its appeal—the view was never very exciting anyway. Still, you might want to take the train up into the New Territories just for the experience. It costs only HK$5.40 (70¢) and takes only 30 minutes to go to the end of the line—and as I've said, there are interesting stops you can make on the way up and back.

Leaving every 3 to 20 minutes from the Kowloon railway sta-

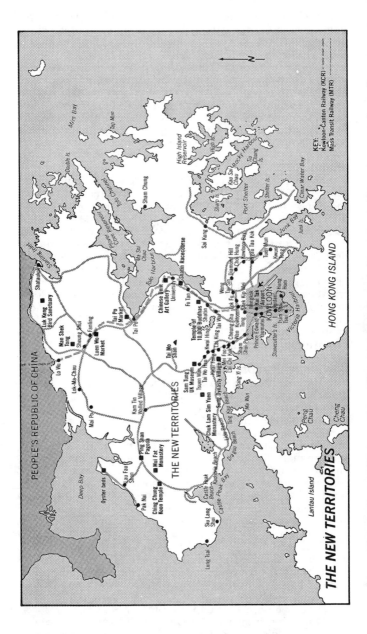

THE NEW TERRITORIES

tion in Hung Hom, the Kowloon–Canton Railway will take you along 20 miles of track, passing through towns like Shatin, University Station, Tai Po Kau, and Fanling before reaching Sheung Shui about a half hour later. Sheung Shui is your last stop unless you have a visa to go farther into China. Altogether the train makes eight stops along the way, making it possible to get out and do some exploring on your own. If I were making a day's experience of the journey, I would first go to Shatin and then all the way to Sheung Shuin, followed by a stop at Luen Wo Market before heading for University Station. After lunch, I would visit the museum and then board a ferry for a cruise through Tolo Harbour.

Shatin

Shatin is Hong Kong's prime example of a budding satellite town. It's also home to Hong Kong's new and modern racetrack and a huge mall called the New Town Plaza. The most interesting thing for the tourist here, though is the **Temple of 10,000 Buddhas,** located on a hill west of the Shatin railway station. It will take about a half hour's energetic walk to get there—with more than 300 steps to climb before reaching the top. The temple was founded by a monk named Yuet Kai, who wrote 96 books on Buddhism. He's still at the temple—well, kind of still there. He's been embalmed and covered in gold leaf and sits behind a glass case for all to see. The other attractions there are the Buddha statues—12,800 of them lining the walls, and no two are exactly alike. Also on the grounds is a nine-story pink pagoda. The temple affords a good view of the surrounding countryside.

University Station

This stop, which is still actually within the boundaries of budding Shatin, serves students going to Chinese University. But your main interest will probably be its art museum and a ferry ride through Tolo Harbour.

The main collection of the **Art Gallery** at the Institute of Chinese Studies, Chinese University, New Territories (tel. 6952218), contains more than 1,000 paintings and examples of calligraphy by Guangdong artists, dating from the Ming period to the present. Also in the gallery are bronze seals, rubbings of stone inscriptions, jade flower carvings, and Chinese ceramics. The gallery consists of four levels and a central courtyard with a Chinese garden. Special exhibitions of art on loan from China's museums are sometimes mounted.

The museum is open Monday through Saturday from 10am to 4:30pm (on Sunday and holidays from 12:30 to 4:30pm). It's closed New Year's Eve and New Year's Day, the first three days of the Chinese New Year, Easter Sunday, Christmas Eve, and Christmas Day. Admission is free. To get there, catch a "University" bus from University Station, getting off at Sir Run Run Shaw Hall.

University Station is also where you get off if you want to take a ferry around **Tolo Harbour.** From the station it's a five-minute walk to Ma Liu Shui, where you board the ferry for a leisurely trip to six villages around the harbor. The ferry leaves only two times a day, at

7:25am and 3:15pm. Since the first ferry may be a little too early for you and doesn't allow you to disembark for sightseeing, I suggest taking the afternoon cruise. This ferry makes a stop at Tap Mun at 4:50pm, goes on to some other villages, and then returns to Tap Mun about 45 minutes later. This gives you a little time to do some sightseeing, but make sure you make it back to the Tap Mun ferry dock by 5:45pm because there are no hotels here. The ferry gets back into Ma Liu Shui at 7:10pm.

Tai Po Market

The **Tai Ping Carpet Factory** allows visitors to come watch the intricate process of producing Oriental carpets. You can buy ready-made carpets there as well as order custom-made ones. Visiting hours are 2 to 4pm only, Monday through Thursday. You have to make an appointment here, which you can do by calling 6565161, extension 211. The factory is located on Lot no. 1687, Tai Ping Industrial Park, Ting Kok Road (the road leading to Plover Cove Reservoir), Tai Po Market.

Fanling

The **Luen Wo Market** in the middle of Fanling (included in "The Land Between" Tour) is interesting if you've never seen a Chinese country market. Covering one square block, this indoor market is a maze of tiny passageways and various stalls selling everything from live chickens to deer heads. There are also vendors of fruit, herbs, goldfish (bred to astonishing varieties and thought to bring good luck), tea, fish, flowers, and soy beans. Many of these vendors also display wares at an open-air market down the street. The best time to visit the market is between 10:30am and noon, when it's at its busiest. To reach it, take bus 78K from Fanling railway station to Luen Wo Road, which runs right alongside the market.

Sheung Shui

Sheung Shui Heung is an ancient village located about 300 yards north of the main town. Although much of its charm has been lost with the construction of modern buildings all around it, it's still more peaceful than other old villages that are closer to the beaten path. Look for **Man Shek Tong,** a small ancestral hall belonging to the Liu clan, once the most prominent family of the Sheung Shui district. In 1688 there were as many as 500 members of the Liu clan living in district, and Man Shek Tong was erected in 1751 at the height of the clan's power and wealth. Consisting of a long central courtyard with one main hall and smaller halls on both sides, Man Shek Tong is set in a pleasant garden in the middle of the old village and boasts wood-carvings, traditional Chinese mural paintings, and pottery figurines on the ridge of the roof.

Where to Eat

I suggest that you eat at the same place the HKTA selected for its "The Land Between" Tour, **Yucca de Lac Restaurant,** in a part of sprawling Shatin called Ma Liu Shui (tel. 6921835). The easiest way to get here is by taxi, from either the University or Shatin station. This Cantonese restaurant has more than 200 items on its menu, including duck, pigeon, pork, beef, chicken, seafood, and tofu dishes. You might want to try fried chicken with lemon sauce, diced pork with cashew nuts, or fried filet of garoupa with green pepper. Dishes range from HK$38 to HK$90 ($4.95 to $11.75). If it's fine weather, you'll want to sit outside on its terrace overlooking the harbor, which gives the restaurant a slightly European atmosphere. The restaurant is open daily from 11am to 11pm.

THROUGH KOWLOON TO THE NEW TERRITORIES BY MTR

Hong Kong's Mass Transit Railway (MTR) can whisk passengers from the heart of Central or Tsimshatsui to the outermost limit of Kowloon in a mere 30 minutes.

Jordan

A part of Kowloon rather than the New Territories, this is the first stop after Tsimshatsui and contains both the Jade Market and Temple Street Night Market, described in Chapter VIII under "Markets."

Mongkok

If you're a bird-lover just as many Chinese are, you might want to visit **Hong Lok Street** with its markets of caged birds. It's a five-minute walk from Mongkok Station. Walk westward along Argyle Street until you reach Hong Lok Street. If you backtrack and walk eastward on Argyle Street, you'll reach **Tung Choi Street** in about 10 minutes, popularly known as Lady's Market. Stalls here sell clothing, shoes, and accessories, including scarves, belts, and hats. It's open from about 10am to late afternoon daily.

Mei Foo

Both the Sung Dynasty Village and Lai Chi Kok Amusement Park are located about a 10-minute walk from Mei Foo Station. Consult Chapter VII for more information.

Tsuen Wan

The last stop on the western line of the MTR, Tsuen Wan is also a convenient jumping-off point for bus trips through the New Territories, especially to the Kam Tin Walled Village.

Just a few minute's walk from Tsuen Wan Station, the **Sam Tung Uk Museum,** Kwu Uk Lane, Tsuen Wan, New Territories (tel. 4412001), is actually a restored Hakka walled village. Built in the 18th century by members of the farming Chan clan, it's typical of a rural walled village and is a tiny oasis of tile-roofed houses in the midst of modern high-rise housing projects. It contains four houses restored to their original condition, an ancestral hall, two rows of side houses, and an exhibition hall. On display are farm implements and traditional Chinese furniture, including elegant blackwood furniture. The museum is open Wednesday through Monday from

9am to 4pm; closed Tuesday, December 24 and 25, January 1, and the first three days of the Chinese New Year. Admission is free.

KAM TIN WALLED VILLAGE

Traveling in the New Territories, you quickly notice women wearing wide-brimmed hats with black fringes and pajamalike clothing, and many of them have gold-capped teeth as well. These are Hakka women, as are most of the farmers of the New Territories. They keep to themselves, preserving their customs and dialect. While most hate to have their photographs taken because they think it steals something from their spirit, some will oblige for money. In fact, don't be surprised if you're instantly approached by Hakka women and asked to take their picture—they've learned that it's an easy way to make an extra couple of Hong Kong dollars (be sure to settle on a price before you start clicking away).

At any rate, during the Ming Dynasty (1368–1644) some of the Hakka clans in the area of the New Territories built walls around their homes to protect themselves against roving bandits and invaders. A handful of these still exist today, and are still homes of the Hakkas. Before visiting any of the walled villages, you should first stop off at the Sam Tung Uk Museum in Tsuen Wan, described above. It will make your visit to a lived-in walled village more enriching. What's more, Tsuen Wan is the logical starting point for a trip to a walled village.

Hakka walled villages include Kut Hing Wei, Shui Tau, Kam Hing Wai, Kam Tsin Wai, and Shek Tsin Wai. Of these, Kut Hing Wei is the most famous. Popularly known as Kam Tin, it's home of about 400 descendants of the Tang clan, who built the village back in the 1600s. The village is completely surrounded by 18-foot-thick walls, and there is only one narrow entrance. Admission to Kam Tin is HK$.50 (6¢).

To reach Kam Tin, take bus 51 from the Tai Ho Road overpass, which is located above the Tsuen Wan MTR station. Your bus will take you over the hills along scenic Route Twisk. Get off at the last stop and then continue walking in the same direction the bus was going. Kam Tin is less than five minutes away, on your left.

---

2. The Outlying Islands

In addition to Hong Kong Island there are 235 outlying islands, most of them barren and uninhabited. Because construction in the New Territories is booming, the islands of Hong Kong now offer the best opportunity for observing rural Chinese life. What's more, they're also easy to get to—all you have to do is hop on a ferry in Central and then sit back and enjoy the view.

Three of the most accessible islands are Lantau, Cheung Chau, and Lamma. Ferries depart approximately every hour or so from the Central District on Hong Kong Island. Those bound for Lantau or Cheung Chau depart from the Outlying Districts Services Pier, while those heading for Lamma leave from the Central Harbour Services Pier. Both piers are located about a five-minute walk west from the Star Ferry concourse (if you're getting off the Star Ferry, turn right and then walk along the waterfront).

You can purchase your ticket at the piers before departure, but remember to avoid going on a Sunday, when ferries are packed with city folks on family outings. Fares are also slightly higher on Sunday, although the most you'll ever pay for a ticket is HK$12 ($1.55), which is for deluxe class on Sunday. Only ferries to Lantau and Cheung Chau have deluxe class, and I highly recommend them. They have an open deck out back, which is a great place to sit when the weather is fine, sipping on a coffee or beer and watching the harbor float past. Fares for ordinary class are HK$4 to HK$6 (50¢ to 80¢) one way.

On Saturday afternoon and Sunday there is additional ferry service from Tsimshatsui's Star Ferry concourse to Lantau and Cheung Chau. Tickets for these, however, must be purchased in advance at Ticketmate counters of MTR stations (there's one at the Tsimshatsui MTR station) and service is less frequent. For inquiries, call 5423081.

For information on ferry schedules, drop by the HKTA for a copy of their free timetables. In addition, be sure also to pick up a copy of the "Outlying Islands" leaflet provided free by the HKTA. If you plan on doing extensive hiking on the islands, inexpensive maps of the trails are available at the Government Publications Centre, located right by Central's Star Ferry terminal.

LANTAU

Twice the size of Hong Kong Island, Lantau is the colony's largest island. But whereas Hong Kong Island has a population of more than a million, Lantau has about 16,000. County parks make up about half of the island, with 43 miles of marked hiking trails. Lantau is an island of high peaks, remote and isolated beaches, small villages, temples, and monasteries. Inhabited since Neolithic times, Lantau supported people engaged in fishing, salt making, and lime burning for centuries.

Taking a ferry from Hong Kong Island, you'll arrive in about an hour at Silvermine Bay, known as Mui Wo in Chinese. It has a hotel fronting the bay and some outdoor restaurants (more on these later), but otherwise there isn't much of interest here. In front of the ferry pier is where you can catch buses going to other parts of the island, including Po Lin Monastery, Tung Chung, Tai O, Pui O, and Cheung Sha.

What to See and Do

The most famous attraction on Lantau is the **Po Lin Monastery** (tel. 9855113), largest and best known of the 135 Buddhist monasteries located on Lantau. Situated on the plateau of Ngong Ping at an elevation of 2,460 feet, the monastery was first established near the turn of the century by reclusive monks, with the present buildings dating from 1921. The main temple is very ornate and houses three magnificent bronze statues of Buddha. The land-

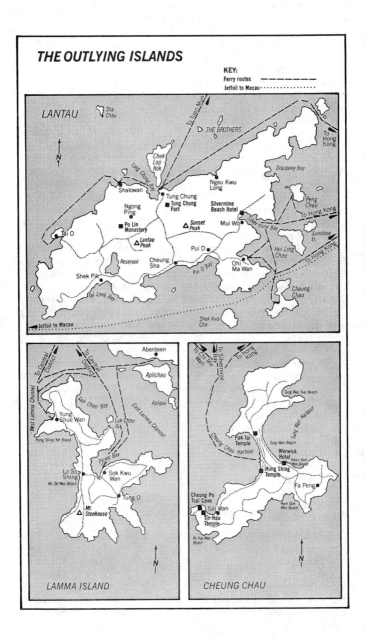

THE OUTLYING ISLANDS

KEY:
Ferry routes — — — — —
Jetfoil to Macau · · · · · · · · ·

LANTAU

Sha Chau

To Tuen Mun

THE BROTHERS

To Hong Kong

Discovery Bay

Chek Lap Kok

Tung Chung Bay

Ngau Kwu Long

Shalowan

Tung Chung
Tung Chung Fort

Silvermine Beach Hotel

Peng Chau

To Hong Kong

Ngong Ping

Po Lin Monastery

Sunset Peak

Mui Wo

Silvermine Bay

Sunshine Is.

Tai O

Lantau Peak

Pui O

Hei Ling Chau

To Hong Kong

Reservoir

Cheung Sha

Ohi Ma Wan

Shek Pik

Pui O Bay

Cheung Chau

Tai Long Bay

Shek Kwu Cha

Jetfoil to Macau

Aberdeen

To Central Cheung

To Central District

West Lamma Channel

Aplichau

Aplipai

Luk Chau Bay

Yung Shue Wan

Luk Chau Is.

East Lamma Channel

Hung Shing Yeh Beach

Picnic Bay

Lo So Shing

Sok Kwu Wan

Mo Tat Wan Beach

Tung O

Mt. Stenhouse

LAMMA ISLAND

To Ohi Ma Wan

To Silvermine Bay

To Hong Kong

Tung Wan Tsai Beach

Luk Wan Harbour

Pak Tai Temple

Tung Wan Beach

Warwick Hotel

Cheung Chau Harbour

Kwun Yam Wan Beach

Hung Shing Temple

Fa Peng

Cheung Po Tsai Cave

Nam Tam Wan Beach

Sai Wan

Tin Hau Temple

Po Yue Wan Beach

CHEUNG CHAU

scape around the monastery is empty and peaceful, good for long solitary walks; and if you want, you can climb to Lantau Peak (3,064 feet above sea level). Close to the monastery is a tea plantation, and that monstrosity on the side of hill is Southeast Asia's tallest Buddha, more than 100 feet tall, weighing 250 tons, and costing HK$68 million ($8.8 million).

But the main reason people come to Po Lin is to eat. It's famous for its vegetarian lunches, served in a big dining hall. And if you don't mind austere surroundings, you can also spend the night here (see "Where to Eat and Stay" below).

From Po Lin you can catch a bus, or, as I suggest, walk the two hours to the village of **Tai O,** Lantau's most interesting village. Tai O wraps itself around the muddy waters of a bay on the west coast of the island. Although parts of the outskirts of town are being developed, the old core of the village has no cars on its narrow, twisting streets, no neon signs, no high-rises of concrete and steel. Instead there are one-story wooden houses resting on stilts above the mud of the bay. Life is unhurried and relaxed. You can hear the click-clicking of adults playing mah-jongg all day long.

Once the center of Lantau's salt-panning industry, the village is divided in two by a creek, and the only way to get across is by a flat-bottom boat which is pulled along a rope strung across the water. The women working the boat charge HK$0.20 (2¢) for the trip. There are several temples in Tai O, the best known of which is Kwan Tai, on Market Street, dedicated to the god of war and righteousness. Another popular temple is Hau Wong, facing the sea at the end of Market Street. There are also some fish-processing shops and open-fronted stores selling Chinese herbs and hardware.

If you're interested in old forts, go to Tung Chung on the north shore of Lantau (buses go there rather infrequently from Silvermine Bay, and you can also walk there from Po Lin Monastery in about three hours). The fort here was built in 1817 and its ruins today hold six cannon.

As for **beaches,** two that have lifeguards on weekends in the summer, changing rooms, and toilets are Pui O and Cheung Sha. The most accessible, Cheung Sha, is a two-mile-long white sandy beach on the south side of the island, about a 15-minute bus ride from Silvermine Bay.

Where to Eat and Stay

▪ **Po Lin Monastery,** Ngong Ping (tel. 9855113). *Prices:* Fixed-price lunch HK$33 ($4.30).

This is the most famous place to eat or spend the night on the island. Only one fixed-price meal is served, which includes soup, vegetarian dishes, and rice. Buy your lunch ticket from the monastery's office, located to the right after entering the temple grounds and across from the dining hall. Your main dishes will be brought to your table, but you should help yourself to soup and rice at the front of the dining hall.

As for accommodations, it's nothing more than hard bunk

beds, and you can expect breakfast to look pretty much like the dinner you had the night before. It was lights out at 6:30pm the night I was there, with breakfast served at 7:30am. If you want, you can climb Lantau Peak to watch the sunrise.

Open: Lunch served daily noon–6pm.

RATES FOR OVERNIGHT STAY: HK$145 ($18.75), including three meals.

- **Silvermine Beach Hotel,** Silvermine Bay (tel. 9848295). 78 rms. `A/C` `FRIDGE` `TV` `TEL`

Located about a seven-minute walk from the ferry pier in Silvermine Beach, this is one of Lantau's few hotels and is the most easily accessible. It faces the waterfront and its restaurant serves Cantonese and Western dishes. Selections include shark's fin, bird's nest, abalone, pigeon, seafood, chicken, duck, pork, beef, and vegetable dishes, most in the HK$40 to HK$60 ($5.20 to $7.80) range. Rooms, simple and a bit dull, are discounted 20% Sunday through Thursday.

Facilities: One restaurant, one outdoor swimming pool.

RATES: HK$360–HK$420 ($47–$54) double; extra bed HK$50 ($6.50).

- **Sang Lee,** Chung Hau Rd., Silvermine Bay (tel. 9848478). *Prices:* Most dishes HK$15–HK$30 ($1.95–$3.90).

This is probably the most fun and festive place to dine in Silvermine Bay, and it's outdoors to boot. It specializes in fresh seafood, including barbecued fish, squid fried with spiced salt, fried rice Singapore style, steamed fish, crab, and clams. To reach it, take a right out of the ferry dock and follow the sidewalk next to the water. The restaurant is soon on your left, easily recognizable by its string of white lights. It's open throughout the year.

Open: Daily 11am–midnight. SEAFOOD

- **Tai O Seafood Restaurant,** 15 Wing On St., Tai O (tel. 9857094). *Prices:* Meals average HK$60–HK$130 ($7.80–$17).

At the other end of the island on the main street of Tai O, this simple restaurant serves Cantonese food as well as seafood, specializing in clam dishes. This place opens early for all those early-rising fisherfolk.

Open: Daily 5am–midnight. CANTONESE

CHEUNG CHAU

If you have only a few hours to spare and don't want to worry about catching buses and finding your way around, Cheung Chau is your best bet. About an hour's ride from Central, it's a tiny island only a square mile in area, but more than 20,000 people live here in a thriving fishing village. There are no cars on the island, making it a delightful place for walking around and exploring.

Inhabited for at least 2,500 years by fisherfolk and serving as a haven for smugglers and pirates until as recently as the 1920s, Cheung Chau still supports a sizable population of fishing families. The waterfront where the ferry lands, known as the Praya, buzzes with activity as vendors sell fish, lobster, and vegetables.

What to See and Do

About 10% of Cheung Chau's people live on junks in the harbor, and one of the things to do here is take a *kai do,* or water taxi, past the junks to Sai Wan—it should cost no more than HK$5 (65¢) and may even be cheaper than that; board it at the public pier next to the ferry pier. I like this harbor more than Aberdeen, and I find it amazing how many families keep dogs on board their boats. At Sai Wan there's a temple dedicated to **Tin Hau,** goddess of the sea and protectress of fisherfolk. From here it's about a 30-minute walk back to the Praya.

As for the village itself, it's threaded through with tiny alleyways and with shops offering noodles and rice, teakwood coffins, and haircuts. Through open doors you can see tailor shops, basket weaving, soy sauce manufacturing, and jade carving. Junks are built on Cheung Chau after a design hardly changed in centuries, entirely from memory and without the aid of blueprints. If you walk down narrow **Tung Wan Road** (almost in front of the ferry and leading away from the Praya), you'll pass lots of open-fronted shops, as well as a gnarled old banyan tree, considered the dwelling place of the spirit of health and fertility. At the end of Tung Wan Road is **Tung Wan Beach,** the most popular beach on the island. One more place of interest is **Pak Tai Temple** at the northern end of the village and built in 1783.

Where to Eat and Stay

• **Warwick Hotel,** Tung Wan Beach, Cheung Chau (tel. 9810081). 70 rms. A/C TV TEL

If you want to spend a few nights away from the hustle and bustle of Hong Kong to unwind and relax, this may be the place to do so. It's located on the south end of Cheung Chau's most popular beach, and next to the hotel is a place where you can rent windsurfing boards and paddleboats. It's also a good place for a meal, with two restaurants serving Western and Chinese food. A meal at either averages about HK$85 ($11). In the summer you can dine on the terrace with a view of the beach.

As for rooms, those facing the beach are slightly more expensive, but they're worth it.

Facilities: Outdoor swimming pool, bar, two restaurants.

RATES: HK$460–HK$520 ($60–$68), single or double; **15%** more on Saturday nights. AE, DC, MC, V.

• **Amego Café,** 31 Praya St. (tel. 9810710). *Prices:* Most dishes less than HK$16 ($2.10).

Easy to find right on Cheung Chau's waterfront (and located just to the right as you disembark from the ferry), it serves easy-to-prepare snacks and Western dishes, including sandwiches, spaghetti, omelets, hamburgers, fried rice, ice cream, shakes, and daily specials. Cheap and simple.

Open: Daily 11:30am–11pm. SNACKS/SANDWICHES.

• **Bor Kee Restaurant,** 16 Tung Wan Rd. (tel. 9812328). *Prices:* Meals average HK$50 ($6.50).

Located on the village's main passageway that links the Praya with Tung Wan Beach, this is a Cantonese restaurant with an open façade and a cafeterialike appearance. There are also some tables outside. It doesn't look like much, but what it lacks in character is more than made up for by its seafood. It has a long menu, but most prices aren't given so it's best just to ask what's fresh and available. There are usually also pigeon, chicken, and duck selections.

Open: Daily 10am–10pm. CANTONESE

- **Frog and Toad,** Tai Long Village, Lantau (tel. 9892300). *Prices:* Average meal HK$60 ($7.80).

Although it's actually located on nearby Lantau Island, this restaurant/bar is most easily reached from Cheung Chau via a 20-minute sampan ride. Simply tell the sampan driver "Tai Long Wan," which means Big Wave Bay. Cost of the trip will be about HK$50 ($6.50), but be sure to bargain and settle the fee beforehand. You'll find yourself deposited at a pier on a seemingly deserted beach, but if you follow a trail leading inland from the middle of the beach (where you'll also see a sign), you'll soon come to a tiny settlement and the Frog and Toad.

Owned by several expatriates, this mellow establishment serves as a day-trip getaway for people in the know, many of whom come here to relax in the rural setting. It serves a barbecue which includes ribs, chicken wings, sausage, and salad. If you want seafood, order it in advance. There's a veranda where you can sit outside on fine days, and when you're ready to leave, simply tell the man behind the bar. He'll call Cheung Chau and have a sampan sent on its way.

Open: Daily 11am–"when the last customer leaves." Telephone before coming, to make sure they're open. BARBECUE

- **Garden Café Pub,** 84 Tung Wan Rd. (tel. 9814610). *Prices:* American breakfast HK$33 ($4.30); most dishes and snacks HK$12–HK$30 ($1.55–$3.90).

Located on the village's main passageway between the Praya and the beach, this simple café is the local foreigner hangout and serves European food. Its specialty is a steak-and-mushroom pie or its pork pie, and other selections include sandwiches, fish and chips, chicken or beef curry, omelets, salads, and snacks. Some of the best things about this place are its tables outside and the small beer garden across the street.

Open: Daily 10am–midnight. WESTERN

- **King's Café,** 25 Praya St. (tel. 9810878). *Prices:* Most dishes HK$11–HK$35 ($1.45–$4.55).

This simple establishment is on the Praya, to the left as you disembark from the ferry. It serves Western-style food and snacks such as spaghetti, curry rice, soups, omelets, salads, ice cream, shakes, and beer. Although the food isn't great, prices are low, and there are some tables and chairs outside where you have a wonderful view of the action on the Praya and on the junks anchored close by.

Open: Thurs–Tues noon–midnight. *Closed:* Wed. SNACKS

- **Sea Pearl,** Cheung Chau Harbour (tel. 9818153). *Prices:* Meals HK$30–HK$110 ($3.90–$14.25).

A gaily painted floating restaurant anchored in Cheung Chau's harbor, it specializes in fresh Cantonese seafood, but also serves such dishes as roast chicken or pigeon, sweet-and-sour pork, or sliced beef with noodles. Very popular with vacationing Chinese, it's reached via a free shuttle service from the public pier (located to the right as you disembark from the ferry from Hong Kong Island). The shuttle boat won't have any English sign on it, but look for the yellow flag with red Chinese characters hoisted on its roof.

Open: Daily noon–9pm. CANTONESE

LAMMA

Lamma is the island to visit if you want to do some pleasant hiking or eat fresh seafood on a peaceful waterfront. The closest of the outlying islands and only 45 minutes by ferry from Central, Lamma is Hong Kong's third-largest island and has a population of only 3,000, with much of its area still undeveloped. There are no cars on the island, and a two-hour hiking trail connects Lamma's two main villages, Sok Kwu Wan and Yung Shue Wan, both served by frequent ferries from Hong Kong Island.

What to See and Do

Yung Shue Wan, which translates as "Banyan Tree Bay," is Lamma's main town. It used to be small and undeveloped, but new houses and shops have sprung up the past decade on its hillsides, and the town is unfortunately overshadowed by an unsightly power station.

At any rate, as you hike out of Yung Shue Wan, you'll pass vegetable patches and green quilts of neatly cultivated fields, watered by villagers who balance two watering cans on a pole slung across their shoulders. After about 30 minutes you'll pass one of Lamma's three beaches, **Hung Shing Yeh,** which has changing facilities, showers, toilets, and lifeguards on duty in the summer. However, since it's close to that power station, you may wait until you reach Lo So Shing or Mo Tat Wan Beach.

As you continue hiking, the path climbs higher onto barren and windswept hills, finally giving way to lush and verdant valleys and then **Sok Kwu Wan.** The hike takes about 1½ hours and is a true delight. If you feel like hiking farther, pass through Sok Kwu Wan and continue about 20 minutes to the east, where you'll eventually reach **Mo Tat Wan Beach.** There are, however, no lifeguards here. While you're in the area, check out the village of **Mo Tat,** about 400 years old and the oldest settlement on the island. It consists of a handful of crumbling old houses inhabited mainly by old people and sits inland, picturesquely amid banana trees and lush countryside.

As for Sok Kwu Wan, it's famous for its open-air seafood restaurants. They're lined up one after the other along the small waterfront, extended over the water on stilts and offering views of the harbor. I suggest that you simply walk along the waterfront and choose one that strikes your fancy, but if you want a specific recommendation, here are some to choose from.

Where to Eat

- **Peach Garden Sea Food Restaurant,** 11 Sok Kwu Wan, waterfront of Sok Kwu Wan (tel. 9828581). *Prices:* Average meal HK$80 ($10.50).

This waterfront establishment is pleasant, with outside dining, white tablecloths, and a view of the harbor. It serves seafood Cantonese style. Try its baked, buttered lobster or spicy squid. There are also fried prawns with black pepper, crab, fish, scallops, clams, pigeon, and chicken dishes.

Open: Daily 10am–10pm. CANTONESE

- **Shum Kee Restaurant,** 26 1st St., waterfront of Sok Kwu Wan (tel. 9828241). *Prices:* Average meal HK$85 ($11).

Similar to the other restaurants along the waterfront, it offers dining with a view of the water and Cantonese-style seafood. Going also by the name Lamma Hilton, it serves scallops, clams, fish, crabs, lobster, prawns, abalone, squid, chicken, beef, pork, and egg dishes. Specialties include spicy shrimp and chili crab dishes.

Open: Daily 10am–11pm. CANTONESE

- **Man Fung Restaurant,** 5 Yung Shue Wan St., Yung Shue Wan (tel. 9820719). *Prices:* Meals run about HK$60–HK$80 ($7.80–$10.50).

If you end up hungry at the other end of the island, this restaurant near the ferry pier has outdoor seating where you have a view of the sea. Its specialties are pigeon, locally caught seafood, oysters from New Zealand, and dim sum. There's a fixed-price menu for two people for HK$180 ($23.50) which includes steamed fish, locally grown vegetables, fried rice, and a choice of fried crab with ginger and onion or roast pigeon. There are also wines from France, Portugal, and Italy.

Open: Daily 6am–10pm. CANTONESE

- **The Island Bar,** 6 Yung Shue Wan St., Yung Shue Wan (tel. 9821376). *Prices:* Drinks average HK$20–HK$30 ($2.60–$3.90).

Located next to Man Fung Restaurant on the waterfront, this is a bar and a local *gwailo* (foreign) hangout. Owned by a Brit who came to Hong Kong more than a decade ago, it's a comfortable place to wait for the next ferry.

Open: Mon–Fri 6pm–2am; Sat, Sun, and hols noon–2am.

---

3. Trips to China

Hong Kong serves as a major gateway for travelers going to the People's Republic of China. Most visitors to the mainland join organized tours that last anywhere from one day to several weeks. The following are two of the best-known agencies for trips to China.

If you want to go to China on your own, **China Travel Service,** 77 Queen's Rd., Central District (tel. 5252284), and 27-33 Nathan Rd., Tsimshatsui (tel. 2113311), can arrange for your visa, and it's best to make your visa application at least two working days prior to departure. However, there is same-day visa service if you get your application in early in the morning. Visas cost HK$100 ($13), except for same-day visas which cost HK$200 ($26). CTS also organizes tours and makes hotel reservations in China. The Central District office is open Monday through Friday from 9am to 5:30pm and on Saturday from 9am to 5pm. The Tsimshatsui office is also open Sunday and holidays from 9am to 1pm and 2 to 5pm.

A large travel agency, **Swire Travel Ltd.,** 18th Floor, Swire House, 9 Connaught Rd., Central (tel. 8448482), organizes a wide range of tours of China, ranging from 1 to 20 days. Stop by their office for one of their colorful booklets. It's open Monday through Friday from 9am to 5:30pm and on Saturday from 9am to noon.

MACAU

Macau is something of an anomaly in Asia. For one thing, it still serves as Portugal's last stronghold in Asia, though that will change when the territory reverts to Chinese authority in 1999. Still, it's a wonder Macau has lasted this long. Hanging from China's gigantic underbelly on its southeastern coast, Macau is all of six square miles. Portugal's other Asian strongholds, Goa and Malacca, have long been claimed by neighboring powers. And although Portuguese is the official language, 95% of its 400,000 residents are Chinese, which means that you hardly ever hear the official language. In fact, you're probably better off with English than with Portuguese. Architecturally, Macau is a cross between Chinese and Portuguese.

According to the 1989 *Guinness Book of World Records,* Macau is the most populous territory in the world, with 63,225 people living per square mile (Hong Kong is listed as the most populous colony). And yet Macau does not seem crowded. Compared to Hong Kong, it's a small and unpretentious provincial town, reminding oldtimers of what Hong Kong used to look like 40 years ago.

With its mixture of Portuguese and Chinese influences, Macau has a charm all its own. Somehow it *feels* different from Hong Kong, different from China, different from anywhere else. Maybe it's the jumble of Chinese signs and stores mixed in with crumbling colonial-style buildings, the temples alongside Catholic churches, the flair of Portugal blended with the practicality of the Chinese. In any case, Macau makes for an interesting excursion of a day or more.

Although its casinos are undoubtedly its main attraction, especially for Hong Kong's Chinese, there are also churches, fortresses, temples, and gardens to explore—but don't expect grand edifices or any of the world's great wonders. If, on the other hand, one of your favorite traveling pastimes is simply wandering through neighborhoods and absorbing the daily life, Macau is sure to grow on you.

What's more, Macau's hotels are much cheaper than their counterparts in Hong Kong, which means that you can live in luxury in Macau for a fraction of what you'd pay in the British colony.

1. A Brief Historical Background

Macau was born centuries before Hong Kong was even conceived. Portuguese ships first landed in southern China in 1513, and in 1557 Portugal acquired Macau from the Chinese. Before long, Macau had achieved a virtual monopoly on trade between China, Japan, and Europe, making the city Portugal's most important trading center in Asia and the Orient's greatest port in the early 1600s.

As the only Europeans engaged in trade in Asia, the Portuguese made a fortune acting as middlemen. Every spring, Portuguese ships laden with Indian goods and European crystal and wines would sail out of Goa, stop in Malacca to trade for spices, drop in on Macau for silk brought down from China, and then travel on to Nagasaki, where the silk would be traded for silver, swords, lacquerware, and other Japanese treasures. Using the monsoon winds, the ships would then sail back to Macau, trade silver for more silk and porcelain, and then return to Goa, where the lacquerware, porcelain, silk, and other exotic Oriental goods were shipped to eager customers in Europe. The complete circuit from Goa and back took several years.

As Macau grew and prospered, it also served as an important base for the introduction of Christianity to China and Japan. Macau became a springboard for Jesuit missionaries, churches were built, and Asian Christians sought refuge on its shores.

Needless to say, because of Macau's obvious prosperity, it soon attracted jealous attention from other European nations. The Dutch tried to invade Macau several times in the first decades of the 1600s, but were repelled each time.

Then, in the 1630s, Japan closed its doors to foreign trade, admitting only the Dutch. Macau's final blow came in 1841, when the British established their own colony on Hong Kong Island, only 40 miles from Macau. As Hong Kong's deep natural harbor attracted the trading ships and Hong Kong leapt into the forefront, Macau lost its importance and slowly sank into obscurity.

Today Macau is experiencing something of a revival, with the growth of several resort hotels and increased transportation service to and from Hong Kong. On December 22, 1999, Portugal's 400 years of rule will come to an end, when Macau becomes a special administrative region of China. Like Hong Kong, Macau will be allowed its own internal government and economic system for another 50 years after the Chinese take over.

---

2. Orientation

Entry procedures into Macau are very simple. If you are American, Canadian, Australian, or British, you do not need a visa for Macau for stays up to 90 days—all you need is your passport. What's more, even though the **pataca** is Macau's official currency, you can use your Hong Kong dollars everywhere in Macau, even in buses and for taxis (though change is likely to be given back in patacas). The pataca is pegged to the Hong Kong dollar at the rate of 103.30 patacas to HK$100, but on the street and in hotels and shops the Macau pataca and Hong Kong dollar are treated as equal denominations. I suppose, therefore, that you could save a minuscule amount by exchanging your money into pataca, but I have never done so and don't consider it worth the hassle. You may wish to exchange a small amount—say, HK$20 ($2.60)—into patacas for taxis, buses, and admission fees, but keep in mind that the pataca is not accepted in Hong Kong. For the sake of simplicity, all prices below are quoted in "HK$," but could equally read "patacas."

The **international telephone country code** is 853.

GETTING THERE

Located only 40 miles from Hong Kong across the mouth of the Pearl River, Macau is easily accessible by ferry, hoverferry, hydrofoil, jetcat, or jetfoil (there is no airport in Macau). Most departures are from the Macau Ferry Terminal, 200 Connaught Road, Central, on Hong Kong Island. On the Kowloon side, there is also limited service by hoverferries, jetfoils, and hydrofoils from the new China Hong Kong Terminal on Canton Road, Tsimshatsui, where boats also depart for China. In any case, the Hong Kong government levies a HK$15 ($1.95) departure tax for those traveling to Macau.

The fastest way to travel is by **jetfoil,** which departs from Central about every half hour until 5 pm in winter and 6 pm in summer and reaches Macau in about 55 minutes. There's even night service, with hourly departures until 2 am. One-way fares are HK$75 ($9.75) for first class and HK$65 ($8.45) for economy class; fares are HK$5 (65¢) higher on weekends and holidays.

As for the other modes of transportation, both the **hydrofoils** and **jetcats** take about 75 minutes and cost HK$46 ($5.95) one way on weekdays, HK$58 ($7.55) on weekends. The longest trips are via **ferry,** which take about 2½ hours and start at HK$12 ($1.55) for a deck chair.

You can make bookings for jetfoil, jetcat, and hydrofoil with VISA, Diners Club, and American Express by calling 8593288. You can also purchase tickets at both Macau ferry piers in Hong Kong and at Ticketmate counters in some MTR stations. If you are going on weekends or holidays, it's wise to buy round-trip tickets well in advance.

TOURIST INFORMATION

Your first stop for information about Macau should be at Hong Kong's Kai Tak Airport, where in the arrivals lobby you'll find a counter for the **Macau Tourist Information Bureau.** Open from 9am to 10:30pm daily, it stocks leaflets and pamphlets about hotels and sightseeing in Macau. There's another Macau Tourist Information Bureau at the Macau Ferry Terminal, Room 305 of the Shun Tak Centre, 200 Connaught Road, in Central. It's open from 9am to 1pm and 2 to 5pm Monday through Friday and from 9am to 1pm on Saturday. Be sure to pick up a map of Macau, as well as a tourist tabloid called *Macau Talk.* If you enjoy do-it-yourself walking tours, be sure to get the free "Macau Walking Tours" pamphlet which gives a street-by-street account of several easy hikes. Its maps are also better than the one given out by the tourist office.

In Macau itself, there's a tourist information counter at the arrivals pier for guidance to your hotel, but your best bet is the **Tourist Information Center** on the ground floor of the Sintra Hotel, avenida da Amizada (tel. 338085, 510670, or 561167). It's open daily from 9am to 6pm.

GETTING AROUND MACAU

Macau is made up of a small peninsula that contains the city of Macau, as well as two small islands called Taipa and Coloane linked to the mainland by bridges.

Because the peninsula is only 2.5 miles in length and a mile at its greatest width, you can **walk** to most of the city's major sights. The main road of the town is avenida de Almeida Ribeiro; the prettiest walk is along rua da Praia Grande and avenida da República.

If you get tired, you can always jump into one of the 585 licensed **taxis,** all painted black and beige and with meters. The charge is HK$4.50 ($5.85) at flagfall and includes the first 5,000 feet. Thereafter it's HK$.60 (8¢) every 825 feet. Luggage costs one pataca, and there's a surcharge of HK$5 (65¢) if you go to Taipa and HK$10 ($1.30) to Coloane. There is no surcharge, however, for the return journey to Macau.

There are **public buses** that run from 7am to midnight, with most fares from HK$.50 to HK$2 (6¢ to 25¢). Bus 3, for example, travels from in front of the ferry pier past the Lisboa Hotel to the main street, avenida de Almeida Ribeiro. Buses going to Taipa and Coloane islands stop for passengers at the bus stop in front of the Hotel Lisboa, located on the mainland near the bridge.

There are also **pedicabs,** tricycles with seating for two passengers. These cyclists charge about HK$40 ($5.20) for an hour of sightseeing, but keep in mind that there are many hilly sights you can't see by pedicab. You should settle on the fare before climbing in.

And finally, if you want to drive around on your own, you can see Macau by **Moke,** which are small, Jeep-like vehicles. Drivers must be at least 21 years old and have held a driver's license for at least two years. Visitors from Australia, New Zealand, the United States, and United Kingdom need only a valid driver's license, but Canadians must have an international driver's license. Mokes rent for about HK$250 ($32.50) per day on weekdays and HK$310 ($40.25) per day on weekends and holidays. They are available from **Macau Mokes** (tel. 378851), located right next to the Macau pier, or can be delivered to your hotel. In Hong Kong, you can obtain information about Mokes by calling 5434190. Driving in Macau is on the right.

---

3. What to See and Do

THE TOP ATTRACTIONS

The most famous structure in Macau is the ruin of **St. Paul's Church,** on rua de São Paulo. Crowning the top of a hill in the center of the city and approached by a grand sweep of stairs, only its ornate façade remains. It was designed by an Italian Jesuit and built in the early 1600s with the help of Japanese Christians who had fled persecution in Nagasaki. In 1835, during a typhoon, the church caught fire and burned to the ground, leaving only its now-famous façade.

There's a good view from the top steps of St. Paul, but if you walk just a few minutes farther uphill you'll have an even grander view from the nearby **Citadel of São Paulo do Monte,** also called Monte Fort. It was built by the Jesuits about the same time as St. Paul, to guard the city from Western enemies and was capable of withstanding a siege for two years. The cannons were used only once, however, in 1622 when Macau was attacked by the Dutch. In its one moment of glory, the fort's cannons fired a shot that landed right on a Dutch powder keg. At any rate, Monte Fort was largely destroyed by the same fire that consumed St. Paul, but there are still wall remnants and cannon here, and it has been turned into a public park that is open from dawn until dusk. As for that lighthouse you see in the distance, that's part of Guia Fort, which occupies the highest point of Macau.

For Portuguese colonial architecture, the most outstanding building is considered to be the **Leal Senado** (Loyal Senate) at largo de Senado in the heart of the city. You can enter to see the carved stone plaques, wrought-iron gate, garden, and the public library. Another historical building is the **Luís de Camões Museum,** located on Praca Luis de Camões, which dates from the 18th century and served as the headquarters of the East India Company Select Committee. Named after Portugal's most famous poet, the museum contains porcelain, paintings by Guangdong masters and Westerners, and portraits of Mandarins and their wives. The museum is open every day except Wednesday from 11am to 5pm and admission is HK$1 (15¢). Adjacent to the museum is the **Camões Garden and Grotto.**

As for Chinese influences, there are many temples in Macau. One of the most important is the **Temple of Kun Iam,** on avenida do Coronel Mesquita. Its present buildings date from 1627, but the most important historical event that took place at this largest and wealthiest of Macau's Buddhist temples was the 1844 signing of the first treaty of trade and friendship between the United States and China. The round granite table where the treaty was signed is still here. The stairs of the main temple are guarded by stone lions, and it's said that if you turn the stone ball they hold in their mouths three times to the left you'll have good luck. The temple contains images of Buddha, as well as the goddess of mercy dressed in the costume of a Chinese bride. There's also, curiously enough, a small gold lacquer statue of Marco Polo with bulging eyes and a moustache; he was considered one of the 18 wise men of China. Behind the temple is a landscaped Chinese garden, with four banyan trees with intertwined branches, popularly known as the Lovers' Tree.

Another important temple is the **Temple of A-Ma,** situated at the bottom of Barra Hill at the entrance to the Inner Harbour. It is Macau's oldest Chinese temple, with parts of it dating back more than 600 years. This temple is dedicated to A-Ma, goddess of seafarers, and it was after this temple that the Portuguese named their city —A-Ma-Gao—or Bay of A-Ma; it's been shortened to Macau now, of course. The temple contains images of A-Ma and stone carvings of a Chinese junk.

Lou Lim Iok Garden, located on estrada de Adolfo Loureiro, is Macau's most flamboyant Chinese garden. It was built in the 19th century by a wealthy Chinese merchant and modeled after the famous gardens in Soochow. Tiny, with narrow winding paths, bamboo groves, and a nine-turn zigzag bridge that crosses a pond of carp, it's a nice escape from the city.

Taipa and Coloane Islands

And of course, don't forget Macau's two islands, Taipa and Coloane. They are the city's breathing space, Macau's playground, a good place to get away from it all. Closest to the mainland and connected by bridge is **Taipa,** known for its firecracker factory, temples, the United Chinese Cemetery, and the raceway of the Macau Trotting Club, Asia's first harness-racing track.

But for lovers of history and architecture, the place to visit is the **Taipa Folk Museum,** located on avenida da Praia in Taipa Village (tel. 001853). It consists of five colonial-style buildings that once belonged to Portuguese families at the turn of the century. Combining both European and Chinese designs, the houses contain large dining and living rooms, ball rooms, rooms for playing cards and other games, and large verandas that face banyan trees and the sea, reflecting the fact that most entertaining in this small colonial outpost was done at home. These homes are filled with furniture, paintings, and personal artifacts of the times. The museum is open Tuesday through Sunday from 9am to 1pm and 3 to 5:30pm, but hours are known to vary so it's wise to telephone in advance. The easiest way to reach Taipa Village is via the bus that stops in

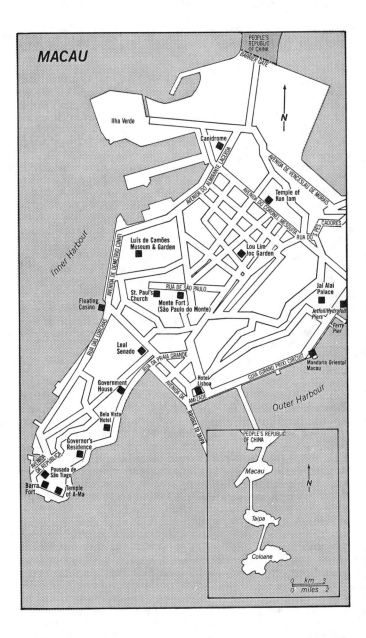

MACAU

People's Republic of China

BARRIER GATE

Ilha Verde

Canidrome

AVENIDA DE VENCESLAU DE MORAIS

AVENIDA DO ALMIRANTE LACERDA

AVENIDA DO CORONEL MESQUITA

Temple of Kun Iam

RUA DO ... PES

CADORES

Inner Harbour

AVENIDA DE DEMÉTRIO CINATTI

Luís de Camões Museum & Garden

Lou Lim Ioc Garden

St. Paul's Church

RUA DE SÃO PAULO

Jai Alai Palace

Floating Casino

Monte Fort (São Paulo do Monte)

Jetfoil/Hydrofoil Piers

RUA DAS LORCHAS

Ferry Pier

Leal Senado

RUA DA PRAIA GRANDE

GUIA (GRAND PRIX CIRCUIT)

Mandarin Oriental Macau

Government House

AVENIDA DA

Hotel Lisboa

Bela Vista Hotel

AMIZADE

Outer Harbour

Governor's Residence

BRIDGE TO TAIPA

People's Republic of China

AVENIDA DE REPÚBLICA

Pousada de São Tiago

Macau

Barra Fort

Temple of A-Ma

Taipa

Coloane

0   km   3
0   miles   2

front of the Hotel Lisboa near the bridge on the mainland or by taxi.

Farther away and connected to Taipa via causeway, **Coloane** is known for its beaches and pine trees. Two of the most popular **beaches** are Cheoc Van and Hac Sa. Both beaches have lifeguards on duty in the summer, as well as nearby public swimming pools that are open until 10pm. For a bit of greenery, visit **Coloane Park,** a 50-acre expanse with a walk-in aviary, Chinese-style pavilions, and barbecue facilities. The park, open from 9am to 7pm daily, charges HK$5 (65¢) for admission and can be reached by taking bus 21A from in front of the Hotel Lisboa. And finally, you might wish to stop off by the **Chapel of St. Francis Xavier** to pay homage to this important saint. This chapel contains an arm bone of St. Francis Xavier, as well as bones of Christian Portuguese and Japanese martyrs killed in Nagasaki in 1597 after Japan outlawed Christianity.

For more information on Taipa and Coloane, pick up a free pamphlet from the Macau tourist office called "Macau, Outlying Islands."

THE GAMBLING AND SPORTING SCENES

The Chinese so love gambling that it's often said that if two flies are walking on the wall, the Chinese will bet on which one will walk faster. It's not surprising, therefore, that Hong Kong Chinese make up about 80% of the four million visitors who come to Macau annually. And since the only forms of legal gambling in Hong Kong are the horse races and mah-jongg, you can bet that most of the Chinese come to Macau to gamble, whether it's at the casinos, jai-alai games, or the tracks.

Casinos

Altogether there are six casinos in Macau. The three most sophisticated are in hotels, in the **Macau Oriental, Hyatt Regency,** and the **Hotel Lisboa.** All three are open 24 hours and include one-arm bandits (slot machines), roulette, boule, baccarat, and blackjack, as well as Chinese games. The other casinos, which cater largely to Chinese, are **Casino Kam Pek,** located on avenida de Almeida Ribeiro; the **Casino Jai-Alai,** located in the Jai-Alai Palace; and the **Floating Casino,** moored in the Inner Harbour at rua das Lorchas near avenida de Almeida Ribeiro. Ornately decorated, the Floating Casino is worth strolling through for a look at Chinese gambling.

Jai-alai

The most popular spectator sport on the island, other than perhaps the races, is jai-alai, one of the world's fastest and oldest ball games. Originating in Spain where it is called Basque pelota, the game involves players who hurl the ball from a wicker basket strapped to one arm at speeds of up to 150 miles per hour. Played in a three-walled court measuring 181 feet long and 53 feet wide, the game objective is to fling the ball in such a manner that the opponent is unable to return it, either on the fly or on the first bounce. And of course, you can bet on the outcome. Games are held in the Jai-Alai Palace near the ferry terminal from 7:30pm to midnight on weekdays and on Saturday and Sunday afternoons at 2pm. Admission is HK$1 (15¢).

Racetracks

On Taipa Island is the track for the **Macau Trotting Club** (tel. 27211), which features harness racing most Sundays. Transportation is provided by both public bus and air-conditioned coaches that depart from in front of the Hotel Lisboa; tickets for the coach and raceway are available in the hotel's lobby. The grandstand is air-conditioned and admission starts at HK$3 (40¢). Call for more information.

For racing of a different sort, check out the greyhound races, held on weekends and sometimes on weekdays at 8pm at the **Canidrome,** avenida General Castelo Branco, located near the border gate with China. Admission starts at HK$2 (25¢).

---

4. Where to Stay

In addition to the room rates given below (which are the same whether you pay in Hong Kong dollars or in patacas since all hotels treat them as equal denominations), both a 10% hotel service charge and a 5% government tax will be added to your bill. Since most of Macau's hotels have reservations facilities in Hong Kong, I've included the Hong Kong reservation telephone numbers. For more complete information about hotel restaurants, see the "Where to Dine" section, below.

EXPENSIVE

• **Hyatt Regency Macau,** estrada Almirante Marquês Esparteiro, Taipa Island (tel. 321234; or 5590168 for reservations in Hong Kong). 335 rms, 21 suites. A/C MINI-BAR TV TEL

If you're looking for a resort getaway with extensive recreational facilities, great restaurants, and comfortable rooms, this hotel is a good choice. Located on Taipa Island near the trotting track, the hotel adjoins the Taipa Island Resort, a sprawling complex with an outdoor heated pool open year round, tennis and squash courts, fitness rooms, and more. The hotel's guest rooms, which were shipped in units from the United States and then assembled in Macau like pieces of a jigsaw puzzle, are bright with Mediterranean pastels, mainly in powder blue, and with all the usual amenities. Rooms face either the water and Macau across the harbor or inland, with ocean views costing the most. If you really feel like splurging, you might want to stay in the Regency Club, an executive floor offering free continental breakfast, cocktails, and canapes. The hotel's disco, the Green Parrot, is one of Macau's most popular nightspots. In short, you could easily spend days here, unwinding and relaxing.

Dining/Entertainment: Afonso's specializes in Portuguese food, while the Flamingo is a Macanese restaurant in a tropical hot-pink setting. There's a swim-up bar in the swimming pool, a cocktail lounge, the Green Parrot disco, and a casino.

Services: Laundry service, babysitting, doctor.

Facilities: Outdoor heated swimming pool, four tennis courts, two squash courts, jogging track, putting green and driving cage, fitness center, sauna, Jacuzzi, massage, hair salon, games room, children's playground, child-care center.

RATES: HK$750–HK$860 ($97–$112), single or double; HK$970 ($126) Regency Club; from HK$1,650 ($214) suite. AE, DC, MC, V.

- **Mandarin Oriental Macau,** avenida da Amizade (tel. 567888; or 5587676 for reservations in Hong Kong). 406 rms, 32 suites. A/C MINI-BAR TV TEL

A companion hotel of the Mandarin Oriental in Hong Kong and the Oriental in Bangkok, this is one of Macau's most exclusive hotels, at a price much lower than what you'd pay in Hong Kong. It's a beautifully designed hotel, elegantly decorated throughout with imports from Portugal, including blue and white tiles, chandeliers, tapestries, and artwork. Its marble lobby features a carved teak staircase leading up to the second floor, where you'll find the hotel's small but sophisticated casino. Rooms are decorated in soft pink or green with Portuguese fabrics and natural teak, and bathrooms are marbled and spacious. The best rooms are those on the top three floors that face the sea and feature large balconies, and the hotel offers more suites than any other hotel in Macau. Conveniently located about a five-minute walk from the ferry terminal, the hotel takes advantage of its waterfront location with an outdoor swimming pool right beside the water and a sunny, outdoor terrace great for a snack or drinks.

Dining/Entertainment: The Grill is the hotel's premier European restaurant, small and intimate with views of the water. At the Dynasty you can eat dim sum and other Cantonese food, while the Cafe Girassol specializes in Macanese cuisine and light meals. Bar da Guia features a live band every night except Tuesday from 8:30pm, while the casino is open 24 hours.

Services: 24-hour room service, car rental, medical clinic, parcel and packing service, same-day laundry and dry cleaning, shuttle-bus service.

Facilities: Outdoor swimming pool, sauna, Jacuzzi, massage, tennis courts, squash courts, business center, book kiosk.

RATES: HK$670–HK$1,080 ($87–$140), single or double; from HK$1,800 ($234) suite. AE, DC, MC, V.

- **Pousada de São Tiago,** avenida da República (tel. 78111; or 8108332 for reservations in Hong Kong). 23 rms and suites. MINI-BAR TV TEL

Built around the ruins of the Portuguese Fortress da Barra, which dates from 1629, this is a delightful small hotel guaranteed to charm even the most jaded of travelers. The entrance to the hotel is very dramatic—a flight of stone stairs leading through a cavelike tunnel. Once in the hotel, guests are treated to the hospitality of a Portuguese inn, with bedroom furniture imported from Portugal. Its Garden Terrace is a great place to while away an afternoon, and most of the rooms have balconies. This place is a true find, perfect for a romantic getaway.

Dining/Entertainment: The Grill Fortaleza is one of Macau's finest and most elegant restaurants, with a drawing-room ambience and serving classic Portuguese and Continental cuisine. The Garden Terrace, a tree-shaded outdoor patio with glimpses of the sea, serves snacks and light meals until midnight. For drinks, there's the Cascata Bar, as well as the Beer Garden, which is open in summer and located beside the road against an original fort wall.

Services: Babysitting, fitness room, laundry and dry-cleaning service, medical and dental service, newspaper delivery to rooms, parcel and postal service, room service till midnight.

Facilities: Outdoor swimming pool.

RATES: HK$970–HK$1,100 ($126–$143), single or double; from HK$1,320 ($171) suite. AE, CB, DC, MC.

MODERATE

• **Bela Vista,** 8 rua Comendador Kou Ho Neng (tel. 573821; or 5408180 for reservations in Hong Kong). 23 rms. A/C TEL

Built in 1892 and hardly changed a bit since then, this hostelry is a rambling, eccentric-looking hotel standing on a hill overlooking the water. Very old world, it's a bit moldy in places, with worn carpets, cracked walls, and blistering paint, but it still remains one of my very favorite places in Macau and is the place to stay if you're at all nostalgic. Its outdoor veranda, where you can sit and watch the slow boats pass in the ocean beyond, is absolutely one of the best places for a glass of cheap Portuguese wine. Rooms are adequate and simple, and the best in the house is Room 39, a corner room with a dramatically high ceiling and its own private veranda overlooking the water.

Services: Postal services, laundry service.

Facilities: One restaurant with indoor and veranda seating.

RATES: HK$250 ($32) single; HK$310–HK$470 ($40–$61) double or twin. AE, DC, MC, V.

• **Hotel Guia,** estrada do Engenheiro Trigo (tel. 513888). 79 rms, 10 suites. A/C MINI-BAR TV TEL

Located on a hill near the Guia Lighthouse, this is one of Macau's newer medium-range hotels. Opened in 1989, it's small and personable, with a friendly staff and a young, enthusiastic manager who used to work for the Mandarin Oriental. There are various rooms available, ranging from those that face inland to those with little balconies that face the sea. The only drawback to its peaceful and quiet location is that it's a bit far from the action, but a free shuttle bus makes runs every half hour or so to and from the boat pier and the Hotel Lisboa.

Services: Room service, laundry service, shuttle bus.

Facilities: One Cantonese restaurant, sauna, nightclub.

RATES: HK$380–HK$550 ($49–$71), single or double; from HK$660 ($86) suite. AE, MC, V.

• **Hotel Lisboa,** avenida da Amizade (tel. 77666; or 5591028 for reservations in Hong Kong). 750 rms and suites. A/C TV TEL

You can't get much closer to the action than this flashy hotel, which has a tendency toward the garish and is very popular with tour groups from Japan and Australia, making its lobby rather noisy and crowded. Its casino, one of the largest, never closes, and there are a number of restaurants and nighttime diversions, including the Crazy Paris Show with its revue of scantily clad European women. A plus to staying here is that buses to the outlying islands and to other parts of Macau stop in front of the hotel. As for the rooms, they're located in an older wing and a newer wing, but they all seem rather old-fashioned and the favored decorating colors are beige, pink, and orange. Still, this is the place to be if you want to be in the thick of it.

Services: 24-hour room service, banks.

Facilities: Restaurants serving European, Portuguese, Japanese, Korean, Chiu Chow, Cantonese, and Shanghainese cuisine; plus cocktail lounges, nightclub, casino, bowling alley, outdoor swimming pool, sauna and massage, children's playground, shopping arcade, disco, games room.

RATES: HK$230–HK$280 ($30–$36) single; HK$370–HK$700 ($48–$91) twin; from HK$1,000 ($130) suite. AE, CB, DC, MC, V.

BUDGET

- **Hotel Central,** 26-28 avenida de Almeida Ribeiro (tel. 77700). 163 rms. A/C TV TEL

This hotel, right on Macau's main road, first opened about 30 years ago and looks it. Although some of the rooms on the seventh and eighth floors have been renovated and have tiled bathrooms, other rooms may look old and run-down, with discolored and peeling wallpaper. In addition, some rooms don't have windows. Ask to see a room first, though be aware that the renovated rooms are more expensive.

RATES: HK$170 ($22) single; HK$200–HK$280 ($26–$36) double or twin. AE, MC, V.

---

5. Where to Dine

As a former trading center for spices and a melting pot for Portuguese and Chinese cultures, it's little wonder that Macau developed its own very fine cuisine. Influenced by Portugal's far-flung outposts, the Portuguese settlers brought with them sweet potatoes, peanuts, and kidney beans from Brazil, piri-piri peppers from Africa, chilis from India, and codfish, coffee, and vegetables from Europe. In turn, the Chinese introduced rhubarb, celery, ginger, soy sauce, lychees, and other Asian foods. The result is Macanese cuisine, the most popular of which is African chicken or prawns, grilled or baked with chilis and peppers. Other favorite dishes in Macau include bacalhau (codfish), Macau sole, caldeirada (seafood stew), spicy giant shrimp, baked quail and pigeon, curried crab, and feijoada (a Brazilian stew of pork, kidney beans, cabbage, and spicy sausage). And don't forget Portuguese wine, inexpensive and a great bargain.

Restaurants will add a 10% service charge to your bill.

EXPENSIVE

- **Afonso's,** Hyatt Regency Hotel, Taipa Island (tel. 321234). *Prices:* Most meals average HK$100–HK$200 ($13–$26). AE, DC, MC, V.

This cheerfully done restaurant specializes in Portuguese food, with an emphasis on fresh seafood. It offers daily specials and a great dessert buffet, and chefs from Lisbon dish out such authentic dishes as plain grilled fresh tuna steak with seasonal vegetables and marinated pork with clams, coriander, and paprika. There's live music in the evenings.

Open: Daily noon–3pm and 7–11pm. PORTUGUESE

- **Flamingo,** Hyatt Regency Hotel, Taipa Island (tel. 321234). *Prices:* Entrées HK$40–HK$100 ($5.20–$13); average meal HK$150–HK$200 ($19.50–$26). AE, DC, MC, V.

Decorated in hot pink, this restaurant has a great Mediterranean ambience, with ceiling fans, swaying palms, and a terrace overlooking a duck pond. The bread is homemade, and the specialties are Macanese and Portuguese, including spicy king shrimp with chili sauce, curry crab, African chicken, and grilled sardines. There are also beef, lamb, and Oriental selections, and in the evenings there's live entertainment.

Open: Daily noon–3pm and 7–11pm. MACANESE/ PORTUGUESE

- **The Grill,** Mandarin Oriental, avenida da Amizade (tel. 567888). *Prices:* Executive luncheon from HK$108 ($14); average dinner HK$250–HK$350 ($32.50–$45.50). AE, CB, DC, MC, V.

This European restaurant, with only 60 seats and very attentive waiters, is decorated in simple old-world elegance. For appetizers, try the sliced beef carpaccio with tomatoes, mozzarella cheese, and olive-oil dressing, or the homemade noodles with fresh goose liver, wild mushrooms, and parmesan cheese. The mousseline of lobster with sweetbread croutons is divine. Steaks and seafood make up most of the restaurant's main courses, and for dessert you'd be foolish to pass up the hot soufflé (your choice of ginger, passion fruit, or almond).

Open: Tues–Sun 12:30–3pm and 6:30–11pm. *Closed:* Mon. EUROPEAN

- **Grill Fortaleza,** Pousada de São Tiago Hotel, avenida da República (tel. 78111). *Prices:* Entrees HK$55–HK$100 ($7.15–$13). AE, CB, DC, MC.

Small and intimate, with seating for only 40 diners, this half-oval room with heavy red curtains and a drawing-room ambience serves both Portuguese and Continental cuisine. Specialties include shredded cod, spicy king shrimp, duck terrine with cherry sauce, spicy African chicken, Macau sole, and grilled U.S. sirloin.

Open: Daily noon–3pm and 7–11pm. PORTUGUESE/
CONTINENTAL

MODERATE AND BUDGET

- **Bela Vista,** Bela Vista Hotel, rua Comendador Kou Ho Neng
(tel. 573821). *Prices:* Entrees HK$55–HK$80 ($7.15–$10.50).
AE, DC, MC, V.

With its sweeping views of the ocean, tugboats, and barges, the
veranda of the Bela Vista is a great place to while away an afternoon
or eat a meal when the weather is balmy. There is, however, also an
indoor restaurant, rather old-fashioned and quaint. It offers African
chicken, spicy king prawns, curries, steaks, moussaka, and seafood
dishes, as well as a house Portuguese wine priced at HK$41 ($5.30)
for three-fourths of a liter.

Open: Daily 11am–10:30pm (3–6pm drinks and snacks only).
PORTUGUESE/EUROPEAN

- **Estrela do Mar,** 11 travessa do Paiva (tel. 81270). *Prices:*
Lunch HK$30 ($3.90); dinner HK$50 ($6.50).

Located off the Praia Grande on a small side street, this small,
unpretentious restaurant dishes out inexpensive Portuguese cuisine. The menu lists soups, salads, Portuguese or African chicken,
roast quail, crabs with curry, spicy fried shrimps, pork chops, steak,
bacalhau, rabbit, and lamb dishes.

Open: Daily noon–midnight. PORTUGUESE

- **Fat Siu Lau,** 64 rua da Felicidade (tel. 573585 or 573580).
Prices: Meals average HK$55–HK$90 ($7.15–$11.75).

This is Macau's oldest restaurant, dating from 1903, but its
three floors of dining have been renovated in upbeat modern art
deco, with a very pleasant color scheme of peach and turquoise blue.
Macanese cuisine is served here, including roasted pigeon marinated in a 75-year-old secret recipe, spicy African chicken, and
grilled king prawn.

Open: Daily 11am–1:30am. MACANESE

- **Garden Terrace,** Pousada de São Tiago Hotel, avenida da
República (tel. 78111). *Prices:* Meals average HK$55–HK$80
($7.15–$10.50). AE, CB, DC, MC, V.

This tree-shaded brick terrace faces the sea and offers informal
dining. It serves a wide range of light meals and snacks, including
soups, salads, sandwiches, seafood, and such international selections as Indonesian satay, Thailand's hot-and-sour prawn soup,
Japanese fried noodles, and grilled African spring chicken.

Open: Daily 7am–midnight. INTERNATIONAL

- **Henri's Galley Maxim's,** 4 avenida da República (tel. 76207).
Prices: Meals average HK$100 ($13).

This popular establishment is owned by Henri Wong, a jovial
and friendly man who used to be a chief steward on a galley job at
sea and has decorated his restaurant as though he were still aboard
ship. The staff is attentive and there are a few seats outside under
umbrellas. Specialties of the house include fried Macau sole, African
chicken, Portuguese baked chicken, bacalhau, fresh crab curry,

steaks, stuffed crabmeat in its shell, spaghetti, and sandwiches.

Open: Daily 11am–11pm. MACANESE/INTERNATIONAL

■ **Long Kei,** 7B largo de Senado (tel. 573970). *Prices:* Average meal HK$100 ($13).

If you're in the mood for Cantonese food, this well-known Chinese restaurant is located in the heart of town, right off avenida de Almeida Ribeiro. The menu includes shark's fin, bird's nest, abalone, chicken, frog, duck, seafood, and vegetable dishes. Try the double-boiled shark's fin with chicken in soup, fried fresh milk with crab, or the minced quail with lettuce.

Open: Daily 11am–11pm. CANTONESE

■ **Poolside Terrace,** Mandarin Oriental Hotel, avenida da Amizade (tel. 567888). *Prices:* Entrees less than HK$60 ($7.80). AE, CB, DC, MC, V.

This is the Mandarin Oriental's outside terrace, a dazzlingly white patio with hanging ferns and potted palms and a view of the water. Very Mediterranean in appearance and atmosphere, it offers light meals and snacks, including pizza, pasta, king prawns, Greek lamb kebab, club sandwiches, and satay. Cocktails are priced at HK$29 ($3.75). If you have an hour or so to kill waiting for a hydrofoil, this is the place to do so, since it's only a five-minute walk to the ferry pier.

Open: Daily 8am–7pm (lunch noon–3pm). INTERNATIONAL

■ **Solmar,** 8-10 rua da Praia Grande (tel. 574391). *Prices:* Meals average HK$120 ($15.50).

This is a typical Portuguese café/restaurant, the place everyone comes to socialize and gossip. One of Macau's oldtimers, it specializes in seafood and African chicken, and its menu includes Portuguese vegetable soup, prawns in hot sauce, bacalhau, steaks, spaghetti, and of course, Portuguese wines. Often crowded, it's located between the Sintra and Metropole hotels.

Open: Daily 11am–10:30pm. PORTUGUESE

CURRENCY CONVERSIONS

At this writing, HK$7.70 = $1 U.S., and this is the rate of exchange used to calculate the dollar values in this book (rounded off). This rate, of course, fluctuates from time to time and may not be the same when you travel to Hong Kong. Therefore the following table should be used only for guidance.

HK$	U.S.$	HK$	U.S.$
.25	.03	150	19.48
.50	.06	200	25.97
1	.13	250	32.47
2	.26	300	38.96
3	.39	350	45.45
4	.52	400	51.95
5	.65	450	58.44
6	.78	500	64.94
7	.90	550	71.42
8	1.04	600	77.92
9	1.16	650	84.42
10	1.30	700	90.91
15	1.94	750	97.40
20	2.60	800	103.90
25	3.25	850	110.39
30	3.90	900	116.88
35	4.55	1,000	129.87
40	5.19	1,250	162.34
45	5.84	1,500	194.80
50	6.49	1,750	227.27
75	9.74	2,000	259.74
100	12.99	2,250	292.21

CLOTHING SIZE CONVERSIONS

Hong Kong makes clothing for countries all over the world. Thus the labels in those garments you inspect may show sizes quite different from those you are used to at home.

The sizes shown in the tables below are *for your guidance only*, as the equivalents are not exact. Therefore, if your clothing is not being made to order, it is wise to try on all clothes before you purchase them to be sure that they fit properly.

WOMEN'S DRESSES, COATS, AND SKIRTS

American	3–4	5–6	7–8	9–10	11	12	13	14	15	16	18
Continental	36	38	38	40	40	42	42	44	44	46	48
British		8	10	11		12	13	14	15	16	17	18	20

WOMEN'S BLOUSES AND SWEATERS

American	10	12	14	16	18	20
Continental	38	40	42	44	46	48
British	32	34	36	38	40	42

WOMEN'S SHOES

American	5	6	7	8	9	10
Continental	36	37	38	39	40	41
British	3½	4½	5½	6½	7½	8½

CHILDREN'S CLOTHING

American	3	4	5	6	6X
Continental	98	104	110	116	122
British	18	20	22	24	26

CHILDREN'S SHOES

American	8	9	10	11	12	13	1	2	3
Continental	24	25	27	28	29	30	32	33	34
British	7	8	9	10	11	12	13	1	2

MEN'S SUITS

American	34	36	38	40	42	44	46	48
Continental	44	46	48	50	52	54	56	58
British	34	36	38	40	42	44	46	48

MEN'S SHIRTS

American	14½	15	15½	16	16½	17	17½	18
Continental	37	38	39	41	42	43	44	45
British	14½	15	15½	16	16½	17	17½	18

MEN'S SHOES

American	7	8	9	10	11	12	13
Continental	39½	41	42	43	44½	46	47
British	6	7	8	9	10	11	12

WEIGHTS AND MEASURES

Like almost every country in the world (the major exception is the United States), Hong Kong uses the metric system of weights and measures. Thus you may find the following information useful. I suggest that you become familiar with the rough equivalents given below, or you can use the formulas if you need more exact conversions.

LENGTH
1 millimeter = 0.04 inches (*or* less than $\frac{1}{16}$ inch)
1 centimeter = 0.39 inches (*or* just under $\frac{1}{2}$ inch)
1 meter   = 1.09 yards (*or* about 39 inches)
1 kilometer = 0.62 mile (*or* about $\frac{2}{3}$ mile)

To convert kilometers to miles, take the number of kilometers and multiply by .62 (for example, 25km × .62 = 15.5 miles).

To convert miles to kilometers, take the number of miles and multiply by 1.61 (for example, 50 miles × 1.61 = 80.5 km).

CAPACITY
1 liter = 33.92 ounces
        = 1.06 quarts
        = 0.26 gallons

To convert liters to gallons, take the number of liters and multiply by .26 (for example, 50 l × .26 = 13 gal).

To convert gallons to liters, take the number of gallons and multiply by 3.79 (for example, 10 gal × 3.79 = 37.9 l).

WEIGHT
1 gram   = 0.04 ounce (*or* about a paperclip's weight)
1 kilogram = 2.2 pounds

To convert kilograms to pounds, take the number of kilos and multiply by 2.2 (for example, 75kg × 2.2 = 165 lbs).

To convert pounds to kilograms, take the number of pounds and multiply by .45 (for example, 90 lb × .45 = 40.5kg).

AREA

1 hectare (100m^2 = 2.47 acres

To convert hectares to acres, take the number of hectares and multiply by 2.47 (for example, 20ha × 2.47 = 49.4 acres).

To convert acres to hectares, take the number of acres and multiply by .41 (for example, 40 acres × .41 = 16.4 ha).

TEMPERATURE

°C −18° −10   0   10   20   30   40

°F   0° 10   20   32   40   50   60   70   80   90 100

To convert degrees C to degrees F, multiply degrees C by 9, divide by 5, then add 32 (for example 9/5 × 20°C + 32 = 68°F).

To convert degrees F to degrees C, subtract 32 from degrees F, then multiply by 5, and divide by 9 (for example, 85°F − 32 × 5/9 = 29°C).

INDEX

GENERAL INFORMATION

ACCOMMODATIONS

Hong Kong

*Key to Abbreviations: B = Budget; E = Expensive; M = Moderate; R-B = Rock-Bottom; VED = Very Expensive Deluxe; YH = Youth Hostel

Outlying Islands

Macau

FROMMER BOOKS
PRENTICE HALL TRAVEL
15 COLUMBUS CIRCLE
NEW YORK, NY 10023
212-373-8125

Date_____

Friends:
Please send me the books checked below:

FROMMER™ GUIDES

(Guides to sightseeing and tourist accommodations and facilities from budget to deluxe, with emphasis on the medium-priced.)

☐ Alaska	$14.95		☐ Germany	$14.95
☐ Australia	$14.95		☐ Italy	$14.95
☐ Austria & Hungary	$14.95		☐ Japan & Hong Kong	$14.95
☐ Belgium, Holland & Luxembourg	$14.95		☐ Mid-Atlantic States	$14.95
☐ Bermuda & The Bahamas	$14.95		☐ New England	$14.95
☐ Brazil	$14.95		☐ New York State	$14.95
☐ Canada	$14.95		☐ Northwest	$14.95
☐ Caribbean	$14.95		☐ Portugal, Madeira & the Azores	$14.95
☐ Cruises (incl. Alaska, Carib, Mex, Hawaii, Panama, Canada & US)	$14.95		☐ Skiing Europe	$14.95
			☐ South Pacific	$14.95
☐ California & Las Vegas	$14.95		☐ Southeast Asia	$14.95
☐ Egypt	$14.95		☐ Southern Atlantic States	$14.95
☐ England & Scotland	$14.95		☐ Southwest	$14.95
☐ Florida	$14.95		☐ Switzerland & Liechtenstein	$14.95
☐ France	$14.95		☐ USA	$15.95

FROMMER $-A-DAY® GUIDES

(In-depth guides to sightseeing and low-cost tourist accommodations and facilities.)

☐ Europe on $40 a Day	$15.95		☐ New York on $60 a Day	$13.95
☐ Australia on $30 a Day	$12.95		☐ New Zealand on $45 a Day	$13.95
☐ Eastern Europe on $25 a Day	$13.95		☐ Scandinavia on $60 a Day	$13.95
☐ England on $50 a Day	$13.95		☐ Scotland & Wales on $40 a Day	$13.95
☐ Greece on $35 a Day	$13.95		☐ South America on $35 a Day	$13.95
☐ Hawaii on $60 a Day	$13.95		☐ Spain & Morocco on $40 a Day	$13.95
☐ India on $25 a Day	$12.95		☐ Turkey on $30 a Day	$13.95
☐ Ireland on $35 a Day	$13.95		☐ Washington, D.C. & Historic Va. on $40 a Day	$13.95
☐ Israel on $40 a Day	$13.95			
☐ Mexico on $35 a Day	$13.95			

FROMMER TOURING GUIDES

(Color illustrated guides that include walking tours, cultural and historic sites, and other vital travel information.)

☐ Australia	$9.95		☐ Paris	$8.95
☐ Egypt	$8.95		☐ Scotland	$9.95
☐ Florence	$8.95		☐ Thailand	$9.95
☐ London	$8.95		☐ Venice	$8.95

TURN PAGE FOR ADDITONAL BOOKS AND ORDER FORM.

0190

FROMMER CITY GUIDES
(Pocket-size guides to sightseeing and tourist accommodations and facilities in all price ranges.)

☐ Amsterdam/Holland	$7.95	☐ Minneapolis/St. Paul	$7.95
☐ Athens	$7.95	☐ Montréal/Québec City	$7.95
☐ Atlantic City/Cape May	$7.95	☐ New Orleans	$7.95
☐ Barcelona*	$7.95	☐ New York	$7.95
☐ Belgium	$7.95	☐ Orlando/Disney World/EPCOT	$7.95
☐ Boston	$7.95	☐ Paris	$7.95
☐ Cancún/Cozumel/Yucatán	$7.95	☐ Philadelphia	$7.95
☐ Chicago	$7.95	☐ Rio	$7.95
☐ Denver/Boulder*	$7.95	☐ Rome	$7.95
☐ Dublin/Ireland	$7.95	☐ San Francisco	$7.95
☐ Hawaii	$7.95	☐ Santa Fe/Taos/Albuquerque	$7.95
☐ Hong Kong*	$7.95	☐ Seattle/Portland*	$7.95
☐ Las Vegas	$7.95	☐ Sydney	$7.95
☐ Lisbon/Madrid/Costa del Sol	$7.95	☐ Tokyo*	$7.95
☐ London	$7.95	☐ Vancouver/Victoria*	$7.95
☐ Los Angeles	$7.95	☐ Washington, D.C.	$7.95
☐ Mexico City/Acapulco	$7.95	*Available June, 1990	

SPECIAL EDITIONS

☐ A Shopper's Guide to the Caribbean	$12.95	☐ Manhattan's Outdoor Sculpture	$15.95
☐ Beat the High Cost of Travel	$6.95	☐ Motorist's Phrase Book (Fr/Ger/Sp)	$4.95
☐ Bed & Breakfast—N. America	$11.95	☐ Paris Rendez-Vous	$10.95
☐ California with Kids	$14.95	☐ Swap and Go (Home Exchanging)	$10.95
☐ Caribbean Hideaways	$14.95	☐ The Candy Apple (NY with Kids)	$12.95
☐ Honeymoon Destinations (US, Mex & Carib)	$12.95	☐ Travel Diary and Record Book	$5.95

☐ Where to Stay USA (Lodging from $3 to $30 a night) $10.95
☐ Marilyn Wood's Wonderful Weekends (Conn, Del, Mass, NH, NJ, NY, Pa, RI, VT) $11.95
☐ The New World of Travel (Annual sourcebook by Arthur Frommer for savvy travelers) $16.95

SERIOUS SHOPPER'S GUIDES
(Illustrated guides listing hundreds of stores, conveniently organized alphabetically by category.)

☐ Italy	$15.95	☐ Los Angeles	$14.95
☐ London	$15.95	☐ Paris	$15.95

GAULT MILLAU
(The only guides that distinguish the truly superlative from the merely overrated.)

☐ The Best of Chicago	$15.95	☐ The Best of Los Angeles	$14.95
☐ The Best of France	$16.95	☐ The Best of New England	$15.95
☐ The Best of Hong Kong	$16.95	☐ The Best of New York	$14.95
☐ The Best of Italy	$16.95	☐ The Best of Paris	$16.95
☐ The Best of London	$16.95	☐ The Best of San Francisco	$14.95
	☐ The Best of Washington, D.C.	$14.95	

ORDER NOW!

In U.S. include $2 shipping UPS for 1st book; $1 ea. add'l book. Outside U.S. $3 and $1, respectively.
Allow four to six weeks for delivery in U.S., longer outside U.S.
Enclosed is my check or money order for $_____

NAME _____

ADDRESS _____

CITY _____ STATE _____ ZIP _____

0190